What People Are Saying About Our Books...

"Should be in the library—and kitchen—of every serious cook."

JIM WOOD—Food & Wine Editor—San Francisco Examiner

*"An attractive guide to the best restaurants and inns,
offering recipes from their delectable repertoire of menus."*

GAIL RUDDER KENT—Country Inns Magazine

"Outstanding cookbook."

HERITAGE NEWSPAPERS

"Nothing caters to visitors as well as this book does."

TONY TOLLNER—Co-owner, Rio Grill

"It's an answer to what to eat, where to eat—and how to do it yourself."

MONTEREY HERALD

*"I dare you to browse through these recipes
without being tempted to rush to the kitchen."*

PAT GRIFFITH—Chief, Washington Bureau, Blade Communications, Inc.

THE GREAT
CALIFORNIA
COOKBOOK

The Chefs' Secret Recipes

By Kathleen DeVanna Fish

Bon Vivant Press   Monterey, California
Edited by Fred Hernandez
Illustrations by Robin Brickman

Library of Congress Cataloguing-in-Publication Data

THE GREAT CALIFORNIA COOKBOOK
The Chefs' Secret Recipes

First printing, 1993

Fish, Kathleen DeVanna
91-092497
ISBN 0-9620472-5-2
First printing, 1993
$13.95 softcover
Includes indexes
Autobiography page 286

Copyright ©1993 by Kathleen DeVanna Fish

Editorial direction by Fred Hernandez
Cover photography by Robert N. Fish
Illustrations by Robin Brickman
Cover design by Morris Design
Type by Electra Typography
Lone Cypress photo with permission of the Pebble Beach Company.

Published by Bon Vivant Press,
a division of The Marketing Arm
P.O. Box 1994
Monterey, CA 93942

Printed in the United States of America
by Publishers Press

Contents

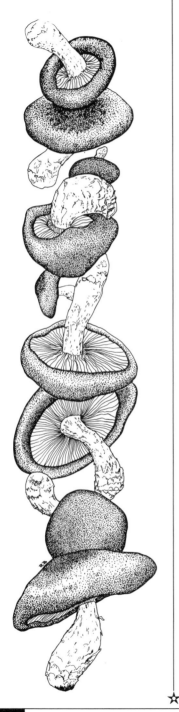

"The Great California Cookbook" is a very personal book. It is filled with personal choices—of great chefs, restaurants and recipes that exemplify the best cooking in California. Nobody paid to be included—the chefs were hand-selected and invited to participate.

It was not an easy task. There are thousands upon thousands of restaurants in this huge state. So narrowing the field to 45 chefs in 14 areas of the state and 225 recipes in 13 categories was particularly difficult. But that's what we've done.

The idea was to help cooks everywhere understand how the professional chefs operate: what they cook, how they do it, their approaches and styles.

Let's begin with the chefs. It was tempting to invite only the most famous of them. While you will recognize many of the big names in this book, we have included some who may be new to you. The requirements: excellence of food, consistency of quality and a flair for beautiful presentation. Some cook in large restaurants, some in smaller venues.

The chefs provided 225 of their kitchen-tested secret recipes for the home cook. To make things easy, we list the recipes in these categories: Starters, Soups, Salads, Breads, Main Dish Meals, Fish and Shellfish, Meats, Game, Poultry, Pasta and Grains, Fruits and Vegetables, Sauces and Condiments and Final Temptations.

Some of the recipes are simple. Some are more complex. We stayed clear of purely trendy food, preferring to stress foods that we know are wonderful. We also tried to provide a wide range of styles and specialties. You'll find dishes with roots in France, Mexico, Italy, the Caribbean, Asia, the Southwest, the Middle East, Russia and Germany. There are vegetarian dishes, seafood, game—and desserts you won't be able to resist.

But we wanted to accomplish more than just listing ingredients and oven times. We wanted to get to know the chefs, to hear what they had to say about cooking, about ingredients, about methods and what they like to eat when they dine out. We wanted to know what ingredients they can't live without. And we wanted to see how they look.

In a section we call Listen to the Chefs, our guest chefs suggest a lot of good quick meals. Some talk about how they got interested in cooking. They talk about the things that many cooks do wrong. They provide insights into their cuisines.

By getting to know the master chefs, all cooks' repertoires are enriched. And this book is for cooks, whether they live in California or not. The intent is to tempt you with the great dishes to be found in California—and the talented people who create them.

To put things into perspective, we have included A Culinary Tour, a section that guides you through the origins of California cooking. Then we take a quick tour of our favorite cities and sights to visit. We include a listing of all the featured restaurants so you'll know where to visit our chefs and taste their creations. A map helps you get there.

We also talk briefly about the great diversity of fresh crops that grow in California. To a large degree, that's why the food is so good here—perfect ingredients.

We also talk about California's wine regions. Most people know a few wines from two or three prime vintage regions. But there are a lot of good wines from regions you may not have considered. Some of our recipes will guide you to particular wines for particular uses.

And in case you're a visitor, we feel you should be prepared for the wide range of climatic conditions in the state. There's no point in being uncomfortable when you're traveling to taste a great chef's food.

Understanding that not all markets are created equal, we include a directory of mail-order food outlets.

The cuisines of California are rich and varied. Ever since the Gold Rush, people have flocked to California. They come from every part of the globe. They bring spices, sauces, exotic ingredients and new ways of looking at food. They settle in a state rich with fruits, vegetables, seafood, game and wines.

They taste one another's food and they cook.

That's the California way.

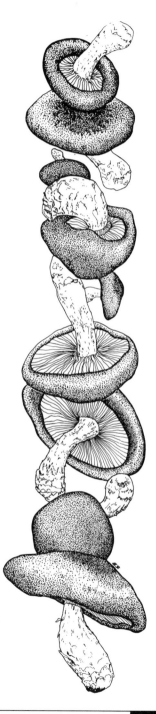

Favorite Restaurant Recipes

Starters

Soups

Salads

Breads

Main Dish Meals

Fish and Shellfish

Meats

Pasta and Grains

Fruits and Vegetables

Sauces and Condiments

Final Temptations

The Best Addresses

SAN DIEGO

CILANTRO'S
Tim Sullivan
3702 Via de la Valle
1½ miles east of Interstate 5
Del Mar, Ca 92014
619-259-8777
SOUTHWESTERN

DELICIAS
Serge Falesitch
6106 Paseo Delicias
Rancho Santa Fe, Ca 92067
619-756-8000
AMERICAN

IL FORNAIO CUCINA ITALIANA
Gianpaolo Putzu
1555 Camino Del Mar
Del Mar, Ca 92014
619-755-8876
ITALIAN

PACIFICA DEL MAR
Scott Kirkwood
1555 Camino Del Mar
Del Mar, Ca 92014
619-792-0476
SEAFOOD

PALM SPRINGS

DOLLY CUNARD'S
Jay Trubee
78045 Calle Cadiz
La Quinta, Ca 92253
619-564-4443
FRENCH

ORANGE COUNTY

THE GOLDEN TRUFFLE
Alan Greeley
1767 Newport Boulevard
Costa Mesa, Ca 92627
714-645-9858
FRENCH CARIBBEAN

J.W.'S
John McLaughlin
Anaheim Marriott Hotel
700 West Convention Way
Anaheim, Ca 92802
714-750-0900
FRENCH

TREES
Russell Armstrong
440 Heliotrope
Near Pacific Coast Highway
Corona Del Mar, Ca 92625
714-673-0910
CALIFORNIA

LOS ANGELES

BORDER GRILL
Susan Feniger and Mary Sue Milliken
1445 4th Street
Santa Monica, Ca 90401
310-451-1655
MEXICAN and CENTRAL AMERICAN

CHEZ MELANGE
William Donnelly
1716 Pacific Coast Highway
Redondo Beach, Ca 90277
310-540-1222
INTERNATIONAL

CITY RESTAURANT
Susan Feniger and Mary Sue Milliken
180 South La Brea Avenue
Los Angeles, Ca 90036
213-938-2155
ECLECTIC INTERNATIONAL

MICHAEL'S
Martin Garcia
1147 Third Street
Santa Monica, Ca 90403
310-451-0843
CALIFORNIA

PARKWAY GRILL
Hugo Molina
510 South Arroyo Parkway
Pasadena, Ca 91105
818-795-1001
CALIFORNIA

PATINA
Joachim Splichal
5955 Melrose Avenue
Los Angeles, Ca 90038
213-467-1108
FRENCH CALIFORNIA

PRIMI
Enrico Glaudo
10543 Pico Boulevard
West Los Angeles, Ca 90064
310-475-9235
ITALIAN

TRUMPS
Michael Roberts
8764 Melrose Avenue
West Hollywood, Ca 90069
310-855-1480
AMERICAN

SANTA BARBARA

DOWNEY'S
John Downey
1305 State Street
Santa Barbara, Ca 93101
805-966-5006
CALIFORNIA

YOSEMITE

ERNA'S ELDERBERRY HOUSE
Erna Kubin-Clanin
48688 Victoria Lane
Off Highway 41
Oakhurst, Ca 93644
209-683-6800
FRENCH

MONTEREY PENINSULA

CENTRAL 159 RESTAURANT
& CATERING
David Beckwith
159 Central Avenue
Pacific Grove, Ca 93950
408-372-2235
CALIFORNIA

EL COCODRILO
Julio Ramirez
701 Lighthouse Avenue
Pacific Grove, Ca 93950
408-655-3311
AMERICAN-CARIBBEAN

THE FISHWIFE
Julio Ramirez
1996 Sunset Drive
Pacific Grove, Ca 93950
408-375-7107
SEAFOOD

PACIFIC'S EDGE
Brian Whitmer
Highlands Inn
Highway 1
Carmel, Ca 93921
408-624-0471
CALIFORNIA

POST RANCH INN
Wendy Little
Highway 1
Big Sur, Ca 93920
408-667-2200
CALIFORNIA

EAST BAY

CHEZ PANISSE
Alice Waters
1517 Shattuck Avenue
At Cedar
Berkeley, Ca 94709
510-548-5525
MEDITERRANEAN

S.F. PENINSULA

HONG KONG
FLOWER LOUNGE
Philip Lo
51 Millbrae Avenue
At El Camino Real
Millbrae, Ca 94030
415-692-6666
CHINESE

SAN FRANCISCO

ACQUERELLO
Suzette Gresham-Tognetti
1722 Sacramento Street
Near Van Ness and Polk
San Francisco, Ca 94109
415-567-5432
ITALIAN

BISTRO ROTI
Cindy Pawlcyn
155 Steuart Street
In the Hotel Griffon
San Francisco, Ca 94105
415-495-6500
AMERICAN

BIX
Cindy Pawlcyn
56 Gold Street
At Montgomery
San Francisco, Ca 94133
415-433-6300
AMERICAN

CHINA MOON CAFE
Barbara Tropp
639 Post Street
Between Taylor and Jones
San Francisco, Ca 94109
415-775-4789
CHINESE

CYPRESS CLUB
Cory Schreiber
500 Jackson Street
At Montgomery
San Francisco, Ca 94133
415-296-8555
AMERICAN

FLEUR de LYS
Hubert Keller
777 Sutter Street
Near Jones
San Francisco, Ca 94109
415-673-7779
FRENCH

FOG CITY DINER
Cindy Pawlcyn
1300 Battery Street
At Embarcadero
San Francisco, Ca 94111
415-982-2000
AMERICAN

GREENS
Annie Somerville
Fort Mason, Bldg. A
San Francisco, Ca 94123
415-771-6222
VEGETARIAN

MASA'S
Julian Serrano
648 Bush Street
Near Stockton
San Francisco, Ca 94108
415-989-7154
FRENCH

SQUARE ONE RESTAURANT
Joyce Goldstein
190 Pacific Avenue
Near Front
San Francisco, Ca 94111
415-788-1110
MEDITERRANEAN

STARS
Jeremiah Tower
and Emily Luchetti
150 Redwood Alley
Near Van Ness
San Francisco, Ca 94102
415-861-7827
AMERICAN

MARIN

BUCKEYE ROADHOUSE
Cindy Pawlcyn
15 Shoreline Highway
By Highway 101
Mill Valley, Ca 94941
415-331-2600
AMERICAN

THE LARK CREEK INN
Bradley Ogden
234 Magnolia Avenue
Larkspur, Ca 94939
415-924-7766
AMERICAN

SACRAMENTO

BIBA RESTAURANT
Biba Caggiano
2801 Capital Avenue
Between 28th and 29th Street
Sacramento, Ca 95816
916-455-2422
NORTHERN ITALIAN

CHINOIS EAST WEST
David SooHoo
2232 Fair Oaks Blvd.
Near Howe
Sacramento, Ca 95825
916-648-1961
CHINESE

NAPA

BRAVA TERRACE
Fred Halpert
3010 St. Helena Hwy North
St. Helena, Ca 94574
707-963-9300
CALIFORNIA

THE FRENCH LAUNDRY
Sally Schmitt
Washington and Creek Street
Yountville, Ca 94599
707-944-2380
CONTEMPORARY FRENCH

MUSTARDS GRILL
Cindy Pawlcyn
7399 St. Helena Highway 29
Yountville, Ca 94558
707-944-2424
CALIFORNIA

TERRA
Hiroyoshi Sone
1345 Railroad Avenue
St. Helena, Ca 94574
707-963-8931
CALIFORNIA

TRA VIGNE
Cindy Pawlcyn
1050 Charter Oak
At Highway 29
St. Helena, Ca 94574
707-963-4444
ITALIAN

SONOMA

JOHN ASH & CO. RESTAURANT
John Ash
4330 Barnes Road
Santa Rosa, Ca 95403
707-527-7687
CALIFORNIA

MADRONA MANOR
Todd Muir
1001 Westside Rd.
Healdsburg, Ca 95448
707-433-4433
CALIFORNIA

PIATTI
Donna Scala
405 First Street West
El Dorado Hotel
Sonoma, Ca 95476
707-996-2351
ITALIAN

SONOMA MISSION INN
Michael Flynn
18140 Sonoma Highway 12
Boyes Hot Springs, Ca 95416
707-938-9000
CALIFORNIA WINE COUNTRY

NORTH COAST

CAFE BEAUJOLAIS
Margaret Fox
961 Ukiah Street
Mendocino, Ca 95460
707-937-5614
CALIFORNIA

Shasta Lake

NEVADA

Mendocino

South Lake Tahoe

SACRAMENTO

Sonoma • Napa

Mono Lake

Berkeley

SAN FRANCISCO

Yosemite National Park

Palo Alto

San Jose

Santa Cruz

Monterey

Fresno

Carmel

Big Sur

Death Valley
National Monument

San Simeon

San Luis Obispo

Santa Barbara

Ventura

Simi Valley

Santa Monica

Palm Springs

LOS ANGELES

Anaheim

Long Beach

San Diego

California is like no other place on Earth. From the very beginning, it was conceived as exotic, as a place where one could not avoid being wealthy. The name of California originates in "The Exploits of Esplandian," a 16th century novel by Garcia Ordonez de Montalvo. The romantic novel described California as a mythical island inhabited by Amazon women, protected by steep cliffs—and here comes that first flourish of fantasy—the only metal to be found on the whole island was gold.

The first European visitors were Spanish, English and Russian, some seeking empire, some seeking wealth, some interested merely in otter pelts. And there were plenty of native Americans already living in California, thriving on the bounty of plentiful game, fish, indigenous plants and plentiful water. But then came the Great Gold Rush and everything changed rapidly.

When James Marshall discovered gold at Sutter's Mill on January 14, 1848, he shouted "Eureka! I have found it!" And that was the shout heard around the world. The dreamers came from everywhere, seeking quick riches and new lives. And while a few lucky prospectors hit it big, most pried barely enough to live on from the reluctant soil. Transportation was very slow in those days, so the dreamy diggers kept flocking to California for years and years. They abandoned their old ways of life to search for the fabled riches. They came expecting to get rich quick. What most found were harsh realities: cold winters in the Sierra gold fields, primitive living conditions, high prices—and relatively little gold. But the miners all shared the exhilaration of going to town to sample the good life, even if for only a few days.

Towns grew quickly and scrambled to get their share of the 49ers' gold. The miners were too preoccupied with seeking gold to bother with the amenities. But they were willing to pay for them. Saloons, stores, hotels, blacksmiths, houses of ill repute, liveries and outfitters sprang up everywhere.

And restaurants.

This was an extraordinary colonization. In most places, settlers came to farm, to raise livestock, to build homes and live off the land. But the tens of thousands who responded to the Gold Rush came expecting to get rich. And when they left the hills, they drifted into the towns and cities to spend what they had accumulated. After all, there was more where that came from.

The first restaurants were rather crude. But soon more sophisticated cooking evolved. Food was abundant because of the proximity to the sea, lush farmlands, ranches and game forests. And there were cooks from all over the world: Chinese, Italian, Mexican, German, Spanish, English and French. And each people brought not only their cuisine, but their spices and methods.

So here we are today, on the brink of the 21st century. It is a huge state, with over 158,000 square miles. Its population is over 25 million—and growing every day. If California were a separate country, it would rank twelfth in the value of international trade, eighth in gross national product, and it would be the seventh largest agricultural producer in the world.

California is home to the major dream factories of Hollywood, Disneyland, and attractive tales of the legendary California lifestyle. You can mention California in any part of the world and they'll know what you're talking about. So the dreamers still arrive every day.

Let's take a look at what California has to offer. Let's start with the cities. Most of the population of California lives in a 40 mile-wide belt on the coast, from just north of San Francisco to south of San Diego. Our quick tour begins at the south and works its way north:

SAN DIEGO: Boasting a superb natural harbor, it accommodates about 30 percent of the entire U.S. Naval fleet. San Diego also offers a world-class zoo, California's first mission (San Diego de Alcala), access to beautiful Coronado and the northern border of Mexico, Sea World in Mission Bay Park, Old Globe Theater, Old Town and Point Loma.

LOS ANGELES: An area so big, so diverse that we can only touch on some highlights. The L.A. vicinity's greatest draws are Disneyland, the Universal Studio Tours, Knott's Berry Farm and Six Flags Magic Mountain. Also popular are ritzy Rodeo Drive in Beverly Hills, Olvera Street's taste of Mexico, Forest Lawn Cemetery in Glendale, Hollywood Bowl and La Brea Tar Pits. An international motion picture and television production Mecca, L.A. is also the most important business center on the West Coast. And it is a world-class location for people-watching and dining—sometimes at the same time.

SANTA BARBARA: A beautiful coastal city rich in Spanish colonial architecture. Home of historic Mission

Santa Barbara, this resort city boasts magnificent mansions and villas tucked away in the surrounding hillsides.

SAN SIMEON: Site of the fabulous home of late newspaper magnate William Randolph Hearst. The Hearst San Simeon State Historical Monument includes a magnificent castle set amid 127 acres. The castle contains about $50 million worth of antiques and art treasures of all kinds. Highlights include the stunning Neptune Pool, a castle-sized dining room (catsup was served at all meals), tapestries, furnishings and ancient statuary. Many tours are available, but reservations are required.

BIG SUR: The stunning beauty of Big Sur extends 75 miles from Santa Lucia, just north of San Simeon, to Point Lobos, just south of Carmel. That stretch along Highway 1 includes spectacular ocean vistas from the cliff-hugging road, redwood trees creeping toward the coast, isolated beaches and coves and Esalen, a world-class spa. It's a beautiful drive, but be aware that it's a curvy road.

MONTEREY-CARMEL: In 1770, six years before the Declaration of Independence was signed, Monterey was declared the capital of California. The Monterey area includes quaint Carmel with its many unique shops and galleries and home to former mayor Clint Eastwood. Also in the area is Pebble Beach, the posh playground that is home to the famed golf courses of Pebble Beach, Spanish Bay and Cypress Point. Other features of the area: 17-Mile Drive and its elegant homes, Cannery Row, the Monterey Bay Aquarium, Carmel Mission, Fisherman's Wharf and the showcase Victorians of Pacific Grove. Santa Cruz, with its seaside amusement park, is 45 miles north.

SAN JOSE: The center of Silicon Valley, San Jose also was the state capital at one time. Home of the Rosicrucian Egyptian Museum, Winchester Mystery House and a revitalized downtown area.

SAN FRANCISCO: The San Francisco Bay Area includes Oakland and Berkeley. San Francisco attractions include the Golden Gate Bridge, Coit Tower, Fisherman's Wharf, Chinatown and the cable cars. Oakland attractions include Lake Merritt, Jack London Square and the Oakland Museum. Berkeley, home of the largest campus of the University of California, features coffee houses, street musicians and many cultural events. Outlying areas include Marin County across the Golden Gate Bridge and Alcatraz Island in the middle of the bay.

NAPA: A prestigious wine center, the fertile Napa Valley boasts beautiful vineyards, elegant wineries and the mud baths and geothermal springs of Calistoga. Enjoy a drive along the Silverado Trail or delight in the many galleries and restaurants.

SONOMA: The Sonoma County region was the birthplace of the California wine industry, boasting 150 winemakers. The fertile Sonoma, Santa Rosa and Russian River valleys add much to the quality of life of California. Bountiful crops include apples, prunes and, of course, wine grapes. Home to the famed San Francisco Solano Mission and the residence of General Mariano Vallejo.

MENDOCINO: A quiet, beautiful town on the North Coast. Home to many artists, Mendocino is a popular getaway spot and honeymoon destination. The coastline is particularly beautiful, dotted with tiny coves and inns.

SACRAMENTO: The most inland of all the cities on this quick tour, Sacramento is the state capital. The site of Sutter's Fort, it also was the western terminus for the Pony Express. Attractions include the State Capitol and Old Town.

California boasts many natural wonders, too. Here are three you may want to visit:

YOSEMITE: This national park is one of the scenic wonders of the world. Its granite walls were carved by glaciers about 1 million years ago. Established in 1890, the national park contains not only famed Yosemite Valley, but 1,189 square miles of spectacular mountains, giant waterfalls, sheer cliffs, forest, lakes, abundant wildlife and redwood trees.

DEATH VALLEY: This national monument occupies almost 3,000 square miles of dramatic desert terrain. Harsh and even dangerous in the summer, Death Valley is a popular destination in the spring and winter. Features include the lowest elevation in the U.S., Scotty's Castle and Zabriskie Point.

LAKE TAHOE: A popular ski area and gambling Mecca. Gambling casinos thrive on the portions of the lake situated in the state of Nevada. Ringed by rugged mountains, the magnificent lake is extremely deep and is a popular vacation destination, summer or winter.

Because this book focuses on good food, a word on the state's agriculture is in order here. The rich, fertile valleys of the state—the Central Valley, the Salinas Valley and the

Imperial Valley—are among the most fertile places in the world. And that's one of the reasons that cooking has flourished so much in California: the finest ingredients. California farmers sell nearly 300 varieties of produce, from asparagus to zucchini blossoms. The varied climates allow the cultivation of such diverse crops as lettuces, kiwifruit, ginger, artichokes, tomatillos, bok choy, melons, persimmons, pomegranates and horseradish. Plus rich harvests of more familiar ingredients. That bounty translates into fine food. Because if you listen to the chefs, you'll see that perfect ingredients are their strongest allies.

Then there are the wines of California. Many people associate California wines with the Napa and Sonoma regions, with good vintages from Monterey, Mendocino and Santa Barbara counties. But the fact is that wine grapes are grown in 45 of California's 48 counties. Gaining in recognition are wines from the Sierra Nevada foothills, the Temecula Valley north of San Diego and the Paso Robles area. The state produces over 80 varieties of wine grapes. It's no coincidence that great restaurants tend to spring up in great wine-producing areas. Good food and good wine are the best of friends.

And let's not forget the fabled California climate. To begin with, California is so big, contains so many varied areas, that there is no one single climate. Southern California, which largely is reclaimed desert land, boasts sunny summers and mild winters. The Central and Northern California coasts are more foggy in the summer and enjoy sunny autumns. The North Coast gets more rain that the rest of the 840-mile coastline. And then there's Death Valley, with the lowest altitude (282 feet below sea level). The Sierra Nevada range draws a large snowpack. And the great Central Valley, bound by four major mountain ranges, has hot summers, perfect for agriculture.

Just look at these weather records and you'll see how varied the climate is in California. The highest temperature ever recorded in the United States, 134°F, was registered in Death Valley in 1913. A temperature of 45° below zero was recorded in Boca, (Nevada County), in 1957. The driest years in the U.S.—not one measurable drop of rain fell in 1913 in Bagdad (San Bernadino County) or in 1929 at Greenland Ranch (Inyo County). But 258 inches of rain fell in one year at Camp Six (Del Norte County). And Hoegees (Los Angeles

County) survived 26 inches of rain one day in 1943. In short, it's a huge state—with many climate zones—most of them pleasantly moderate. But don't assume you will find sunshine every day in every location. It's best to check ahead.

Everybody wants to come to California. And it's been like that for a long time. That's how all the residents got here—from someplace else.

California has become the gateway to the world: Asia, the Pacific Islands, Mexico, Central and South America, the Caribbean, throughout the United States, the Mediterranean and Africa, the Middle East and northern Europe.

The flavors of the Earth meet in California. Savor them.

☆

Chicken drumettes,
jalapeño honey mustard

Chicken on sugarcane

Stuffed charred chiles
with tomato salsa

Garlic custard with mushroom sauce

Stuffed baked eggplant bundles

Eggplant dumplings

Roasted garlic

Sweet pea guacamole

Terrine of eggplant, peppers,
goat cheese

Grilled mozzarella

Mussels in serrano cream

Mussels with chile vinaigrette

Red potatoes stuffed
with smoked trout mousse

Grilled zesty prawns

Salmon in a corn pancake

Scallop and salmon terrine

Sweet corn tamales

Pickled tongue
with Italian parsley sauce

Smoked trout pâté

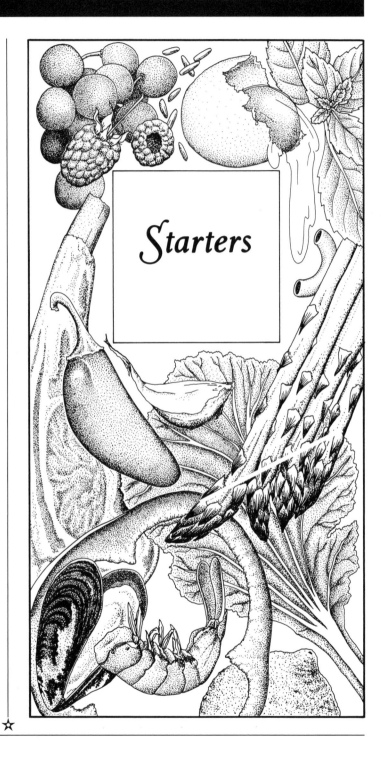

Starters

Spicy Chicken Drumettes with Jalapeño Honey-Mustard Sauce

Boil jalapeños in water for 5 minutes. Cool, discard stems. Set aside.

Liquefy sugars by placing in a saucepan with water, bringing mixture to a boil.

In a blender, combine the jalapeños, sugar, honey, vinegar, mustard and turmeric. Blend until all ingredients are puréed.

Trim excess fat off chicken drumettes. Toss chicken with ½ cup sauce and place on a cookie sheet, baking for 20 to 30 minutes, or until golden brown, turning once or twice.

Serve with sauce on side for dipping.

Serves 4
Preparation Time:
45 Minutes
Pre-heat oven to 400°

11 **jalapeños**
½ **cup sugar**
½ **cup brown sugar**
2 **Tbsps. water**
½ **cup honey**
¼ **cup rice wine vinegar**
2 **cups Dijon mustard**
¾ **tsp. turmeric**
20 **chicken drumettes**

Tim Sullivan
Cilantro's
Del Mar
★

Chicken on Sugarcane with Sweet Chile Sauce

Yield: 24 appetizers
Preparation Time:
  25 Minutes
(note refrigeration time)

¼ cup sugar, granulated
½ cup water
½ cup white vinegar
½ tsp. salt
6 garlic cloves, finely
  chopped
3 to 5 fresh red chile
  peppers, seeded,
  chopped fine
2 lbs. chicken meat,
  ground
½ lb. bacon, ground
¼ cup water chestnuts,
  chopped
½ tsp. salt
1 Tbsp. brown sugar
1 tsp. baking soda
¼ tsp. red chile pepper
  flakes
2 Tbsps. mint leaves or
  parsley, chopped
6 long sugarcanes, canned
  Chaokoh brand
  Chopped peanuts as
  garnish
  Mint leaves as garnish

Prepare the sweet chile sauce in a stainless steel pot. Combine the granulated sugar, water, white vinegar, salt, 4 garlic cloves and red chile peppers over low heat until well blended. Remove from heat and allow to cool before pouring into a glass jar. Set aside.

In a large mixing bowl, combine the chicken, bacon, water chestnuts, 2 garlic cloves, salt, brown sugar, red chile pepper flakes and mint. Chill mixture in the refrigerator.

Cut sugarcane along lengths to make 24 sticks. With wet hands, mound 3 Tbsps. chicken around one end of the sugarcane. Deep-fry in 350° fryer until set and lightly browned.

Refrigerate immediately. You can store in a refrigerator for up to 3 days.

Finish when guests arrive by grilling over charcoal or baking in 500° oven for 8 minutes. Serve with sweet chile sauce garnished with chopped peanuts and mint leaves.

David SooHoo
Chinois East West
Sacramento

Stuffed Charred Chiles with Tomato Salsa

O ver a grill or open flame, char chiles until skin blisters and becomes black. Cool. Then carefully peel skin off, keeping chiles intact.

In food processor, blender or mixing bowl, blend all cheeses together, until smooth. Place mixture in pastry bag without a tip and carefully stuff the chiles with cheese so as not to overfill and burst them. Chill.

Prepare the salsa by mixing the tomato, onion, radishes, jalapeño pepper, cilantro, lemon juice, salt and pepper. This will make one cup of salsa.

Pre-heat oven to 400.° Place chiles on an oven-proof platter and bake for about 10 minutes. Watch carefully and remove from oven before cheeses melt and run out. The spiciness of the dish compensates for the temperature; it does not have to be steaming hot.

Place chiles on warmed plates, placing ¼ cup of salsa between them. Garnish with cilantro leaves.

Serves 4
Preparation Time:
 30 Minutes
(note refrigeration time)

 8 large Anaheim chile
   peppers
⅛ lb. gorgonzola cheese
¼ lb. fontina cheese
¼ lb. bel paese cheese
¼ lb. Parmesan cheese,
   grated
¼ lb. cream cheese
 1 large tomato, seeded,
   chopped
 1 small onion, finely
   chopped
 2 radishes, finely chopped
 1 jalapeño pepper,
   minced
 4 Tbsps. fresh cilantro,
   finely chopped
   Juice of 1 lemon
   Salt and pepper to taste
   Cilantro leaves for
   garnish

Jay Trubee
Dolly Cunard's
La Quinta

☆

33

Garlic Custard with Mushroom Sauce

Serves 4
Preparation Time:
1 Hour
Pre-heat oven to 270°

1 **pt. whipping cream**
12 **garlic cloves**
4 **egg yolks**
Freshly ground nutmeg
to taste
Salt and pepper
8 **large shiitake**
mushrooms, sliced
8 **other wild mushrooms,**
sliced
3 **scallions, minced**
4 **Tbsps. sweet butter**
2 **cups chicken stock**
Salt and white pepper
to taste
3 **Tbsps. chives, minced**
⅔ **cup walnuts, toasted**

 o make the custard, slowly simmer the whipping cream and garlic until the cream is reduced by ⅓ and the garlic is soft. Run this through a food mill and stir in the egg yolks, nutmeg, salt and pepper. Mix thoroughly.

Butter eight 2 oz. ramekins or soufflé or custard cups and fill with the custard mixture. Cover the ramekins with buttered parchment and bake in a water bath for 40 minutes.

Meanwhile, make the sauce. Sauté the mushrooms and scallions in enough butter to coat the bottom of a skillet. When soft, add chicken stock. Over high heat, reduce the liquid by ⅓ and season with salt and pepper. Remove from heat.

When the custard is done, turn it out onto the center of a small plate. Reheat the mushroom sauce, stir in 1 Tbsp. soft butter, add the chives and walnuts.

To serve, spoon mushroom sauce around the garlic custard.

Cindy Pawlcyn
Bistro Roti, Bix, Buckeye Roadhouse, Fog City Diner,
Mustards Grill, Tra Vigne
San Francisco, Mill Valley, Napa

Stuffed, Baked Eggplant Bundles

Peel the eggplant and trim the ends. Cut it lengthwise into ¼″ thick slices. Place the slices in a large dish and sprinkle with salt. Let stand at room temperature for 30 to 40 minutes. The salt will draw out the eggplant's bitter juices. Pat the slices dry with paper towels.

Combine the bread crumbs and Parmesan cheese in a bowl. Dip the eggplant slices into the egg and coat them lightly with the bread crumb mixture.

Heat ½″ oil in a large skillet over medium-high heat. When the oil is hot, fry a few slices of eggplant at a time, until they are lightly golden on both side. Drain on paper towels. The dish can be prepared up to this point several hours ahead.

Preheat the oven to 375°. Place one slice of prosciutto and one of fontina cheese over each eggplant slice. Roll up loosely into a bundle. Secure each bundle with a toothpick.

Spread 2 Tbsps. olive oil in a baking pan. Add the bundles and bake 6 to 8 minutes or until the cheese is melted and the bundles are nice and hot. Serve warm.

Serves 4
Preparation Time:
 45 Minutes

- 1 medium size eggplant
  Salt
- 1½ cups dry, unflavored bread crumbs
- ½ cup freshly grated Parmesan cheese
- 2 eggs lightly beaten in a bowl
  Frying oil
- ⅓ lb. prosciutto, thinly sliced
- ⅓ lb. fontina cheese, thinly sliced
- 2 Tbsps. olive oil

Biba Caggiano
Biba Restaurant
Sacramento

Eggplant Dumplings

Serves 4
Preparation Time:
  45 Minutes

  1 **large eggplant**
  1 **cup olive oil**
  2 **eggs**
  ¼ **cup Parmesan cheese,**
     grated
  1⅓ **cups flour**
     Dash of oregano
     Salt and pepper to
     taste

eel eggplant, then cut into cubes. Sauté eggplant in olive oil for approximately 15 minutes over low heat, but don't let the eggplant turn brown. Drain eggplant on paper towels and cool.

In a mixing bowl, combine the eggs, Parmesan cheese, flour and oregano. Season with salt and pepper. Add the cooled eggplant and place mixture into a pastry bag.

In a large pot, bring water to a boil. Squeeze the eggplant mixture out of the pastry bag and cut into ¾" pieces. Drop into boiling water for 2 minutes each. The dumplings will rise to the top of the water when they are cooked.

Remove and serve with your favorite tomato or basil sauce.

Enrico Glaudo
Primi, Valentino
Los Angeles, Santa Monica

Roasted Garlic

Cut each head of garlic half way down from top to expose tops of each clove. Place cloves in a pan where they can fit together quite tightly. Drizzle each bulb liberally with olive oil. If desired, sprinkle a little salt directly onto cloves, but not onto oil between them. Sprinkle fresh pepper and fresh thyme directly onto garlic, if desired.

Cover pan with foil. Bake for 1 hour or more, or until just tender. Remove from oven and spread the soft, roasted garlic on the sourdough baguette and serve.

Serves 6
Preparation Time:
 1 Hour
Pre-heat oven to 300°

6 **heads of garlic**
 Olive oil
 Coarse salt, optional
 Fresh thyme, optional
 Freshly ground pepper
 Sourdough baguette,
 sliced

Cindy Pawlcyn
Bistro Roti, Bix, Buckeye Roadhouse, Fog City Diner,
Mustards Grill, Tra Vigne
San Francisco, Mill Valley, Napa

Sweet Pea Guacamole

Serves 8
Preparation Time:
  15 Minutes

  2 Tbsps. virgin olive oil
  2 Tbsps. fresh lime juice
  ¼ bunch cilantro,
    trimmed of long stems
  1 jalapeño pepper,
    seeded, or 2 serrano
    peppers, seeded
  1 lb. frozen peas,
    defrosted
  ¼ tsp. ground cumin
  ¾ tsp. salt
  ¼ medium red onion,
    finely diced

C ombine oil, lime juice, cilantro and pepper in a blender or food processor and blend until cilantro and peppers are roughly puréed. Add peas, cumin and salt and blend until smooth. There will still be some lumps, but this adds to the textural interest of the guacamole.

Spoon guacamole into a mixing bowl and add the onion. Serve as a dip with tortilla chips or use to accompany tamales.

©*Secret Ingredients*

Michael Roberts
Trumps
Hollywood

Terrine of Eggplant, Peppers and Goat Cheese

Peel eggplants, slice thin and sauté lightly in olive oil. Set aside

Roast red and yellow peppers then skin and seed. Cut into 3″ × 4″ rectangles. Set aside

Make a tomato aspic by first softening the gelatin in cold water. Heat together with the tomato juice until dissolved and well incorporated. Set aside.

Line a terrine mold with plastic wrap and pour in a very thin layer of tomato aspic, just enough so the eggplant slices will adhere. Layer the eggplant slices until the bottom is covered. The eggplant can overlap slightly if necessary. Add another brushing of aspic, then eggplant, repeating until there are 4 layers of eggplant. Brush again with aspic then place one layer of roasted red pepper, then aspic, then yellow pepper. Place an even layer of crumbled goat cheese, then pesto.

Repeat the entire process again, starting with the eggplant. As you add layers, press them into the terrine so they are condensed but not mashed. Do not put aspic next to the pesto layer. Finish the terrine with 4 layers of eggplant. Wrap the entire terrine in plastic as tightly as possible. Heat in a water bath at 350° for 45 minutes to 1 hour. Remove from heat, fold a piece of cardboard to fit on top of ingredients inside terrine. Place a heavy weight on top, then refrigerate for a minimum of 4 hours.

Serves 4
Preparation Time:
  1½ Hours
(note refrigeration time)

  3 **large firm eggplants**
1¾ **cups tomato juice**
  5 **sheets gelatin**
  4 **medium red peppers**
  4 **medium yellow**
    peppers
1¼ **cups goat cheese,**
    crumbled
  1 **cup pesto**

Brian Whitmer
Pacific's Edge, Highlands Inn
Carmel

☆

39

Grilled Mozzarella

Serves 4
Preparation Time:
  15 Minutes

  4 large romaine leaves
  **1 lb. fresh mozzarella, cut
    into 4 squares
    Salt and pepper**
**⅛ lb. prosciutto, diced
    Olive oil**

 lanch the romaine leaves in boiling salted water for 30 seconds. Remove and immediately immerse in ice water to stop the cooking process. Drain, then pat the leaves dry.

Lay out the leaves, rib side down. Place a square of cheese in the middle of each leaf. Sprinkle with salt and pepper, then top each piece of cheese with ¼ of the diced prosciutto. Fold in the edges of the leaves like an envelope. Brush with oil.

Grill over a medium to hot flame until the cheese begins to weep. Serve immediately.

Cindy Pawlcyn
Bistro Roti, Bix, Buckeye Roadhouse, Fog City Diner,
Mustards Grill, Tra Vigne
San Francisco, Mill Valley, Napa

Mussels in Cilantro & Serrano Cream Sauce

I n a large sauté pan, heat the olive oil and butter. Add the shallots, garlic, mussels and wine. Cover and allow to cook over medium heat for 3 minutes or until mussels open. Remove the lid and discard any mussels that haven't opened.

Reduce by half the remaining liquid in the pan. Add cream, tomato, onion, cilantro and chiles. Continue cooking for 2 minutes.

Remove the mussels from the pan and arrange them on a serving plate. Continue cooking the cream sauce until it is reduced by half.

Pour the sauce over the mussels and serve.

Trade Secret: This is a wonderful appetizer served with warm French bread.

Serves 4
Preparation Time:
 20 Minutes

12 New Zealand green lip
   mussels, cleaned
 1 Tbsp. olive oil
 2 Tbsps. butter
 1 tsp. shallots, minced
 1 tsp. garlic, minced
 ½ cup white wine
 ¼ cup heavy cream
 1 tomato, chopped
 ½ red onion, chopped
 1 Tbsp. fresh cilantro,
   chopped
 1 serrano chile, minced

Julio Ramirez
The Fishwife, El Cocodrilo
Pacific Grove

Mussels with Chile Vinaigrette

Serves 6
Preparation Time:
  1 Hour

½ jalapeño chile, finely
  chopped with a few
  seeds
½ small red bell pepper,
  chopped
½ Tbsp. olive oil, to sauté
  the peppers
½ cup cider vinegar
1 shallot, minced
1 tsp. Dijon mustard
1 tsp. Worcestershire
  sauce
  Salt and pepper to taste
1 cup olive oil
  Small bunch parsley,
  chopped
  Small bunch cilantro,
  chopped
3 lbs. medium sized fresh
  mussels
1 cup white wine
  (Riesling is good for this)
3 bay leaves
3 shallots
1 tsp. whole black
  peppercorns
  Spinach leaves, washed,
  stemmed

n a small pan, gently sauté the chopped jalapeño and bell peppers in the oil, for a few minutes.

Combine the vinegar, shallot, mustard, Worcestershire, salt and pepper in a small mixing bowl. Whisk in the olive oil slowly. Add the parsley, cilantro and sautéed peppers. Allow to stand for at least 1 hour. Stir again and correct the seasonings if necessary. Depending on personal preference, you may want to add extra jalapeño peppers, but be careful. This recipe yields 2 cups vinaigrette.

Discard any mussels that are open. A gentle tap may cause some to close—those will be fine. Scrub the shells well and remove the beard, pulling it sharply to detach the part that is inside the shell.

Place the wine, bay leaves, shallots and peppercorns in a kettle with a close fitting lid. Simmer the broth for 5 minutes. Add the mussels and increase heat to high. Boil with the lid on until the mussels open, about 5 minutes. If some of the mussels have not opened, return those to the kettle for a little longer, but any that continue to stay closed should be discarded. Carefully remove the mussels from their shells. If sand is present wash both the shells and the mussels.

To serve, arrange the half-shells on a plate like the spokes of a wheel. Place a small spinach leaf in each shell, then place a mussel on top of the leaf. Spoon chile vinaigrette generously over the mussels.

John Downey
Downey's
Santa Barbara

Small Red Potatoes Stuffed with Smoked Trout Mousse and Caviar

Boil potatoes in salted water until soft. Plunge imme-diately into ice water. When cold, remove and pat dry. Cut in half and cut a small slice off the bottom of each piece so they sit nicely on a plate. Scoop out a small amount of potato with melon baller. Sprinkle potatoes with salt and pepper and set aside.

In a food processor, soften cream cheese. Add trout, horseradish, dill, salt, pepper and lemon juice. Place mousse in a pastry bag fitted with fluted tip and pipe onto the pota-toes. Garnish with a small amount of caviar and a dill sprig.

Serves 4
Preparation Time:
  45 Minutes

12 **egg-sized red potatoes**
 1 **side smoked trout**
½ **cup cream cheese**
 1 **Tbsp. prepared**
   horseradish
 1 **tsp. dill, chopped**
   Squeeze of lemon juice
 2 **Tbsps. American caviar**
   Dill sprigs for garnish

Wendy Little
Post Ranch Inn
Big Sur

43

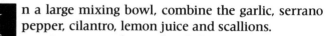

Grilled Zesty Prawns

Serves 6
Preparation Time:
 10 Minutes
(note marinating time)

  4 garlic cloves, peeled,
     chopped
  1 roasted serrano chile
     pepper, peeled, seeded
  1 bunch cilantro,
     chopped
     Juice of 3 lemons
  1 bunch scallions, diced
  1 Anaheim or ancho chile
     pod
  2 cups peanut or olive oil
24 jumbo prawns

In a large mixing bowl, combine the garlic, serrano pepper, cilantro, lemon juice and scallions.

Cut or tear the ancho chile into the marinade mixture and toss. Add half the oil and pour over prawns. Add remaining oil only if necessary to evenly coat the prawns. Marinate for 2 hours.

Grill for 2 minutes on each side before serving.

Trade Secret: Do not float the prawns in the marinade; that will dilute the flavors.

David Beckwith
Central 159 Restaurant & Catering
Pacific Grove

Salmon in a Corn Pancake Topped with Golden Caviar and Watercress Sauce

Wash the watercress and trim off the leaves. Discard the stems. Cook the leaves in a pot of boiling salted water until tender, about 3 minutes. Drain in a strainer, refresh under cold water and squeeze out moisture. In a small saucepan, heat butter and sauté the shallots until golden. Deglaze with white wine and reduce until almost dry. Add veal glaze or chicken stock and cream. Bring to a boil and reduce to a simmer. Add the cooked watercress leaves and blend well.

Slice evenly and thinly 8 slices of salmon. On a plate, spread the salmon pieces with a tsp. of caviar. Fold in half so that the caviar is sealed between the two layers of salmon. Season with salt and pepper on both side. Set aside.

Bring 4 qts. salted water to a boil. Add the corn and boil for 5 minutes, then quickly dip in cold water. Cut the kernels from the cobs. In a food processor, combine the corn, eggs, flour, salt and pepper. Pour the batter into a small mixing bowl.

Grease a crepe pan or a frying pan with oil and heat. Add 1½ Tbsps. of the pancake mixture. Top the mixture with the slices of salmon and barely cover the salmon with another thin layer of corn mixture. Cook until golden brown on both sides.

To serve, garnish pancakes with cooked asparagus tips. Top the pancakes with sour cream and caviar. Sprinkle with chopped chives.

Serves 4
Preparation Time:
  45 Minutes

 1 **bunch watercress**
½ **Tbsp. butter**
 1 **Tbsp. shallots, chopped**
 2 **Tbsps. dry white wine**
 2 **Tbsps. veal glaze or 1**
   Tbsp. chicken stock
¾ **cup heavy cream**
⅓ **lb. fresh Norwegian**
   salmon
 3 **oz. golden caviar or**
   sturgeon caviar
 3 **ears corn, cleaned**
 3 **eggs**
 2 **Tbsps. flour**
   Salt and pepper
 2 **Tbsps. cooking oil**
16 **pieces asparagus tips,**
   cooked
 2 **Tbsps. sour cream**
 1 **Tbsp. chives, chopped**

Hubert Keller
Fleur de Lys
San Francisco

Sea Scallop and Salmon Terrine

Yield: 12 thin slices
Preparation Time:
 1½ Hours

1 **bunch red chard**
1 **lb. scallops, very cold**
6 **egg whites**
1 **cup cream**
 Salt and pepper to taste
 Juice of 1 lemon
3 **tsps. dry Vermouth**
3 **cloves garlic, peeled,**
 crushed
2 **bunches spinach,**
 washed, dried
¾ **lb. salmon, cut in**
 1″ strips

ash chard and remove entire stem. Blanch in lightly salted boiling water for 10 seconds. Remove quickly and place in a bowl with ice water. When cooled, pat dry with kitchen towel.

Dampen the inside of a 12″ terrine pan with water and line with plastic wrap. Line wrap with blanched chard leaves. Set aside.

In a food processor, combine ½ amount of scallops and egg whites. Gradually add ½ cup cream while processor is operating. Add salt, pepper, juice of half a lemon 1½ tsps. of Vermouth and garlic to taste. Set aside.

Take remaining scallops, egg whites and add spinach to processor. Again, slowly add the ½ cup cream and 1½ tsps. vermouth and garlic to taste. Blend until smooth and silky. Season with juice of half lemon, salt and pepper and garlic to taste.

Fill the two mousse mixtures into two separate large pastry bags. Take prepared terrine pan and pipe in mousse mixture alternately, starting with scallop mousse, then spinach mousse. In center, place salmon strips, then cover with spinach mousse and scallop mousse. Finish by covering with remaining chard. Top terrine with well buttered aluminum foil. Seal edges well.

Place terrine in a a roasting pan half filled with hot water and cook in oven for 50 minutes at 350° Let cool for about 1 hour, slice to desired portions.

Erna Kubin-Clanin
Erna's Elderberry House
Oakhurst

Sweet Corn Tamales

Remove the corn husks and save for the tamales. With a knife, shave the corn kernels from the cobs. Place the kernels in a blender and purée. Place the corn purée in a mixing bowl and add the corn meal and masa harina. Add the salt and margarine and mix thoroughly.

Take the corn husks, with the silk removed, and put enough dough in each to make a finger-size tamal, then fold the husk around the filling, making a neat, secure "envelope."

Steam the tamales in standing position for 1¼ hours. Serve with black beans and crème fraîche.

Trade Secret: The corn meal and the masa harina are to tighten up the mixture and give proper consistency to the dough. Add more or less depending on the moistness of the corn purée.

Serves 8
Preparation Time:
 1½ Hours

 6 ears of fresh corn
½ cup corn meal
½ cup masa harina (finely ground corn meal)
 1 tsp. salt
½ cup margarine
 Black beans, optional
 Crème fraîche, optional

Julio Ramirez
The Fishwife, El Cocodrilo
Pacific Grove

Pickled Tongue with Italian Parsley Sauce

Serves 10
Preparation Time:
  2 Hours
(note marinating time)

  1 beef tongue, about
    3 lbs.
2½ cups salt
1½ cups firmly packed
    brown sugar
1½ cups granulated sugar
1½ gallons water
  2 Tbsps. crushed black
    peppercorns
  1 Tbsp. whole cloves
  1 Tbsp. juniper berries,
    crushed
  3 bay leaves
  2 garlic cloves, peeled
  1 rib celery, chopped
  1 carrot, chopped
  ½ onion, chopped

  ½ cup parsley, chopped
  ½ cup fresh bread
    crumbs
  ¼ cup capers, rinsed
2½ Tbsps. shallots,
    chopped
  2 Tbsps. fresh dill,
    chopped
1½ Tbsps. garlic, minced
  ½ Tbsp. sugar
  1 cup olive oil
  ¼ cup red wine vinegar
    Salt and freshly ground
    black pepper

 o make the brine, combine all ingredients except the tongue in a large, non-corrosive pot. Bring to a simmer, remove from heat and cool.

Prick tongue with a fork or skewer. Place in brine, weigh it down to keep it submerged. Cover and refrigerate up to 5 days. Then place tongue in a large pot of water with celery, carrot and onion. Bring to a boil, then reduce heat to maintain a simmer. Simmer until tongue reaches 180,° about 2 hours. Drain, remove skin while warm and chill tongue.

To serve, slice thin and accompany with baby lettuces, tomato and salsa verde (recipe below).

Salsa Verde

In bowl, combine parsley, bread crumbs, caper, shallots, dill, mint, garlic and sugar. Whisk in oil and vinegar. Season to taste with salt and pepper

Suzette Gresham-Tognetti
Acquerello
San Francisco

Smoked Trout Pâté

This is a wonderful spread for croutons, tastes good on avocados and makes a rich sandwich spread when paired with sliced cucumber and watercress on dark rye or pumpernickel bread.

Remove the heads and skin from the trout and bone carefully, to yield ½ lb. of smoked filets after cleaning. Put the trout in a food processor and pulse until chopped. Transfer to a bowl and fold in the rest of the ingredients.

Trade Secret: To make a homemade mayonnaise, blend 3 egg yolks and ¼ cup lemon juice until creamy. Slowly add 2 cups of a mild olive oil, not virgin, until desired consistency.

Serves 4
Preparation Time:
 15 Minutes

1½ lbs. smoked trout
 ½ cup white or yellow
   onion, finely diced
 ½ cup chives, chopped
 1 cup mayonnaise
   Salt and pepper
   to taste
   Lemon juice to taste

Joyce Goldstein
Square One Restaurant
San Francisco

Soups

Chilled Avocado Soup

In a large mixing bowl, mash avocados, add lime juice, then the other ingredients. Whisk until smooth, then to consistency of thick cream, using extra stock or milk if needed. Taste for seasoning. Use plenty of black pepper. Chill.

To serve, garnish each bowl with chopped chives, including the chive blossom.

Trade Secret: The soup can be made several hours in advance. The lime juice keeps it from darkening.

Serves 4
Preparation Time:
20 Minutes

4 ripe avocados, peeled
¼ cup lime juice
1 cup chicken stock
2 cups buttermilk
1 cup light cream
½ cup white onion, minced fine
Fresh black pepper, coarsely ground
Chives for garnish

Sally Schmitt
The French Laundry
Yountville

Butternut Soup

Serves 6
Preparation Time:
45 Minutes

2 Tbsps. butter
1 medium yellow onion,
   peeled, chopped
2 stalks celery, chopped
2 medium carrots, peeled,
   chopped
1 medium butternut
   squash, peeled and
   seeded
4 bay leaves
1 tsp. thyme, dried
   or fresh
½ tsp. anise seed
1 tsp. marjoram
4 cups chicken stock
   Salt and white pepper
   to taste
½ cup heavy cream
   Marjoram leaves or
   cranberries as garnish

elt the butter in a 3 qt. saucepan. Add the onion, celery and carrots. Cook slowly without browning until softened. Add the butternut squash, cut into chunks, then the herbs, the chicken stock and a little salt and pepper. Cover and bring to a boil. Reduce heat and simmer until butternut squash is tender.

Purée the soup in a food processor fitted with steel blades, a blender, or pass through a fine strainer. Return to a clean saucepan and bring to a boil. Remove from heat and stir in the cream. Correct seasoning with salt and pepper to taste.

Serve in hot bowls garnished with fresh marjoram leaves or warm cranberries.

John Downey
Downey's
Santa Barbara

Chicken Stock

Place all ingredients into a 6 qt. pot. Bring to a boil. Skim the gray foam off and reduce heat. After 15 minutes, skim foam off again. Simmer for 2½ hours, partially covered.

Strain, remove as much fat as possible with a large spoon and chill overnight. Remove the rest of the fat fastidiously before using.

Yield: 8 cups or 2 qts.
Preparation Time:
  2½ Hours

10 **cups water**
 4 **lbs. chicken parts**
 2 **onions, cut into**
   quarters
 2 **stalks celery, cut into**
   chunks
 2 **carrots, cut into slices**
   Several parsley sprigs
 2 **bay leaves**
   Freshly ground pepper
 ⅛ **lemon**

Margaret Fox
Cafe Beaujolais
Mendocino

Boston Clam Chowder

Preparation Time:
45 Minutes
Yield: One gallon

2 lbs. Manila clams,
washed
2 qts. water
1 lb. clams, chopped
¼ cup oil
4 stalks celery, chopped
1¼ medium onions,
chopped
¼ tsp. thyme
2 bay leaves, crushed
1 cup light roux (oil or
butter mixed with
flour in equal amounts
over low heat)
4 medium potatoes,
peeled, diced
2 qts. heavy cream or
half and half

lace the Manila clams in a large pot with water and bring to a boil. When clam shells open, remove from pot, drain and discard the shells. Save the clam broth, set aside.

In another large pot, heat the oil and add the celery, onions, thyme and bay leaves. When vegetables and herbs are soft, add both the chopped clams and the steamed clams. Add the clam broth. (Be careful not to add any sand that may have settled to the bottom of the broth.)

Cook until the clams are tender. Add the roux, gently stirring it in. When the mixture is smooth, add the potatoes. Continue cooking for 15 minutes. As soon as the potatoes are cooked, add the cream or half and half, heating gently.

Trade Secret: This soup can be made in advance and refrigerates well without the cream. As you use it, add 2 cups of cream or half and half for each quart of clam base that you plan to serve.

Julio Ramirez
The Fishwife, El Cocodrilo
Pacific Grove

Corn & Potato Chowder with Cheddar Cheese Fritters

Prepare the fritter batter by mixing together the flour, cornstarch, baking powder, parsley and onion. Salt and pepper to taste.

Blend together the water, peanut oil, egg and cheddar cheese and fold into the dry ingredients. Mix well and let stand. This can be made up to 4 hours before using.

Cut up the shaved corn ears and mix the corn ears with the carrots, onions and celery.

Melt butter in a heavy saucepan and add the vegetable mixture. Sweat over low heat for 10 minutes with cover on. Add chicken stock and cream and bring to a simmer. Reduce this mixture for 20 minutes. Strain through a sieve. Add diced potatoes and shaved corn to saucepan and pour the strained stock back into pan. Let simmer for 5 minutes.

Dice the red pepper into 1″ squares and add with the parsley leaves into the soup. Season to taste with salt and pepper.

Fry 2 fritters per serving in oil and place in center of individual soup bowls.

Serves 6
Preparation Time:
2 Hours

1½ cups cake flour
2 Tbsps. cornstarch
1 tsp. baking powder
¼ cup parsley, chopped
2 Tbsps. white onion, grated
Salt and pepper to taste
¾ cup water
1 tsp. peanut oil
1 whole egg
½ cup Tillamook cheddar cheese, grated
6 ears of corn, (shave off kernels and save ears for stock)
1 cup carrots, chopped
1 cup onion, chopped
1 cup celery, chopped
3 Tbsps. butter
5 cups chicken stock
2 cups heavy cream
4 russet potatoes, peeled, cut into ½″ cubes
2 red peppers, roasted, skinned, peeled
1 cup fresh parsley leaves
1 qt. vegetable oil for frying (heat to 325°)

Cory Schreiber
Cypress Club
San Francisco

★

Smoked Trout Chowder

Serves 6
Preparation Time:
45 Minutes

2 Tbsps. butter
¼ cup peanut oil
3 garlic cloves, finely chopped
2 carrots, peeled, chopped
1 medium red onion, diced
1 large red bell pepper, diced
1 large green bell pepper, diced
2 medium leeks, diced
1 small jalapeño pepper, skinned, seeded
1½ cups white wine
1½ cups fish or chicken stock
1 lb. smoked trout, coarsely chopped
6 small red potatoes, cooked
3 Tbsps. fresh thyme
2 cups milk
2 cups half and half
Garlic croutons, Italian parsley or roasted garlic, as garnish

 n a 4 qt. pot, melt butter in the peanut oil over high heat. Add the garlic, carrots, onion, peppers, leeks and jalapeño. Cook until tender.

Add white wine and cook 5 minutes.

Add stock, trout and potatoes, let simmer 10 minutes.

Add thyme, milk and half and half and cook for 30 minutes.

Pour into oversized bowls and serve with garlic croutons, fresh chopped Italian parsley or with a float of roasted garlic.

Trade Secret: This chowder makes a great entree by itself with a loaf of crusty sourdough bread.

David Beckwith
Central 159 Restaurant & Catering
Pacific Grove

Cream of Corn Soup with Crayfish Butter

Shuck the corn, remove all the silk from the ears, and slice downward on the ears between the cob and the kernels to remove the kernels without getting any of the cob.

Melt the butter in a saucepan and add the corn, marjoram and a few tablespoons of the stock. Cover and sweat over very low heat for 5 minutes. Boil the remaining stock and pour over the corn. Bring the corn back to a boil and remove from heat. As soon as it is cool enough to handle, purée it through the fine-mesh disk of a food mill or in a food processor; then press it through a sieve to get a fine purée.

Whip the crayfish essence and ½ cup of cream in a bowl to soft peaks.

When you are ready to serve, reheat the corn purée with the remaining cream. Check the seasoning and pour into soup plates. Spoon the shellfish cream on the center of the soup.

©*Jeremiah Tower's New American Classics*

Serves 4
Preparation Time:
  25 Minutes

  8 **ears fresh young corn**
  2 **Tbsps. butter**
  ½ **Tbsp. fresh marjoram**
    leaves
  2 **cups chicken stock**
  ¼ **cup crayfish or**
    shellfish essence
  1½ **cups heavy cream**
    Salt and freshly ground
    pepper

Jeremiah Tower
Stars
San Francisco

Spicy Southwestern Corn Chowder

Serves 6
Preparation Time:
 3 Hours

16 **ears of sweet yellow**
  corn
 2 **jalapeños**
 1 **stick or 8 Tbsps. sweet**
  butter
 1 **yellow onion, chopped**
 8 **garlic cloves, chopped**
 2 **cups Chardonnay**
 1 **qt. heavy cream**
  Juice of 2 limes
 1 **bunch cilantro leaves,**
  chopped
 1 **pt. half and half**
  Salt and white pepper

 Remove corn from ears with sharp knife. Place kernels from 11 ears in one bowl, place kernels from remaining 5 ears in separate bowl.

Roast jalapeños over open flame or grill. You want to blacken the skins, turning jalapeños often so the meat of the pepper is not charred. Once skin is blistered, put jalapeños in brown paper bag.

Over medium heat, melt butter in a soup pot or kettle. Add onions and garlic, stirring constantly to avoid burning. Add corn kernels of 11 ears and stir well. When corn has a glaze to it, add the wine and reduce by ⅔. Add heavy cream and reduce by ⅓ on low heat.

Remove soup from heat and purée in an electric mixer or food processor. Pass though a medium fine sieve and return to soup pot over low heat.

In a separate pot, cook remaining corn kernels in boiling water over high heat. Once corn is cooked, add to soup.

Remove jalapeños from bag and rinse under cold water. Remove skins and seeds and finely chop.

Add the jalapeños, lime juice and cilantro to the soup. Check the consistency. If soup is too thin, cook longer and reduce to desired consistency. If soup is too thick, dilute gradually with half and half. Salt and pepper to taste.

Scott Kirkwood
Pacifica Del Mar
Del Mar

Purée of Garlic Soup

Separate the heads of garlic into cloves, but don't bother to peel them.

Heat the olive oil in a 2 qt. pot over medium heat. Add the garlic and cook, stirring occasionally for 15 to 20 minutes or until the skins start to turn golden. Add the onion and cook until soft, another 5 minutes.

Add the stock or broth, then the lemon juice, bay leaves and thyme. Increase heat to high and bring to a boil. Lower heat to medium and simmer for 30 minutes.

Remove from heat, place contents of the pot in a food processor or blender and purée. Strain the soup through a strainer, or pass soup through a food mill.

Place garlic purée in a medium pot over medium heat. Add milk, cover and bring to a boil. Immediately reduce heat to low and simmer for 10 minutes.

Place in a soup tureen and serve piping hot.

Serves 8
Preparation Time:
  1 Hour

1 **lb. garlic, about 8 medium garlic heads**
3 **Tbsps. olive oil**
2 **medium onions, peeled, diced**
3 **cups chicken stock or canned low-sodium chicken broth**
  Juice of 1 lemon
4 **bay leaves**
4 **sprigs thyme or ½ tsp. dried thyme**
4 **cups milk**

Michael Roberts
Trumps
Hollywood

Shellfish Gazpacho

Serves 4
Preparation Time:
  25 Minutes
(note refrigeration time)

  4 **Tbsps. olive oil**
  8 **large scallops**
  8 **shrimps**
  8 **small clams (little neck**
     or Manila)
  8 **mussels**
  1 **cup white wine**
  2 **Tbsps. sherry vinegar**
  1 **small onion, chopped**
  2 **Tbsps. + 1 tsp. garlic,**
     minced
  1 **medium cucumber,**
     peeled, seeded
  2 **or more dashes Tabasco**
     sauce
  3 **cups tomato juice**
  ¼ **cup mayonnaise**
     Salt and pepper to taste
  2 **large red peppers**
  8 **rounds of French bread**

eat 2 Tbsps. olive oil in a skillet over medium heat and add scallops and shrimp. Cover and cook until shellfish are cooked, about 4 minutes. Remove from heat and refrigerate.

Add clams, mussels, white wine, vinegar, onion and 2 Tbsps. garlic to skillet. Cook over high heat until the shells open, about 5 minutes. Remove skillet from heat, remove the shells and refrigerate the clams and mussels. Transfer the remaining juices to a food processor or blender. Add the cucumber, Tabasco, 1 tsp. garlic and one cup tomato juice and blend until smooth. Add the mayonnaise and blend until incorporated. Season with salt and pepper. Pour the mixture into a bowl, add remaining tomato juice and place in the refrigerator to chill.

Roast the peppers, remove the skin and seeds and place in the refrigerator to chill.

Brush the rounds of bread with the remaining olive oil and toast them under a broiler, then set aside to cool.

To serve, arrange 2 shrimps and 2 scallops in a pepper half and place in soup bowls. Spoon gazpacho around the peppers and arrange the clams and mussels in the soup. Place the croutons on the peppers. Serve well chilled.

© *What's for Dinner*

Michael Roberts
Trumps
Hollywood

☆

Lobster Gazpacho

Combine all ingredients in a large bowl. Adjust seasonings, add chile to taste.

Let sit 4 hours to blend flavors. Correct seasonings and serve in well chilled bowls.

Serves 4
Preparation Time:
  20 Minutes
(note refrigeration time)

2 Maine lobsters, 1 lb. each, cooked, chilled, minced
1 cucumber, diced
1 yellow bell pepper, diced
1 red bell pepper, diced
½ sweet onion, diced
2 ripe tomatoes
1 small jalapeño chile, minced
3 Tbsps. balsamic vinegar
6 Tbsps. olive oil
  Salt and freshly ground pepper
  Pinch of salt
  Juice of one lemon
1 bunch cilantro

Alan Greeley
The Golden Truffle
Costa Mesa

Lobster & Coconut Milk Soup with Ginger and Garden Vegetables

Serves 4
Preparation Time:
   1¼ Hours

   5 cups fresh or canned, unsweetened coconut milk
   1 celery stalk, diced
   4 fresh lemon grass stalks, crushed
   ¾ cup ginger, peeled, finely chopped
   6 Tbsps. lemon juice
   1 Tbsp. garlic, chopped
   4 Tbsps. cilantro, finely chopped
   1 cup dry white wine
   1 live lobster, 1½ lbs.
   1 Tbsp. olive oil
   1 medium onion, sliced thin
   1 medium carrot, peeled, sliced thin
   1 small leek, julienne
   10 shiitake mushrooms, stems removed, minced
   Salt and pepper
   16 basil leaves, coarsely chopped
   2 Tbsps. chives, finely chopped
   ½ cup French green beans, blanched, cut into 1″ pieces
   1 large tomato, peeled, seeded, diced

his dish has a pretty contrast of colors and delightful taste that comes from the richness of the lobster and the coconut broth blended with all the fresh herbs and vegetables.

Pour coconut milk in a large sauce pan. Add the celery, crushed lemon grass, ginger, lemon juice, garlic, cilantro and wine. Bring to a boil and season with salt and pepper. Add the lobster and poach for 10 minutes. Remove the lobster and strain the coconut broth through a fine sieve.

When the lobster has cooled, break it in two where the tail meets the body. With scissors, cut the soft part of the tail and remove the meat in one piece. Set aside. Break off the claws and carefully crack the shells and remove the meat. Dice the lobster meat into small pieces.

Heat the olive oil in a sauce pan and add the onion, carrot, leek and shiitake mushrooms, cooking for 2 minutes. Add salt and fresh ground pepper. Pour in the strained coconut broth and bring to a boil. Then lower the heat to barely simmering and continue cooking for 3 to 5 minutes.

Add the basil, chives, blanched green beans, tomato and lobster meat to the vegetables and broth and bring to a boil over high heat. Stir slightly. Taste and adjust with salt and pepper if necessary. Gently transfer in a serving tureen and serve at once.

Trade Secret: I have found the canned version of coconut milk quite acceptable and a lot less work. Look for the ones from Thailand or Malaysia. You can find them in Asian specialty markets, usually in 14 fluid ounce cans. Shake the cans well before opening.

Hubert Keller
Fleur de Lys
San Francisco

☆

Leek & Potato Soup with Thyme

In a large soup pot, sauté the leeks and celery gently with the oil until they are softened. Do not allow to brown.

Add the chicken stock, a little salt and pepper and the herbs.

Peel and slice the potatoes and add to the soup. Bring the soup to a gentle boil, then simmer until the potatoes are well cooked. Remove from the heat, then purée in a food processor fitted with a steel blade. Pass the soup through a fine strainer.

Reboil in a clean pot and correct the seasonings. I like lots of pepper in this soup.

Serve in warm bowls garnished with finely chopped fresh thyme if available.

Trade Secret: This is one of my favorite soups. I love potatoes! It's a soup which seems to evoke the very soul of the garden.

Serves 6
Preparation Time:
  45 Minutes

  1 Tbsp. olive oil or
    canola oil
  2 lbs. leeks, washed,
    sliced
  2 stalks celery, washed,
    sliced
  1½ qts. chicken stock or
    water
    Salt and pepper
  2 tsps. dried thyme
    or 1 tsp. fresh
  ½ tsp. anise seeds
  2 tsps. dried rosemary
    or 1 tsp. fresh
  3 bay leaves
  2 lbs. russet potatoes

John Downey
Downey's
Santa Barbara

Chilled Melon Soup

Serves 6
Preparation Time:
   10 Minutes

6 cups watermelon,
   seeded, puréed
3 cups watermelon,
   diced ¼″
2 cups cantaloupe,
   diced ¼″
1 bunch scallions,
   diced fine
   Juice of 3 limes
   Salt to taste
   Tabasco to taste
3 tsps. fresh mint, chopped
   fine
2 Tbsps. Midori liqueur,
   optional

lace all ingredients into a blender and purée. Serve well chilled.

William Donnelly
Chez Melange
Redondo Beach

Golden Chanterelle Mushroom Soup

In a heavy-bottomed 4 qt. sauce pot, heat ½ cup olive oil on high heat until oil begins to smoke. Add 1½ lbs. chanterelle mushrooms and white mushrooms, stirring for 5 minutes. Add celery, leeks, shallots and garlic, stirring constantly over high heat until all of the vegetable juices have evaporated and mushrooms start to brown, approximately 10–15 minutes.

Add 2½ qts. chicken stock or consommé, stir, add thyme and bay leaves. Bring to a boil, skim off any impurities that come to the top. Reduce heat to a slow boil and reduce by ⅓, approximately 60–90 minutes.

Remove from heat and cool. Remove thyme sprigs and bay leaves. In a blender or food processor, purée soup until smooth and pass through strainer. Season with salt and fresh pepper.

To serve, sauté remaining ¼ lb. chanterelles in 1 Tbsp. olive oil until golden brown. Place mushrooms on the bottom of each bowl and ladle hot soup over them. Top with celery leaves.

Trade Secret: If soup is too thin, put back on stove and reduce. If puréed soup is too thick, use chicken stock to thin. This soup can be prepared 2–3 days in advance.

Serves 6
Preparation Time:
  2 Hours

½ cup olive oil, plus
  1 Tbsp.
1¾ lbs. golden chanterelle
  mushrooms, chopped
½ lb. white mushrooms,
  chopped
3 qts. strong chicken
  stock or strong
  consommé
2 large ribs celery,
  chopped
2 medium leeks,
  chopped
½ cup shallots, thinly
  sliced
4 large garlic cloves,
  thinly sliced
3 sprigs fresh thyme
  or 1 tsp. dried thyme
2 bay leaves
  Salt and pepper
  to taste
  Inner leaves of one
  bunch of celery,
  chopped

Brian Whitmer
Pacific's Edge, Highlands Inn
Carmel

★

Pea and Lettuce Soup

Serves 4
Preparation Time:
  25 Minutes

  2 **Tbsps. unsalted butter**
  1 **cup yellow onion,**
     diced
  4 **cups shelled peas**
2½ **cups chicken stock**
  3 **tightly-packed cups**
     lettuce, julienne
     Salt and pepper
     to taste
     Pinch of sugar,
     optional

elt the butter in a medium-size saucepan over moderate heat. Add the onions and cook for about 8–10 minutes, until tender and translucent. Add the peas and 2 cups of the stock, bring to a full boil. Lower heat and simmer for 5 minutes or until the peas are tender. Add the lettuce and cook for 2 minutes until the lettuce is wilted.

Purée the soup in a blender or food processor. Thin with the remaining stock to the desired consistency.

Season the soup to taste with salt and pepper. If the peas are a bit starchy, add a pinch of sugar for balance.

Trade Secret: For the lettuce you may use romaine, butter or an assortment of greens. You do not need much stock. As the lettuce cooks, it gives off quite a bit of liquid. For a garnish you might try a mint cream or a lemon cream and diced prosciutto or fried bread croutons.

Joyce Goldstein
Square One Restaurant
San Francisco

Pimiento Soup with Fried Polenta

In a pot, bring 3 cups water to a rolling boil over high heat, add the salt and whisk in the cornmeal, little by little. Reduce the heat and stir so that the polenta does not stick. Cook for another 4 minutes, stirring often, until the consistency is stiff and somewhat dry. Immediately transfer the polenta to a 10″ × 8″ oiled baking dish. Let the polenta stand for 5 minutes, then cover the dish and refrigerate for 1 hour or until very firm.

Grill the pimientos whole, until their skins blister and char very slightly. Transfer to a plastic bag or a container with a tight-fitting lid and let steam for 20 minutes. Remove the pimientos and peel away the charred skin. Do not rinse under water. Cut the pimientos in half and remove the seeds and stems.

Melt the butter in a 6 qt. pot and cook the onions for 10 minutes. Add the pimientos and the water and stew together for 10 minutes, uncovered. Add the stock, bring to a boil and reduce the heat. Simmer for 20 minutes.

Remove the polenta from the refrigerator. Invert the baking dish onto a cutting board and cut the polenta into short sticks, approximately ½″ wide and 2″ long. Heat oil in a 10″ cast-iron skillet and carefully add the polenta sticks to the hot oil to deep-fry them. Let the sticks brown evenly. When the polenta has turned a rich brown all over, remove it from the oil and let it drain on a towel-lined plate. Let cool slightly, then separate the sticks.

Transfer the soup in batches to a blender and purée for 2 minutes. Pass through a medium-fine sieve into another pot. Season to taste with salt, pepper and a little balsamic vinegar.

Serve the soup in warm bowls and garnish each bowl with several polenta sticks.

©Chez Panisse Cooking

Serves 8
Preparation Time:
  One Hour
(note refrigeration time)

  4 cups water
¼ tsp. salt
  1 cup coarse cornmeal
  2 lbs. pimientos
  3 Tbsps. unsalted butter
  2 yellow onions, diced
  4 cups chicken broth
    Salt and pepper
  3 cups neutral flavored oil
    (peanut or vegetable)
    Balsamic vinegar

Alice Waters
Chez Panisse
Berkeley

Pumpkin Soup
with Bleu Cheese Cream & Chives

Serves 8
Preparation Time:
  45 Minutes

2 cups pumpkin, fresh
  or canned
1 yellow onion, sliced
2 Tbsps. butter
3 cups chicken stock
  Salt and pepper to taste
  Nutmeg to taste
  Sugar to taste, optional
  Bleu cheese, garnish
  Chives, garnish

I f using fresh pumpkin, cut pumpkin in half width-wise and remove seeds. Place on a cookie sheet, cut side down, and bake at 325° for 30 minutes or until soft. Cool and spoon out pumpkin meat.

In a 2 qt. pot, sauté onions in butter until soft and lightly browned. Add pumpkin and chicken stock to the onion and bring to a boil, stirring constantly for 5 minutes.

Purée in a blender until smooth. Adjust seasonings by adding stock if needed. Season to taste with salt, pepper, nutmeg and sugar.

Serve warm, garnished with bleu cheese and chives.

Todd Muir
Madrona Manor
St. Helena

Seafood Caldo

Rinse the seafood in cold water, drain and place in a pot. Add the water. Over medium heat, bring the pot to simmer. Continue to simmer until the mussels open, then add the tomatoes, onion, jicama, carrots and chile. Bring the pot to a simmer again, then finish the soup by adding the cilantro and lime juice. Season with salt and pepper to taste.

Serve immediately—the vegetables should be crisp and fresh, not overcooked.

Serves 4
Preparation Time:
  15 Minutes

1 **cup scallops**
1 **cup rock shrimp**
2 **filets snapper or rock cod, 8 oz. each, cut in cubes**
8 **mussels in their shells, cleaned**
4 **cups water**
1 **cup tomatoes, diced**
¼ **cup red onion, diced**
¼ **cup jicama, diced**
¼ **cup carrots, julienne**
1 **serrano chile, minced fine**
2 **Tbsps. cilantro, chopped**
  Juice of 1 lime
  Salt and pepper to taste

Julio Ramirez
The Fishwife, El Cocodrilo
Pacific Grove

⭐

Seafood Gumbo

Serves 4
Preparation Time:
  40 Minutes

½ onion, sliced thin
1 leek, sliced thin
1 green bell pepper,
  diced
½ red bell pepper, diced
½ yellow bell pepper,
  diced
1 stalk celery, sliced thin
1 tsp. garlic, minced
2 tsps. thyme, chopped
  fine
1½ cups ham, diced
  Olive oil
½ cup wine
2 tomatoes, diced
2 qts. clam broth
½ tsp. black pepper
½ tsp. crushed red chiles
1 tsp. salt
  Tabasco to taste
¼ lb. bay shrimp
½ lb. bass or other firm
  fish, cubed
¼ lb. dungeness crab legs,
  shelled
1 Tbsp. brown roux or
  cornstarch
2 Tbsps. gumbo file

In a large soup pot over medium heat, sauté the onion, leek, peppers, celery, garlic, thyme and ham in oil.

When vegetables are soft, add the wine, tomatoes, clam broth, black pepper, chiles, salt and Tabasco.

Bring to a boil and add the shrimp, bass and crab.

Simmer and thicken with either a brown roux or dissolve cornstarch into soup.

Remove from heat and add gumbo file. Serve immediately.

William Donnelly
Chez Melange
Redondo Beach

Spinach and Mint Soup

Bring the chicken stock to a boil. Reduce the heat slightly and add the spinach. Cook for about 30 seconds, then add the mint, lemon juice to taste, tofu and garbanzo beans. Season to taste with salt and pepper.

Pour soup into individual bowls and garnish with lemon slices.

© *The Morning Food Cookbook*

Serves 4
Preparation Time:
  10 Minutes

4 cups chicken stock
4 cups fresh spinach, cleaned
6 tsps. fresh mint, chopped
  Lemon juice to taste
1 cube tofu, cut into squares
½ cup cooked garbanzo beans
  Salt and pepper to taste
4 lemon slices

Margaret Fox
Cafe Beaujolais
Mendocino

Butternut Squash & Leek Soup
with Gruyere Cheese & Thyme

Serves 6
Preparation Time:
   One Hour

 2 **Tbsps. butter**
   White of 2 medium
   leeks, sliced
 4 **garlic cloves, minced**
   Salt to taste
½ **tsp. dried thyme**
½ **cup white wine**
 2 **medium butternut**
   squash or any winter
   squash
   Black or white pepper
   Vegetable soup stock
   (recipe follows)
¼ **lb. Gruyere cheese,**
   grated
 1 **small bunch fresh**
   thyme, chopped

elt the butter in a thick-bottomed soup pot. Add the leeks, garlic, salt and thyme. Cook the leeks until tender. Add the wine and cook until the wine has reduced.

Peel, seed and cut the squash into small cubes, approximately 4 cups. Add the cubed squash to the soup and cover with the stock. Cook over medium heat until the squash takes on a rather smooth consistency. Thin the soup with more stock if necessary to desired consistency. Season to taste with salt and pepper. Sprinkle with grated Gruyere cheese and chopped fresh thyme.

Annie Somerville
Greens
San Francisco

Vegetable Soup Stock

Combine all ingredients in a large pot. Cover with cold water and cook over moderate heat until the stock begins to boil. Turn down the heat and simmer for 30 minutes. Strain stock and discard cooked vegetables.

Yield: 5 cups
Preparation Time:
  45 Minutes

  Tops of 2 medium leeks, chopped
1 carrot, peeled, chopped
1 medium potato, chopped
2 celery stalks, chopped
2 bay leaves
1 Tbsp. fresh marjoram
1 Tbsp. fresh oregano
1 Tbsp. fresh thyme
1 Tbsp. fresh parsley
4 garlic cloves
2 black peppercorns
  Pinch of salt
5 cups cold water

Annie Somerville
Greens
San Francisco

Sweet Mama Squash Soup

Serves 6
Preparation Time:
2 Hours
Pre-heat oven to 400°

3 lbs. hard-skinned yellow squash, "Sweet Mama" our favorite
3 Tbsps. fresh ginger, finely julienne
½ cup and 1 Tbsp. corn or peanut oil
1 small yellow onion, sliced thin
1 Tbsp. fresh ginger, finely minced
1½ tsps. garlic, finely minced
1 thumbnail-size piece cassia or cinnamon bark
1 whole star anise, broken into 8 points
10 cups unsalted chicken or vegetable stock
    Kosher salt, sugar and freshly ground pepper to taste
¼ cup almonds, sliced and toasted
    Fresh whole coriander leaves

Cut squash in half, discard seeds and place cut-side down on a foil-lined baking sheet. Bake until very soft, about 50–60 minutes. Cool and discard peel. Cut squash into chunks.

Fry the julienne ginger threads until golden in oil and drain. Set aside.

In a large non-aluminum stock pot, heat 1 Tbsp. oil over moderate heat, adding the onions, ginger, garlic, cassia and star anise, tossing well to combine. Reduce the heat and cover the pot to "sweat" the onions until very soft and juicy, about 15 minutes. Add squash and stock, bringing soup to a near-boil, stirring occasionally. Discard cassia and anise and purée soup in batches in a blender or food processor.

Before serving, bring the soup slowly to a near-boil over moderate heat. Adjust the tastes with kosher salt, sugar and pepper. Garnish with a hill of ginger threads, a sprinkling of almonds and few strategically placed coriander leaves.

Trade Secret: Leftovers keep beautifully for 3–4 days, refrigerated.

©*The China Moon Cookbook*

Barbara Tropp
China Moon
San Francisco

☆

Tomato Bisque

In a large pot, sauté onions in 6 Tbsps. butter along with dill seed, dill weed and oregano for 5 minutes or until onions are translucent. Add tomatoes and chicken stock.

Make a roux by blending 2 Tbsps. butter and 2 Tbsps. flour, whisking constantly over medium heat for 3 minutes without browning. Add roux to stock and whisk to blend. Add salt and pepper. Bring to a boil, stirring occasionally.

Reduce heat and simmer for 15 minutes. Add chopped parsley, honey, cream and half and half. Remove from heat and purée. Strain.

Serve warm with a dollop of sour cream.

Trade Secret: This is the epitome of a comforting soup. It's creamy and rich and nourishing. Even though I am such a fan of fresh tomatoes, this is the one dish that I think may work even better with canned tomatoes.

©*Cafe Beaujolais*

Serves 4
Preparation Time:
   30 Minutes

   ½ **cup chopped onions**
   ½ **cup unsalted butter**
   1 **tsp. dill seed**
   1½ **tsps. dill weed**
   1½ **tsps. oregano**
   5 **cups canned crushed**
      whole tomatoes
   4 **cups chicken stock**
   2 **Tbsps. flour**
   2 **tsps. salt**
   ½ **tsp. white pepper**
   ¼ **cup parsley, chopped**
   4 **tsps. honey**
   1¼ **cups heavy cream**
   ⅔ **cup half and half**
      Sour cream

Margaret Fox
Cafe Beaujolais
Mendocino

Apple, pear & arugula

Warm cabbage salad

Chinese chicken salad

Southern fried chicken salad

Smoked chicken salad

Duck salad with artichokes

Goose breast with orange,
beets & greens

Greek prawn salad

Greens in honey mustard vinaigrette

Baby lettuce with baked
goat cheese dressing

Lebanese toasted pita bread salad

Lobster ratatouille salad

Warm lobster salad, citrus vinaigrette

Wild mushroom salad with pancetta

Fried oyster & green bean salad,
horseradish salsa

Warm salad with pancetta

Pancetta-wrapped onions with greens

Pasta salad with smoked trout

Pear & walnut salad

Prawns, radicchio, endive,
balsamic vinegar

Smoked salmon rolls
with horseradish cream

Warm scallop, lemon coriander
vinaigrette

Shrimp in an orange vinaigrette

Shrimp and mozzarella
in lemon vinaigrette

Caribbean cole slaw

Crunchy cabbage slaw

Wilted spinach salad

Grilled tuna and red onion

Waldorf salad, bleu cheese,
Dijon vinaigrette

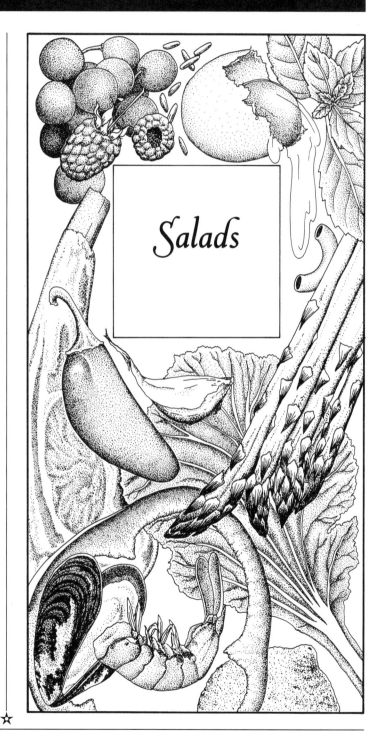

Salads

Apple, Pear & Arugula Salad with Balsamic Vinaigrette

Remove stems, wash and dry arugula. Place in bowl with apples, pears and nuts.

Prepare the balsamic vinaigrette by combining the shallot, garlic, balsamic vinegar, olive oil, salt, pepper and lemon juice. Whisk vigorously until blended.

Toss the salad with the vinaigrette and place on 4 chilled plates. Crumble Gorgonzola on each.

Serves 4
Preparation Time:
  15 Minutes

4 bunches arugula
2 apples, sliced
2 pears, sliced
¼ cup walnuts, toasted
1 shallot, minced
1 garlic clove, minced
⅓ cup balsamic vinegar
½ cup olive oil
  Salt and pepper to taste
1 tsp. lemon juice
¼ lb. Gorgonzola cheese

Michael Flynn
Grille at Sonoma Mission Inn
Boyes Hot Springs

Warm Cabbage Salad with Duck Fat

Serves 4
Preparation Time:
  20 Minutes
Pre-heat oven to 350°

1 **red cabbage**
8 **slices bacon or pancetta**
8 **slices white bread,**
  preferably baguette or
  country bread
½ **cup walnut halves**
1 **garlic clove, peeled,**
  cut in half
2 **Tbsps. red wine vinegar**
  or fresh lemon juice
  Salt and freshly ground
  pepper
¼ **cup rendered duck fat**
4 **one-ounce round fresh**
  white goat cheeses
1 **Tbsp. fresh parsley,**
  chopped

ut the cabbage in half through the root end. Cut out the core from each half. Turn the halves cut side down and slice crosswise into ⅛″ pieces.

Lay the bacon out flat on a rack and bake or grill until crisp. When cool enough to handle, cut into 1″ lengths. Keep warm.

Bake the bread crouton slices and walnuts on a sheet pan for 10 minutes. When the bread is cool enough to handle, rub with the garlic. Keep the croutons warm and let the walnuts cool.

Put the cabbage in a bowl. Add the vinegar or lemon juice and the salt and pepper and toss the cabbage thoroughly.

Heat the duck fat in a pan and put the cabbage in it. Toss quickly but thoroughly for 30 seconds. Add the bacon and walnuts and toss again for 1 minute.

Serve immediately on warm plates. Put the cheese in the center of the cabbage, sprinkle with the parsley and put the croutons on the plate.

©*Jeremiah Tower's New American Classics*

Jeremiah Tower
Stars
San Francisco

Chinese Chicken Salad

Combine the rice vinegar, salad oil, sesame oil, sugar, black pepper and ¼ cup soy sauce to make the salad dressing. This will make enough dressing for 12–15 salads. The leftovers can be stored in the refrigerator indefinitely. Mix well before each use.

Rub a whole chicken with soy sauce liberally. Roast at 350° for about 1 hour or until done. When cool, remove the meat from the bones. Remove the fat and skin. Tear the chicken meat into bite-sized pieces.

Heat 6″ of peanut oil in a pot that is at least 12″ deep, to 350°. Break up the Mai-Fun noodles and cook them in the oil in small batches. They will instantly expand to 4 or 5 times their volume when they hit the hot oil. Remove them from the oil while they are still snow white, not allowing them to brown and toughen. Drain on paper towels.

Julienne the lettuce into pieces ⅛″ to ¼″ thick.

Cut the ginger into thin slices then julienne into hair-like slivers.

Toss the chicken and lettuce together in a large bowl and add enough dressing to coat the salad but not drown it. Add the rice noodles and toss again gently.

To serve, arrange the salad on a chilled plate, garnish with ginger and green onion.

Serves 4
Preparation Time:
   1½ Hours

1 **cup Marakun brand rice vinegar**
1 **cup salad oil**
1 **Tbsp. + 2 tsps. roasted sesame oil**
½ **cup sugar**
1 **tsp. coarse ground black pepper**
¾ **cup soy sauce**
1 **whole chicken Peanut oil**
½ **package Mai-Fun noodles (rice sticks)**
1 **head iceberg lettuce Pickled red ginger and green onion, chopped to garnish**

Russell Armstrong
Trees
Corona del Mar

Southern Fried Chicken Salad with Ranch Dressing

Serves 4
Preparation Time:
 30 Minutes

 3 **cups buttermilk**
¾ **cup mayonnaise**
¼ **cup sour cream**
 1 **small onion, diced fine**
 2 **medium garlic cloves,**
     diced fine
 1 **tsp. thyme**
     Salt and fresh ground
     pepper
 1 **cup all-purpose flour**
½ **tsp. cayenne**
½ **tsp. black pepper**
½ **tsp. Coleman's dry**
     mustard
½ **tsp. granulated garlic**
 2 **chicken breasts,**
     cut into cubes
 1 **head green leaf lettuce**
 1 **head red leaf lettuce**
½ **lb. baby mixed greens**
¾ **cup fresh sweet**
     yellow corn
½ **cup pecans**
 3 **cups peanut oil**
     for frying

repare the ranch dressing by combining 1 cup buttermilk with the mayonnaise, sour cream, onion, garlic, thyme and salt and pepper to taste. This makes 2 cups dressing. Refrigerate.

Prepare the spicy flour mix in a large mixing bowl by combining the flour, cayenne, black pepper, dry mustard and granulated garlic.

Mix together the chicken and 2 cups buttermilk until chicken is well coated. Dredge in spicy flour mixture and fry in hot peanut oil. Remove chicken from heat and drain on paper towels.

Wash the lettuces and tear into bite-sized pieces. Strip the corn kernels from ears and steam corn for 2 minutes, then cool.

In a salad bowl, mix together the lettuces, corn, pecans and fried chicken. Toss with the ranch dressing.

William Donnelly
Chez Melange
Redondo Beach

Smoked Chicken Salad

Prepare the vinaigrette dressing by whisking together the mustard, garlic, vinegar and almond oil to form a light emulsion. Season to taste with salt and pepper. Set aside.

Blanch the asparagus spears in salted boiling water. Remove when al dente. Finely chop the asparagus.

Sauté the shiitake mushrooms in butter. Add a pinch of salt. Cook until tender.

Remove the skin from the cooked chicken meat and shred into small pieces. Combine the chicken meat, pine nuts, asparagus and mushrooms in a sauté pan with the vinaigrette dressing. Cook until the ingredients are hot.

Place 5 spinach leaves on each plate. Mold each salad into a 6 oz. tea cup. Invert onto the spinach. Remove the cup and sprinkle remaining dressing on spinach leaves.

Serves 8
Preparation Time:
  20 Minutes

  1 tsp. Dijon mustard
  1 tsp. garlic, chopped
  2 Tbsps. sherry vinegar
  ½ cup almond oil
    Salt and pepper to taste
  8 asparagus spears
  ½ lb. shiitake mushrooms, sliced
  2 Tbsps. butter, clarified
  1 four-pound chicken, smoked
  2 Tbsps. pine nuts, lightly toasted
40 spinach leaves

John McLaughlin
JW's Restaurant
Anaheim

Duck Salad with Artichokes & Mixed Greens

Serves 8
Preparation Time:
45 Minutes

2 artichokes
1 lemon
2 duck breasts
2 Tbsps. olive oil
   Assorted lettuce:
   green leaf, red leaf, etc.
¼ cup walnut oil
½ Tbsp. balsamic vinegar
½ Tbsp. lemon juice
   White pepper
   Chives, chopped
   Chervil, chopped

lean artichokes and poach in lemon water until cooked. Cut out the heart of the artichoke and slice. Set aside.

Sauté duck breasts in olive oil and cook to medium rare. Slice duck breasts and set aside.

Prepare vinaigrette by mixing walnut oil, vinegar and lemon juice together. Season with white pepper.

Toss salad with vinaigrette and arrange duck and artichoke slices around the salad. Sprinkle with chives and chervil before serving.

Fred Halpert
Brava Terrace
St. Helena

Apple-Smoked Goose Breast with Orange, Beets & Greens

Prepare the vinaigrette by whisking the olive oil and balsamic vinegar together. Add the orange juice, thyme salt and pepper. Set aside.

Place the goose breast in a sauté pan over low heat and begin to render fat off the breast. The skin will turn a blackish color. When desired amount of fat is rendered, portion the breast into 4 pieces. Wrap in plastic and put in freezer for 4 hours. When the goose breast is firm, remove it from the freezer and slice as thin as possible. Five pieces per serving is fine.

Trim the tops off the beets and place in a sauce pan, cover with water. Bring to a simmer and cook until tender, about 30–40 minutes. Cool the beets under cold water and remove skin. Cut each beet into 6 pieces and toss in vinaigrette.

Remove skin from oranges and cut each orange into 5 round slices. Arrange oranges and beets onto plate. Fan the sliced goose breast around the oranges and beets. Toss the greens with desired amount of vinaigrette, bleu cheese, salt and pepper. Place on top of the beets and oranges. Enjoy!

Serves 5
Preparation Time:
  1 Hour
(note refrigeration time)

  1 **cup olive oil**
  ¼ **cup balsamic vinegar**
   Juice of 3 oranges
  1 **tsp. thyme, chopped**
   Salt and pepper
  1 **Hobb's apple-smoked**
   goose breast
  3 **large gold or red beets**
  6 **oranges**
  ¼ **lb. mixed baby lettuces**
  ½ **cup crumbled bleu**
   cheese

Cory Schreiber
Cypress Club
San Francisco

Greek Prawn Salad

Serves 4
Preparation Time:
  15 Minutes

16 large shrimp, deveined
 2 cups baby lettuces
    Oil and vinegar to taste
 4 Roma tomatoes,
    quartered
 1 red onion, sliced
    ⅛" thick
 2 red bell peppers, sliced
    ⅛" thick
 1 red bell pepper, sliced
    ⅛" thick
16 broccoli flowerettes
 2 cucumbers, sliced
    ¼" thick
 1 cup Kalamata olives
 1 Tbsp. garlic, minced
 2 Tbsps. oregano,
    chopped
 1 Tbsp. fresh thyme,
    chopped
⅔ cup extra virgin olive oil
⅓ cup red wine vinegar
    Salt and black pepper
    to taste
 1 cup cooked rice
½ cup ricotta cheese
¼ cup sun-dried tomatoes
 1 cup feta cheese

 lean and steam shrimp until bright pink in color. Rinse in cold water and set aside.

Clean and tear baby lettuces into bite-sized pieces. Toss with oil and vinegar. Set aside.

Mix together the Roma tomatoes, red onion, bell peppers, broccoli, cucumber, olives, garlic, oregano and thyme with the olive oil and vinegar. Season with salt and pepper.

Mix together the rice, ricotta cheese and sun-dried tomatoes.

To serve, place baby lettuce in center of plate and top with the fresh vegetables. Arrange the rice mixture around the rim of plate. Top salad with shrimp and sprinkle with feta cheese.

William Donnelly
Chez Melange
Redondo Beach

★

Mixed Greens with Roasted Pecans and Honey Mustard Vinaigrette

I n a quart jar or bottle, mix the vinegar and mustard, shake well. Add the salt and shake. Add the honey and continue to shake. Add the oil and water and shake until blended. Refrigerate.

On each of four individual plates, arrange a handful of chilled mixed greens. Top each salad with roasted pecans. Dress each salad with the honey mustard vinaigrette.

Serves 4
Preparation Time:
  15 Minutes

¾ cup red wine vinegar
 4 Tbsps. Dijon country-
    style mustard
    Salt to taste
 1 Tbsp. honey
 1 cup peanut oil
 2 Tbsps. water
    Chilled mixed greens
¾ cup roasted pecans

Julio Ramirez
The Fishwife, El Cocodrilo
Pacific Grove
★

85

Baby Lettuce Salad
with Baked Goat Cheese Herb Dressing

Serves 8
Preparation Time:
  20 Minutes
Pre-heat oven to 350°

- 1 lb. goat cheese
- 1 cup bread crumbs
- 1 cup olive oil
- ¼ cup balsamic vinegar
- ½ Tbsp. marjoram, chopped
- ½ Tbsp. sage, chopped
- ½ Tbsp. thyme, chopped
- 8 cups baby lettuce, mixed variety
- 1 red pepper, roasted, julienne
- 1 yellow pepper, roasted, julienne
- Croutons

 oll the goat cheese in bread crumbs. Bake for 10 minutes in 350° oven.

Meanwhile, prepare the herb dressing by combining the olive oil, balsamic vinegar and herbs.

Toss lettuce with the herb dressing. Place the warm goat cheese on top of the lettuce. Garnish with strips of red and yellow peppers and croutons.

Todd Muir
Madrona Manor
Healdsburg

Fattoush–Lebanese Toasted Pita Bread Salad with Citrus Vinaigrette

T o prepare the citrus vinaigrette, blend the olive oil, lemon juice and salt and pepper. Set aside.

Toast the pita bread until it is semi-crisp. Then break it up into 2″ pieces. Do not crumble.

The tomato or cucumber do not need to be peeled. Remove the seeds if cucumber is very seedy.

Toss the romaine with vinaigrette and place it on the salad plate. Toss the diced vegetables, mint, parsley and pita pieces with vinaigrette and mound this mixture on top of the romaine. This may become your favorite summer salad!

Serves 4
Preparation Time:
  15 Minutes

½ **cup olive oil**
 3 **Tbsps. lemon juice**
   Salt and pepper
 4 **whole round pieces of**
   pita bread
 2 **cups tomato, diced**
 2 **cups cucumber, diced**
½ **cup red onion,**
   chopped fine
½ **cup green onions,**
   chopped fine
 2 **Tbsps. mint, chopped**
 2 **Tbsps. parsley, chopped**
 4 **cups romaine lettuce,**
   julienne, loosely packed
   Salt and pepper to taste

Joyce Goldstein
Square One Restaurant
San Francisco

★

Lobster Ratatouille Salad

Serves 6
Preparation Time:
  45 Minutes

3 live lobsters, 1¼ lbs.
  each
  Sprigs of dill or chervil
1 small onion, diced
1 Tbsp. + 1 tsp. garlic
1 medium zucchini, diced
1 small eggplant, diced
2 red bell peppers,
  roasted, peeled, diced
  Olive oil
20 fresh basil leaves,
  chopped
1 tsp. Dijon mustard
1 tsp. shallots, chopped
¾ cup hazelnut oil or extra
  virgin olive oil
3 Tbsps. sherry vinegar
1 Tbsp. lemon juice
3 ripe avocados, halved,
  skinned
3 artichoke bottoms,
  cooked, cut in wedges

 ook the lobsters in boiling, salted water. When the lobsters cool, remove the shell. Set aside.

Prepare the ratatouille by sautéing the onion, 1 Tbsp. garlic, zucchini, eggplant and bell peppers in olive oil. Add the basil leaves, salt and pepper to taste. Set aside.

For the dressing, thoroughly mix the mustard, shallots, ½ tsp. chopped garlic, hazelnut oil, sherry vinegar and lemon juice in a blender or food processor.

To serve, place half an avocado on individual plates. Top avocado with ratatouille, lobster meat and artichokes. Drizzle with dressing.

John McLaughlin
JW's Restaurant
Anaheim

Warm Lobster Salad with Citrus Vinaigrette

T o make the vinaigrette, reduce each juice for one minute individually (reduce lemon and lime together.) Combine juices in a mixing bowl and whisk in the vinegar, olive oil, port and truffle juice. Add salt, white pepper and sugar to taste. Sugar is to soften the acidity of the citrus juices and not to sweeten.

Tie the lobster tail to a wooden stick in order to keep the tail straight after cooking. Poach lobster for 2 minutes in boiling water. Remove lobster from water and allow to cool for 2 minutes. Remove from shell carefully so pieces are not broken. Cut tail meat into ¼″ medallions, holding them together to retain tail shape. Boil the artichokes in the vegetable consommé with juniper berries and thyme. Peel artichoke leaves and slice.

Create a bed of salad for the lobster-shaped presentation. For the head, place the mache leaves in a semi-circle at the top of the plate and on top another semi-circle of red oak lettuce topped with the curly endive. In the center of the plate the slices of artichokes will be a bed for the medallions. Fan out the Belgian endive at the bottom of the plate to create the tail.

Put lobster meat in a sauté pan with some of the dressing, heat and place medallions on the bed of lettuce to make the shape of the lobster. Place the claws on either side of the head section of the salad. Spoon warm salad dressing over entire salad. Garnish with chervil leaves, pink peppercorns and lobster caviar.

Serves 6
Preparation Time:
  45 Minutes

⅛ **cup orange juice**
⅛ **cup lemon juice**
⅛ **cup lime juice**
⅛ **cup pineapple juice**
⅛ **cup sherry vinegar**
2 **cups extra virgin**
  olive oil
  Touch of port
1 **oz. truffle juice**
  Salt and white pepper
1 **tsp. sugar**
8 **Maine lobsters,**
  1 lb. each
3 **artichoke bottoms**
1 **qt. vegetable consommé**
3 **juniper berries**
  Thyme
1 **bunch mache lettuce**
1 **head red oak leaf lettuce**
1 **head curly endive**
1 **head Belgian endive**
  Chervil leaves for
  garnish
8 **pink peppercorns per**
  plate
  Lobster caviar

Julian Serrano
Masa's
San Francisco

Wild Mushroom Salad with Pancetta

Serves 6
Preparation Time:
  20 Minutes

  3 **bunches mache, leaves**
    trimmed
  2 **bunches arugula, leaves**
    trimmed
  2 **heads baby limestone**
    lettuce, leaves trimmed
  1 **head baby radicchio,**
    leaves trimmed
  ¼ **cup walnut oil**
  ½ **lb. each fresh**
    chanterelle, shiitake,
    oyster mushrooms,
    trimmed, cut into
    ½″ pieces
  ½ **oz. pancetta, julienne**
    strips, optional
  ¼ **cup pine nuts**
  2 **large shallots, finely**
    chopped
  2 **medium-size garlic**
    cloves, finely chopped
  ¼ **cup sherry wine vinegar**
  2 **Tbsps. each fresh basil,**
    tarragon, thyme and
    chives, minced
    Salt and fresh ground
    black pepper

Toss all the greens together in a salad bowl.

In a large sauté pan, heat 3 Tbsps. of the walnut oil over high heat until it just begins to smoke. Add the mushrooms and let them sear, without stirring, for about 30 seconds; then sauté them, stirring constantly for about 2½ minutes more, until nicely browned. Add the mushrooms to the salad bowl.

To the same pan, still over high heat, add the remaining 1 Tbsp. oil and sauté the pancetta for about 30 seconds; then add the pine nuts and sauté until golden, about 1 minute. Add the shallots and stir them quickly, then add the garlic and sauté about 30 seconds more. Add the vinegar and stir to deglaze the pan, then stir in the herbs, salt and pepper.

Pour the hot dressing into the salad bowl and toss immediately to coat all the greens. Mound the mixture on salad plates and serve immediately.

Trade Secret: You can substitute a selection of whatever salad greens are available. This is one of those combinations you have to eat the moment it hits the table to extract the maximum taste.

©*Michael's Cookbook*

Martin Garcia
Michael's
Santa Monica

Fried Oyster & Green Bean Salad with Horseradish Salsa

Prepare the horseradish salsa by combining the tomatoes, horseradish, lemon juice, olive oil, salt and pepper. Let stand for 30 minutes before serving.

Steam or cook the green beans until tender. Do not overcook. Set aside.

Bread the oysters with cornmeal. Pan fry until crunchy.

To serve, place the green beans on individual serving plates, top with salsa and fried oysters.

Serves 4
Preparation Time:
  45 Minutes

1 cup chopped ripe
  tomatoes
2 Tbsps. fresh horseradish,
  julienne
  Juice of ½ lemon
2 Tbsps. olive oil
  Salt and pepper to taste
1 lb. green beans, blue lake
  or haricot vert beans
8 oysters, shucked
1 cup cornmeal

Alan Greeley
The Golden Truffle
Costa Mesa

Warm Salad of Winter Greens with Pancetta

Serves 6
Preparation Time:
  15 Minutes

6 cups salad greens
6 thin slices pancetta
6 Tbsps. walnut oil
4 Tbsps. raspberry vinegar
2 Tbsps. honey
2 Tbsps. pine nuts, toasted
  Chrysanthemum petals,
  garnish, optional

ash greens thoroughly and tear into serving-size pieces.

Sauté pancetta in a nonstick skillet until lightly cooked, about 3 minutes, drain and keep warm.

In a large skillet, heat the walnut oil, vinegar and honey. Add greens and stir for a few seconds, until slightly wilted. Do not overcook.

Serve on warmed plates garnished with pancetta, pine nuts and chrysanthemum petals, if used.

Trade Secret: Use a combination of greens such as mustard, kale, spinach, endive and radicchio.

John Ash
John Ash & Co.
Santa Rosa

Pancetta-Wrapped Onions with Greens

In a medium bowl whisk together the balsamic and red wine vinegar, Dijon mustard, herbs and garlic until blended. Slowly whisk in the oil and bacon fat. Set vinaigrette aside.

Place onions in baking pan and drizzle with 5 Tbsps. vinaigrette, stirring to coat onions. Add water to pan and bake until onions are tender, basting occasionally with pan juices, about 45 minutes. Cool and peel onions. Cut into 4 pieces, leaving the core intact.

Increase oven to 400° Wrap each onion quarter in pancetta. Place onions on baking sheet and bake until pancetta is cooked through, about 15 minutes.

Toss greens and red bell pepper in a large bowl with remaining vinaigrette to taste. Divide greens among individual plates and top with cheese. Arrange onions around greens and serve.

Trade Secret: Serve with a wedge of grilled bread rubbed with garlic.

Serves 4
Preparation Time:
  1½ Hours
Pre-heat oven to 325°

¼ cup balsamic vinegar
3 Tbsps. red wine vinegar
1 Tbsp. Dijon mustard
1 Tbsp. each fresh basil, thyme, chopped
1 garlic clove
¾ cup olive oil
¼ cup bacon fat, melted
2 red onions, unpeeled
⅓ cup water
8 paper-thin pancetta slices or regular bacon slices
4 cups mixed greens, bite-size
¼ cup roasted red bell pepper, drained, chopped (available in jars)
16 paper-thin slices Parmesan cheese

Cory Schreiber
Cypress Club
San Francisco

Pasta Salad with Smoked Trout and Fresh Dill

Serves 4
Preparation Time:
  20 Minutes

1 cup rotelle pasta
2 Tbsps. olive oil
1 cup sweet red onion,
  sliced thin
¼ cup fresh dill, chopped,
  or 2 Tbsps. dried
¾ lb. smoked trout, boned,
  skinned, cut into
  ½″ cubes
1 cup ripe Roma
  tomatoes, seeded, cut
  into thin slivers
3 Tbsps. prepared
  horseradish
½ cup buttermilk
½ cup mayonnaise
  Salt and fresh ground
  pepper
  Drops of lemon juice
  to taste
  Arugula or watercress
  sprigs, garnish
1 Tbsp. capers, drained

ook pasta al dente and immediately plunge into cold water to stop the cooking. Drain thoroughly and toss with oil to prevent pasta from sticking.

Lightly toss pasta with remaining ingredients and correct seasonings.

Arrange on a chilled platter on arugula sprigs with capers sprinkled over the top.

John Ash
John Ash & Co.
Santa Rosa

Pear & Walnuts with Romaine Hearts, Watercress & Radicchio

P repare the walnut sherry vinaigrette by mixing together the vinegar, shallot and salt. Whisk in the oils to emulsify. Set aside.

Toast walnuts for 10 minutes, until they begin to brown. Set aside to cool.

Rinse the greens and spin dry. Toss the salad greens, pears and walnuts with the walnut-sherry vinaigrette. Sprinkle with black pepper and serve.

Serves 6
Preparation time:
  15 Minutes
Pre-heat oven to 375°

3 Tbsps. sherry vinegar
1 small shallot, minced
  Salt to taste
4 Tbsps. light olive oil
4 Tbsps. walnut oil
½ cup walnuts, chopped
2 heads romaine lettuce
1 small head radicchio
2 bunches watercress
2 ripe Comice pears, cored, sliced
  Freshly-ground black pepper

Annie Somerville
Greens
San Francisco

★

Salad of Sauté Prawns, Radicchio & Endive with Balsamic Vinegar

Serves 4
Preparation Time:
  15 Minutes

  1 **small head radicchio**
  2 **small Belgian endives**
  1 **small bunch spinach**
  4 **Tbsps. olive oil**
1¼ **lb. medium-size**
     prawns, shelled,
     deveined
     Salt and fresh ground
     pepper
  3 **Tbsps. balsamic**
     vinegar
  ⅓ **cup extra virgin**
     olive oil

Discard any bruised or wilted leaves from the radicchio. Wash the radicchio, endives and spinach leaves under cold running water and dry well with paper towels. Cut the leaves into thin strips and place in a large salad bowl.

Heat the oil in a large skillet over medium high heat. Add the prawns and cook until they are golden on both sides and opaque, 2 to 3 minutes.

With a slotted spoon, transfer the prawns to the salad bowl. Season with salt and pepper. Add the balsamic vinegar and the extra virgin olive oil and mix well. Taste and adjust the seasoning.

Arrange the salad on individual serving dishes and top the greens with the prawns.

Trade Secret: Balsamic vinegar can be found in Italian and many food markets. Keep in mind that balsamic vinegar varies in strength. The older the vinegar the more concentrated and aromatic it becomes and the less you need to use. Also, the older the vinegar, the more expensive it becomes. Substitute with good red wine vinegar if balsamic vinegar is not available.

Biba Caggiano
Biba Restaurant
Sacramento

☆

Smoked Salmon Rolls on Spinach & Radicchio with Horseradish Cream

Prepare the cucumber vinaigrette by blending together the egg, almonds, 1 tsp. shallots, cucumber skin, parsley, rice wine vinegar and both oils in a blender at high speed. The vinaigrette should be emulsified and bright green in color. Set aside.

Prepare the horseradish cream by combining the sour cream, 1 tsp. shallots, dill, horseradish and lemon juice.

In a bowl, toss the raddichio and spinach with some olive oil and balsamic vinegar to taste (3 to 1). Add salt and pepper.

Lay the smoked salmon slices flat and brush the center with horseradish cream. Use ¾ of the spinach and raddichio salad to roll into the salmon slices. The salmon rolls can be cut into 1″ slices for a sushi effect.

The remaining spinach and radicchio salad is placed in the center of the plate for color. Line the outside of the plate with cucumber vinaigrette and serve.

Serves 4
Preparation Time:
  30 Minutes

- 1 **egg**
- 1 **Tbsp. almonds, sliced**
- 2 **tsps. shallots, minced**
   Skin of one cucumber
- ½ **bunch Italian parsley**
- ¼ **cup rice wine vinegar**
- ¾ **cup hazelnut and olive oil combined**
- ½ **cup sour cream**
- 1 **Tbsp. fresh dill, chopped**
- 1 **Tbsp. horseradish**
- 1 **tsp. lemon juice**
- 5 **cups spinach, cut into fine strips**
- 1 **large head raddichio, cut into fine strips**
- 12 **slices smoked salmon**

Serge Falesitch
Delicias
Rancho Santa Fe

✮

Warm Scallop Salad with Lemon Coriander Vinaigrette

Serves Six
Preparation Time:
25 Minutes

1¼ lbs. scallops, ¼" thick
1 cup extra virgin olive oil
½ cup lemon juice
½ cup tomatoes, finely chopped
1 Tbsp. coriander seeds, roasted
Salt and pepper to taste
2 Tbsps. chives, chopped

lace scallops in a serving plate in the broiler until warm, not fully cooked. Remove from heat.

Meanwhile, prepare the vinaigrette by combining the olive oil, lemon juice, tomatoes and coriander seeds over low heat. Salt and pepper to taste.

Pour the warm vinaigrette over the scallops and return to the broiler until the scallops are cooked.

Sprinkle with chives and serve hot.

Hiroyoshi Sone
Terra Restaurant
St. Helena

Drunken Shrimp with Mizuna & Radicchio in Orange Vinaigrette

Marinate the shrimp in 1 cup orange liqueur for about 30 minutes. Refrigerate.

Prepare the orange vinaigrette by combining the lime juice, orange juice, brown sugar, ginger, green onions, red pepper, 3 Tbsps. orange liqueur, peanut oil, salt and pepper. Mix well and set aside.

Remove the shrimp from liqueur. Place liqueur in pot and bring to a boil. Meanwhile peel shrimp. Dump shrimp in boiling liqueur for 20 seconds, then remove. Cool and cut in half lengthwise.

Place mizuna around plate with papaya slices. Spread radicchio and baby garden greens in center of plate topped with shrimp. Drizzle dressing over the top and decorate with edible flowers.

Trade Secret: Flowers make a most appropriate and beautiful garnish for salads. Use your own good sense; some may tend to be too heavily scented and strong-tasting.

Serves 4
Preparation Time:
  25 Minutes
(note marinating time)

- 1 lb. large shrimp
- 1 cup + 3 Tbsps. orange liqueur
- 3 Tbsps. lime juice
- 1 cup orange juice
- 3 Tbsps. brown sugar
- 2 Tbsps. ginger, minced
- 2 Tbsps. green onions, julienne, white part only
- 2 Tbsps. red pepper, julienne
- ½ cup peanut oil
  Salt and pepper to taste
- 2 heads mizuna
- 1 ripe papaya, peeled, cut in diagonals
- ½ cup baby garden greens
- 1 head spotted red radicchio
  Edible flowers, optional

Hugo Molina
Parkway Grill
Pasadena

Salad of Marinated Shrimp, Belgian Endive, Fresh Mozzarella in Lemon Basil Vinaigrette

Serves 4
Preparation Time:
  30 Minutes
(note marinating time)

½ lb. shrimp, peeled
 1 cup extra virgin olive oil
 2 garlic cloves, minced
   Salt and pepper to taste
   Juice of 3 lemons
 1 Tbsp. Italian parsley,
   finely chopped
 1 head endive, sliced into
   strips
½ lb. fresh mozzarella
   cheese, cut into ½"
   cubes
 8 fresh basil leaves
 4 Tbsps. walnuts,
   chopped
 4 lemon quarters, garnish

lace shrimp into boiling water and cook until just pink, about 3 minutes. Remove and cool in ice water to stop cooking. Slice in half lengthwise.

Prepare the marinade by combining ¼ cup olive oil, garlic, salt, fresh ground pepper, 1 Tbsp. lemon juice and chopped parsley. Marinate shrimp for 2 hours.

Prepare the dressing by combining the juice of 2 lemons, salt and pepper in a small bowl. Slowly add ¾ cup olive oil in a thin stream, stirring constantly. Set aside.

Drain shrimp from the marinade and combine with the endive and mozzarella. Add the basil leaves and toss with the lemon vinaigrette. Sprinkle with walnut and garnish with lemon quarters.

Gianpaolo Putzu
Il Fornaio Cucina Italiana
Del Mar

Caribbean Cole Slaw

I n a large bowl, combine the cabbage, onion, green and red bell peppers and chiles with the salt and black pepper. Stir in the vinegar and sugar.

Pack the cole slaw in a lidded container for at least 8 hours before serving to allow the cabbage to "pickle."

Trade Secret: The Caribbean cole slaw will keep for a good week in the refrigerator, so it's a great make-ahead dish.

Serves 4
Preparation Time:
  10 Minutes
(note refrigeration time)

½ **head white cabbage,**
   shredded
½ **medium onion, diced**
½ **green bell pepper, diced**
½ **red bell pepper, diced**
4 **Serrano or jalapeño**
   chiles, finely chopped
   Salt and fresh ground
   black pepper
1 **cup white vinegar**
½ **Tbsp. sugar**

Julio Ramirez
The Fishwife, El Cocodrilo
Pacific Grove

Crunchy Red Cabbage Slaw

Serves 6
Preparation Time:
  15 Minutes
(note refrigeration time)

  1 lb. red cabbage
  ¾ cup pickled ginger juice
  2 Tbsps. pickled ginger,
    minced
    Sugar and kosher salt
    to taste
    Garnish of toasted black
    sesame seeds
  1 green scallion, sliced

At least 12 hours and ideally 2–3 days in advance, make the slaw. Taste the pickled ginger juice if you are using a commercial variety and adjust to your taste with sugar and salt. If you are using "China Moon Pickled Ginger," the flavors are already balanced.

Core the red cabbage and slice crosswise into fine shreds.

Combine the sliced cabbage, pickled ginger juice and pickled ginger. Press the slaw into a glass casserole dish, seal and refrigerate overnight to several days, stirring occasionally. The cabbage will turn a hot pink.

Before serving, garnish with toasted black sesame seeds and green scallion rings.

Trade Secret: The slaw stays delicious for a week or more.

© The China Moon Cookbook

Barbara Tropp
China Moon Cafe
San Francisco

Wilted Spinach Salad

Place garlic, mustard and vinegar in food processor or blender and process until garlic is completely chopped. With the processor running, slowly drizzle in oil continuously until dressing is completely emulsified.

Serve dressing either hot or cold, using ¼ cup of dressing per serving.

Coat spinach leaves completely before serving.

Serves 6
Preparation Time:
10 Minutes

12 garlic cloves, peeled
1½ Tbsps. Dijon mustard
1 cup sherry vinegar
3 cups olive or peanut oil
2 bunches fresh spinach, cleaned, stemmed

David Beckwith
Central 159 Restaurant & Catering
Pacific Grove

Grilled Tuna and Red Onion Salad

Serves 4
Preparation Time:
30 Minutes
(note marinating time)

  1 **large red onion**
1½ **qts. water**
  2 **Tbsps. balsamic**
    vinegar
  4 **Tbsps. extra virgin**
    olive oil
  2 **tsps. salt**
 ¼ **tsp. freshly ground**
    black pepper
12 **oz. fresh tuna, cut into**
    1″ thick slices
    Juice of 1 small lemon
  2 **Tbsps. fresh Italian**
    parsley, chopped

repare a small charcoal fire. While it is burning, prepare the onion. Peel it and cut it in half lengthwise (from root to stem). Cut each half into 8 segments. Separate the layers of each segment.

Bring the water to a boil with 1½ tsps. salt, add the onions and parboil them for 2 minutes. Drain in a colander. Transfer the onions to a bowl. While still hot, dress them with the vinegar, 2 Tbsps. olive oil, ¼ tsp. salt and the pepper.

Lightly oil and salt and pepper the tuna on both sides. Grill tuna to medium-rare, about 2 minutes on each side. Let it cool and break it up into chunks by hand. Season the tuna with ¼ tsp. salt, the lemon juice, and the remaining parsley, and let them marinate together for 1 hour. Add tuna to the red onions and serve at room temperature.

©*Chez Panisse Cooking*

Alice Waters
Chez Panisse
Berkeley

Waldorf Salad with Bleu Cheese in Dijon Vinaigrette

Prepare the Dijon vinaigrette by blending the mustard, vinegar, shallots, salt and pepper slowly in a large bowl. Whisk in the olive oil, until emulsified. Serve at room temperature. Refrigerate between uses.

Combine the greens and dress with half the Dijon vinaigrette. Arrange on a plate.

Combine apples, walnuts and celery. Dress with Dijon vinaigrette and place on bed of greens in the center. Top with a dollop of mayonnaise and sprinkle with parsley and Roquefort crumbles.

Trade Secret: Do not overdress the greens or apple celery mixture.

Serves 4
Preparation Time:
  15 Minutes

  ½ cup Dijon mustard
  1 cup champagne
    vinegar
  4 Tbsps. shallots
  1½ tsps. sea salt
  ¾ tsp. white pepper
  3 cups olive oil
  ¾ cup chicory
  ¾ cup arugula
  ¾ cup butter lettuce
  4 Granny Smith apples,
    chopped
  1 cup walnuts, chopped
  1 celery stalk, minced
  ½ cup mayonnaise
  ½ bunch parsley, minced
  ⅓ cup Roquefort cheese,
    crumbled

Cindy Pawlcyn
Bistro Roti, Bix, Buckeye Roadhouse, Fog City Diner,
Mustards Grill, Tra Vigne
San Francisco, Marin, Napa

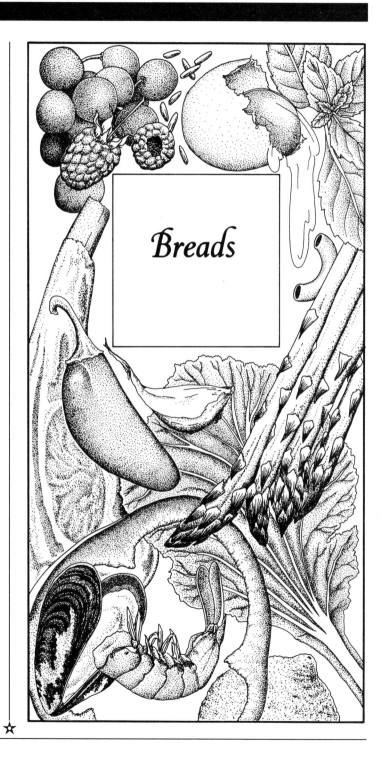

Breads

Tuscan Bread

Stir yeast into ¼ cup warm water, let stand until creamy. Add remaining water and Biga to the yeast mixture. Add flour and salt, mixing until the dough binds well. Knead dough well, making sure to use enough flour to prevent sticking. Place dough in a lightly oiled bowl, cover and let rise until tripled in bulk, about 3 hours. Do not punch down.

To shape loaves, use a generous amount of flour on work surface and hands to prevent sticking. Dust dough with flour and cut in half. Flatten dough out and tightly roll lengthwise into a log shape. Flatten out the log and roll tightly from top to bottom. Shape each piece into a ball by slowly stretching top layer from top to bottom (seamside). Place loaves on baking sheet covered with baking parchment paper, seamside down. Cover with a damp towel and let rise until doubled in bulk, about one hour.

Pre-heat oven to 450° Bake until a deep golden brown and hollow sounding when tapped on the bottom, about 40 minutes.

Yield: 2 large loaves
Preparation Time:
  4 Hours

1¼ tsp. active dry yeast
¼ cup warm water
3 cups water, room
   temperature
⅘ cup or 200 grams Biga
   (recipe follows)
4½ cups all-purpose flour
3 cups bread flour
1 Tbsp. + 1 tsp. salt

Biga

Stir yeast into ¼ cup warm water and let stand until creamy, about 10 minutes. Add remaining ingredients to yeast mixture and mix with a wooden spoon 3–4 minutes. The result will be a loose, sticky dough.

Place dough in a lightly oiled bowl, cover with plastic wrap and let stand at even room temperature for 2 days. Afterwards, keep refrigerated. The dough will keep for approximately 2 weeks. Bring to room temperature before using.

Trade Secret: I recommend using a clay baker or place a pan of hot water on oven bottom for first 15 minutes of baking.

¼ tsp. active dry yeast
¼ cup warm water
¾ cup plus 1 Tbsp. water,
   room temperature
2½ cups all-purpose flour

Suzette Gresham-Tognetti
Acquerello
San Francisco

107

Soda Bread

Yield: 3 small loaves
Preparation Time:
1¼ hours
Pre-heat oven to 425°

3 cups whole wheat
flour
1½ cups bread flour
⅓ cup dark brown sugar
2 tsps. salt
2 tsps. baking soda
2 large eggs, room
temperature
2¼ cups buttermilk, room
temperature
½ lb. unsalted butter, cut
into small pieces

ix all the dry ingredients thoroughly. Using your fingertips, rub the butter pieces into the flour mixture until it has a coarse and sandy texture.

Combine the eggs with the buttermilk. Add the liquid to the dry ingredients and mix well.

Divide the dough into three even pieces and form each into a roll about 16 inches long. Lay the loaves on a lightly floured baking sheet and make several diagonal slashes in the top of each one. Sprinkle generously with white flour and bake immediately at 425° for about 50 minutes.

Trade Secret: Try this bread with crème fraîche and strawberry jam spread on thickly. This is my most requested recipe. Easy to make, tastes great, and freezes well.

John Downey
Downey's
Santa Barbara

Skillet Sun-Dried Tomato & Cheddar Bread

Combine all dry ingredients in a medium mixing bowl. Stir in jalapeño, cheddar and chopped tomato.

In a separate bowl, whisk together eggs and milk. Stir liquids into the dry mixture and then mix in the peanut oil.

Lightly oil and heat an 8" cast iron skillet until very hot. Pour in batter and bake at 400° for approximately 40 minutes. If using an 8" baking pan, add an additional 20 minutes to the cooking time.

Trade Secret: The basics of this recipe come from an old Iowa family cookbook to which I have tried to give a little twist of the kaleidoscope to update for a more modern taste.

Yield: 8–10 servings
Preparation Time:
 1 Hour
Pre-heat oven to 400°

2 cups yellow cornmeal
2 cups all-purpose flour
¼ cup granulated sugar
2 Tbsps. baking powder
1 jalapeño, seeded,
 finely diced
1 cup cheddar cheese,
 grated
½ cup sun-dried tomatoes,
 chopped, drained of oil
2 eggs
2 cups milk
⅔ cup peanut oil

David Beckwith
Central 159 Restaurant & Catering
Pacific Grove

Bruschetta–Grilled Italian Bread

Serves 4
Preparation Time:
 15 Minutes

 1 tsp. garlic, chopped
 1 cup olive oil
 8 ripe Roma tomatoes,
   diced
20 fresh basil leaves,
   julienne
 1 tsp. oregano
   Salt and pepper to taste
 1 garlic bulb
12 slices thick crusty
   Italian bread
   Black olives for garnish

n a mixing bowl, combine the chopped garlic, ½ cup olive oil, tomatoes, basil and oregano. Salt and pepper to taste. Let mixture stand for 30 minutes at room temperature.

Cut garlic bulb in half and rub each slice of bread on both sides. Brush lightly with remaining olive oil.

Toast in oven under broiler, turning slices when golden brown. Finish other side the same way.

Place bread slices on a large platter and top with tomato mixture evenly. Garnish with olives and serve.

Donna Scala
Piatti Ristorante
Sacramento, Napa, Sonoma, Carmel, Montecito, La Jolla

Buckwheat Dill Muffins

Mix dry ingredients in a bowl. Add the fresh dill.
In a separate bowl, mix the remaining ingredients. Carefully combine all ingredients, taking caution not to overmix.

Butter muffin cups and fill ⅔ full. Bake until done, approximately 10 to 15 minutes.

Yield: 12 muffins
Preparation Time:
  20 Minutes
Pre-heat oven to 375°

- 1 cup all-purpose flour
- 1 cup buckwheat flour
- 1 tsp. salt
- ½ tsp. baking soda
- 1½ Tbsps. baking powder
- 4 Tbsps. granulated sugar
- 4 Tbsps. fresh dill, chopped fine
- 2 eggs
- 1¼ cups buttermilk
- ½ cup sweet butter, melted

Bradley Ogden
Lark Creek Inn
Larkspur

★

Name That Muffin

Yield: 18 muffins
Preparation Time:
  45 Minutes
Pre-heat oven to 400°

  2 **cups unsifted white**
    flour
  ¾ **tsp. salt**
  ¾ **tsp. baking soda**
  ¼ **tsp. baking powder**
  2 **eggs**
  ¾ **cup brown sugar**
  ¾ **cup corn oil**
  ¾ **tsp. vanilla extract**
  1⅓ **cups prepared fruit or**
    vegetables
  1½ **tsp. cinnamon**
  1½ **tsp. ground ginger**
  ⅓ **cup poppy seeds**
  ¾ **cup walnuts, toasted,**
    chopped

ift together the flour, salt, baking soda and baking powder. In a separate bowl, whip the eggs with the sugar and oil. Stir in the vanilla, whatever fruits or vegetables you are using, the spices, and the poppy seeds. Then add the flour mixture and the nuts. Do not overmix.

Spoon the batter into greased or papered muffin cups, filling each about ¾ full. Bake for 25 to 30 minutes or until golden brown.

Variations:
Apple or pear: Core and shred them.
Zucchini: Shred them unpeeled
Oranges: Wash well, chop up (skin, pulp and juice) and process in the bowl of a food processor. Add ⅓ cup extra poppy seeds, 1 extra tsp. ginger and ½ tsp. cinnamon.
Pumpkin: Steam fresh pumpkin and cut into small bits.
Tomato: Cut them into small bits.

Trade Secrets: The personality of this muffin changes, depending on the fruit or vegetable that is added to the batter. One interesting option is to divide the batter into several batches and add different fruits or vegetables to each batch.

© *The Morning Food Cookbook*

Margaret Fox
Cafe Beaujolais
Mendocino

Main Dish Meals

Corn blinis, marinated salmon
Chilaquiles
Tomato, white bean, bleu cheese chile
Crab cakes
Cocoa crêpes stuffed with lobster
Blue corn scallop enchiladas
Rock shrimp lasagna
Chile relleno with papaya salsa
California stirfry
Sweet and sour chicken, lobster stirfry
Braised stuffed tofu dumplings
Smoked chicken tostada
Duck tostada
Chicken quesadilla

Corn Blinis Sandwich with Marinated Salmon

Serves 4
Preparation Time:
 30 Minutes
(note marinating time)

 2 lbs. salmon, skin on
 ½ cup kosher salt
 4 Tbsps. sugar
 4 Tbsps. fennel seeds
 1 Tbsp. white pepper
 6 ears corn
 2 Tbsps. butter
 1 shallot, chopped fine
 ½ cup heavy cream
 ½ cup flour
 2 eggs
 3 Tbsps. milk
 ½ bunch parsley, chopped
 3 Tbsps. sour cream
 1 bunch chives, chopped
 1 red bell pepper, roasted,
    peeled, diced

To marinate the salmon, mix together salt, sugar, fennel seeds and white pepper. Place half of the mixture in a pan and place the salmon filet, skin side down, on top. Place the rest of the mixture over the salmon. Place another pan over the salmon to weigh it down. Marinate for 24 hours or until moisture is leached from salmon.

Cut the corn off the cob and blanch in boiling water. Then, sauté corn in butter with the shallots. Add cream and let reduce for 2 minutes.

Mix flour and eggs in blender. Add milk, corn and chopped parsley. Heat a heavy 7″ nonstick skillet until quite hot. Pour in 3 Tbsps. of the batter, then quickly tilt the pan so the batter spreads evenly. Cook until lightly brown, 30 to 45 seconds, then turn and cook another 15 seconds. Repeat, using up all the batter.

To serve, slice the salmon in paper-thin slices and place in sandwich between two blinis. Garnish with sour cream, chopped chives and diced red bell pepper.

Joachim Splichal
Patina
Los Angeles

☆

Chilaquiles

Break the eggs in a mixing bowl and beat them lightly. Cut the tortillas into 8ths and add to the eggs. Let sit 15 minutes.

Cut the avocados in half from tip to stem, and remove the pit. Using a large spoon, scoop the flesh out in one piece. Lay cut side down on a plate, slice and fan out the slices. Cut the tomatoes into slices and lay slices next to the avocado. Drizzle with lime juice, oil and sprinkle with salt and pepper.

Heat the butter in a large skillet over medium heat and add the meat, onion, chile powder and cumin. Cook, stirring occasionally, for 5 minutes. Add the beaten eggs and tortillas and cook, stirring, until eggs are cooked to desired doneness.

Arrange a mound of eggs on each plate next to the avocado and tomato and garnish with some cilantro. Serve immediately.

© *What's For Dinner*

Serves 4
Preparation Time:
25 Minutes

6 eggs
4 corn tortillas
2 avocados
2 tomatoes
4 Tbsps. lime juice
4 tsps. olive oil
2 Tbsps. butter or
   margarine
1 cup cooked beef,
   chicken or pork, diced
   or shredded
2 onions, finely diced,
   about 1½ cups
1 tsp. chile powder
½ tsp. ground cumin
   Salt and pepper to taste
   Cilantro

Michael Roberts
Trumps
Hollywood

Tomato, White Bean and Bleu Cheese Chile

Serves 8
Preparation Time:
 1½ Hours
(note soaking time)

- 2 **cups dried white beans**
- 2 **poblano chile peppers**
- 2 **Anaheim chile peppers**
- 2 **red peppers**
- 2 **Tbsps. vegetable oil**
- 2 **medium onions, diced,**
  about 2 cups
- 2 **jalapeño peppers,**
  seeded, minced
- 3 **Tbsps. garlic, minced**
- 15 **tomatoes, seeded, diced**
  or two 28 oz. cans
  peeled tomatoes
- 2 **dried ancho or pasilla**
  peppers, stems removed
- 2 **tsps. cumin powder**
- ¼ **tsp. ground cinnamon**
- 3 **cups chicken stock or**
  water
  Salt as desired
- ¾ **lb. Roquefort cheese**

he night before, cover beans with water and let stand to soften.

Roast, peel and seed the pasilla, Anaheim and red peppers, then dice them.

Pre-heat oven to 325°. Heat the oil in a large casserole or Dutch oven over medium heat. Add the onions and jalapeño peppers and cook, uncovered, until the onions are translucent, about 5 minutes. Add the garlic, tomatoes, roasted peppers, dried chiles, cumin, cinnamon, drained beans and chicken stock. Cover and place in the oven for 1 hour.

Salt the chile and return it to the oven for another 30 minutes or until the beans are tender. Remove the chile from the oven, mix in the crumbled bleu cheese and spoon into a serving bowl.

Michael Roberts
Trumps
Hollywood

Crab Cakes

Mix all ingredients in a large bowl by hand, breaking up large pieces of crabmeat. Chill 15 minutes in the refrigerator.

Shape crabmeat into 9 balls about 4 Tbsps. each, with wet hands. Flatten to ½″ thick and panfry on hot griddle coated with oil. Brown each side, about 1 minute, but do not cook through.

Immediately wrap with plastic, chill and refrigerate until ready to use. They will keep in refrigerator for two days.

To use, simply put crabcakes on sheet pan and bake in 550° oven for 5 minutes, straight from the refrigerator.

Serve with aioli flavored with sweet-pickled ginger.

Serves 4
Preparation Time:
   20 Minutes

8 oz. prawns, peeled, deveined, coarsely ground
2 oz. scallops, coarsely chopped
2 Tbsps. water chestnuts, minced
1 Tbsp. green onions, diced
4 oz. dungeness crabmeat
   Salt and white pepper
1 tsp. garlic, chopped
1 tsp. sugar
1 tsp. oyster sauce
   Aioli sweet-pickled ginger, recipe page 209

David SooHoo
Chinois East West
Sacramento

Mexican Cocoa Crêpes Stuffed with Lobster

Yield: 9 Crêpes
Preparation Time:
  30 Minutes

- ½ **bar of Mexican chocolate, chopped fine**
- 1½ **cups milk**
- 1 **large egg**
- 2 **Tbsps. black pasilla chile powder**
- 1 **tsp. granulated garlic**
- ¼ **tsp. cayenne pepper**
  Pinch of salt and pepper
- ½ **cup all-purpose flour**
- ½ **cup leeks, white part only, julienne**
- 2 **Tbsps. butter**
- ½ **lb. lobster meat, chopped**
- ½ **cup heavy cream**
- ½ **cup jack cheese, shredded**
- ¼ **cup edible flowers for garnish**

lend the chocolate, milk, egg, chile powder, garlic, salt and peppers until completely smooth. Warm up a crêpe pan or Teflon skillet. Rub with butter and pour about 4 Tbsps. of batter on center of skillet, swirling around to make a thin crêpe. Cook for 1 minute. Keep in warm place.

Prepare the stuffing by sautéing the leeks in butter for 1 minute. Add lobster and sauté for 1 minute. Add cream and jack cheese and cook until it gets very thick.

To assemble, place stuffing on half of each crêpe and fold. Place on center of plate. Decorate with edible flowers if desired.

Hugo Molina
Parkway Grill
Pasadena

Blue Corn Enchiladas Stuffed with Scallops in a Beaujolais Cream Sauce

I n large sauté pan on medium-high heat, put clarified butter or oil and add shallots, garlic and thyme. Add mushrooms, then wine. Reduce by ¾, then add half the cream. Simmer on medium-low heat. Add half the basil and chipotle pepper. Reduce mixture by ⅓. Check consistency and spiciness. The longer you reduce, the spicier the sauce becomes. If too spicy, add more cream. Remove from heat and add remainder of basil and lemon juice. Salt and pepper to taste

Lightly dredge scallops in clarified butter or light cooking oil, salt and pepper. Place on grill.

When cooked, place scallops inside each warmed tortilla, ladle a little sauce inside tortilla then fold over and ladle sauce on top of tortilla. Dribble caviar on top and garnish with red and yellow peppers.

Serves 4
Preparation Time:
  30 Minutes

  4 Tbsps. clarified butter
    or cooking oil
  4 Tbsps. shallots, finely
    chopped
  2 Tbsps. garlic, finely
    chopped
  1 bunch fresh thyme,
    chopped
  ¼ lb. shiitake mushrooms
  3 cups Beaujolais wine
  3 cups heavy cream
  2 bunch fresh basil,
    julienne
  1 Tbsp. chipotle pepper,
    finely chopped
    Juice of 1 lemon
    Salt and white pepper
 40 large sea scallops
  8 blue corn tortillas
  2 Tbsps. salmon caviar
  1 red bell pepper,
    julienne
  1 yellow bell pepper,
    julienne

Scott Kirkwood
Pacifica del Mar
Del Mar

Rock Shrimp Lasagna with Grilled Vegetables

Serves 4
Preparation Time:
 30 Minutes

3 red bell peppers
1 yellow bell pepper
1 leek, cut lengthwise
1 red onion, cut into
    1″ slices
1 Japanese eggplant, cut
    into 3 slices, lengthwise
3 Tbsps. diced tomatoes
½ red onion, minced
1 Tbsp. butter
1 clove garlic, minced
1 Tbsp. sun-dried
    tomatoes, cut into strips
1 small carrot, sliced
½ cup white wine
½ cup heavy cream
    Salt and pepper to taste
¼ lb. rock shrimp
½ tsp. olive oil
1 Tbsp. basil, chopped
¼ cup mozzarella cheese,
    grated
    Twelve 5″ circles of
    pasta cut from a sheet
    of pasta

Lightly coat with oil 1 red bell pepper, yellow bell pepper, leek, sliced red onions and eggplant and grill or barbecue until well marked and cooked through. Dice the vegetables and add the tomatoes. Set aside.

Prepare the sauce by sautéing the minced onion in butter. Add the garlic, sun-dried tomatoes, 2 red bell peppers, sliced carrot and cook for 10 minutes, stirring constantly on high heat. Reduce the heat to medium and add the wine, boiling for 5 minutes. Add the cream and cook until sauce is thick. Transfer the sauce to a blender. Add salt and pepper to taste. If the sauce is too lumpy, add extra chicken stock. Strain through medium strainer holes.

Sauté the rock shrimp for 2 minutes at high heat in olive oil. Add the grilled vegetables and basil. Add the mozzarella cheese and ½ cup of the sauce to bind the mixture.

Blanch pasta circles to al dente.

Assemble the lasagna, starting with the pasta circle, then some of the vegetables and sauce, making 2 layers.

Serve immediately, with sauce surrounding lasagna.

Serge Falesitch
Delicias
Rancho Santa Fe

Chile Relleno with Papaya Salsa

Prepare salsa by sautéing the onion in oil over medium flame, add ginger and curry and cook 5 minutes. Add tomatoes, papayas, lime juice and cook 2 to 3 minutes more, remove from heat and add cilantro and salt. Keep warm.

Fill roasted chiles with each of the cheeses, and place on greased cookie sheet. Bake 10 minutes. Top with salsa, serve bubbling hot.

Trade Secret: This makes a great entree served with black beans and vegetables.

Serves 4
Preparation Time:
  30 Minutes
Pre-heat oven to 350°

  ½ cup red onion, diced
  2 Tbsps. peanut oil
  ½ tsp. ginger, minced
  1 tsp. curry powder
  8 Roma tomatoes,
    blanched, skinned,
    seeded, diced
  4 papayas, peeled,
    seeded, diced
    Juice of 2 limes
  3 Tbsps. cilantro
    Salt to taste
  8 poblano chiles,
    roasted, peeled,
    seeded
1½ cups cheddar cheese
1½ cups jack cheese
  1 cup goat cheese

Tim Sullivan
Cilantro's
Del Mar

California Stirfry

Serves 4
Preparation Time:
15 Minutes

2 Tbsps. oil
1 cup uncooked chicken,
   sliced
¼ cup onion, sliced
¼ cup celery, sliced
¼ cup carrot, sliced
1 cup white mushrooms,
   sliced
2 tsps. garlic, chopped
⅓ cup chopped clams
   with juice (½ small can)
1 cup heavy cream
1 Tbsp. white wine,
   optional
½ tsp. dried thyme
1 cup prawns, peeled,
   deveined
⅓ tsp. salt
⅛ tsp. white pepper
1 Tbsp. oyster sauce
1 Tbsp. lemon juice
2 Tbsps. cornstarch
4 Tbsps. cold water
1 avocado cut into chunks
   Toasted pinenuts,
   garnish

eat a wok until hot and add oil to cover bottom. Stir-fry chicken about 1 minute until lightly browned and add the onions, celery, carrots and mushrooms. Continue to brown the vegetables another 30 seconds and add the garlic. Stirfry 15 seconds until the garlic is aromatic.

Add the clam with its juices, heavy cream, wine, dried thyme and simmer with cover.

After 1½ minutes simmering, add the raw prawns. Again cover and simmer 1 minute longer.

Remove the wok cover and season with salt, pepper, oyster sauce and lemon juice. Thicken using a cornstarch solution of 2 Tbsps. cornstarch in 4 Tbsps. cold water, as needed. Turn off heat and taste.

Mix in fresh avocado chunks and serve garnished with toasted pinenuts.

Trade Secret: I like to marinate the chicken with 1 Tbsp. oil, ¼ tsp. salt, ⅛ tsp. white pepper and 1 Tbsp. cornstarch about 1 hour before using.

David SooHoo
Chinois East West
Sacramento

Sweet and Sour Chicken and Lobster Stirfry

Prepare the sweet and sour sauce in a saucepan over medium heat by combining the sugar, vinegar, soy sauce, 2 Tbsps. sherry, catsup, garlic, sesame oil and pineapple juice. Bring to a boil and add the cornstarch in water. Stir until sauce begins to thicken. Remove from heat and set aside.

Sauté chicken and lobster in oil in a wok until cooked, about 5–6 minutes. Add celery, bell peppers, onion and carrots. Cook 1–2 minutes, then add the pineapple, water chestnuts, snow peas and green onions. Deglaze with 2 Tbsps. dry sherry and stir in the sweet and sour sauce.

Place pineapple shells on plate and mound with stirfy. Garnish with cilantro leaves.

Serves 4
Preparation Time:
  30 Minutes

  5 Tbsps. sugar
  4 Tbsps. white wine
    vinegar
  3 Tbsps. light soy sauce
  4 Tbsps. dry sherry
  3 Tbsps. catsup
  1 Tbsp. garlic, crushed
  1 Tbsp. sesame oil
  ½ cup pineapple juice
  1 Tbsp. cornstarch
    dissolved in 3 Tbsps.
    cold water
  1½ cups chicken, diced
    Four 4 oz. lobster tails,
    cut lengthwise in half
  4 Tbsps. oil
  2 celery stalks, sliced
    thin
  1 red bell pepper, sliced
    thin
  1 onion, sliced thin
  2 carrots, sliced thin
  1 pineapple, cubed
  1 cup water chestnuts
  ½ cup snow peas
    1 green onion, cut thin
  4 pineapple shells for
    serving
  ½ bunch fresh cilantro
    leaves

William Donnelly
Chez Melange
Redondo Beach

★

Braised Tofu Dumplings Stuffed with Shrimp and Crab

Serves 4
Preparation Time:
 40 Minutes

 1 **cup chicken stock or**
   canned chicken broth
   Salt and pepper
¼ **tsp. sugar**
½ **tsp. oyster sauce**
 4 **tsps. cornstarch**
 2 **tsps. cold water**
¼ **lb. raw fresh shrimp**
   meat
   One 16 oz. package soft
   tofu, diced
 1 **oz. fresh crabmeat**
   Dash sesame oil
 1 **sprig fresh cilantro,**
   chopped
10 **large egg whites**
 5 **heads bok choy**
 2 **Tbsps. vegetable oil**

 repare the sauce by combing chicken stock, dash of salt, sugar and oyster sauce in a saucepan and bring to a boil. Mix 1 tsp. cornstarch with cold water and add to chicken stock. Boil for a few seconds, stirring, until sauce clears and thickens. Set aside.

Mince shrimp meat and combine with tofu, crabmeat, 3 tsps. cornstarch, dash of salt and pepper, sesame oil, cilantro and egg whites. Mix well, then fill 12 to 16 tablespoons or soup spoons with the dumpling mixture and steam over simmering water for 5 minutes. Remove dumplings from spoons with a knife tip. Set aside.

Cut bok choy in quarters lengthwise. Pan-fry with oil and dash of salt, about 3 minutes. Drain.

To serve, place dumplings in center of plate and drizzle with sauce. Garnish edges of plate with the bok choy.

Philip Lo
Hong Kong Flower Lounge
Millbrae

✩

Blue Corn Tostada with Smoked Chicken in a Jalapeño Cream Sauce

Prepare the sherry wine vinegar jalapeño cream sauce in a saucepan by combining 1 cup vinegar and 2 Tbsps. shallots over high heat. Reduce until almost no liquid is left. Add chicken stock and reduce by half. Add cream and reduce by half. Add roasted jalapeño, salt and white pepper. Keep warm, set aside.

Prepare the tomato vinaigrette by combining the tomato, 1 Tbsp. shallots, garlic and cilantro. Add lime juice, olive oil and 1 Tbsp. vinegar. Mix together well and season with salt and pepper. Set aside.

To serve, portion the smoked chicken and cheese, topped with the tomato vinaigrette evenly among 4 tortillas. Place tortillas on a cookie sheet and into a pre-heated oven at 375° until cheese melts. Drizzle 4 Tbsps. of sauce on tortillas and serve.

Serves 4
Preparation Time:
  30 Minutes
Pre-heat oven to 375°

  1 cup + 1 Tbsp. sherry
    wine vinegar
  3 Tbsps. shallots,
    chopped
1½ cups chicken stock
  1 cup heavy cream
  1 jalapeño, roasted
    Salt and white pepper
  1 tomato, peeled,
    seeded, chopped
  1 clove garlic, chopped
    fine
  1 Tbsp. cilantro,
    chopped
    Juice of ½ lime
  2 Tbsps. olive oil
  4 blue corn tortillas
  1 smoked chicken,
    julienne
  1 cup white cheddar
    cheese

Scott Kirkwood
Pacifica del Mar
Del Mar

Duck Tostada

Serves 4
Preparation Time:
45 Minutes
Pre-heat oven to 350°

4 **spring roll wrappers**
⅔ **head Napa cabbage,**
chopped
1½ **cups mixed baby**
lettuces
1 **red bell pepper,**
julienne
½ **bunch green onions,**
sliced
2 **Tbsps. sugar**
⅛ **cup + 2 Tbsps. rice**
wine vinegar
2 **Tbsps. lime juice**
3 **Tbsps. vegetable oil**
1 **jicama, peeled, sliced**
thin
½ **red onion, julienne**
1 **mango, peeled, julienne**
½ **tsp. crushed chiles**
¼ **cup pineapple juice**
4 **cups cooked duck or**
chicken meat, cut into
1½″ strips
½ **cup coconut milk**
2 **Tbsps. brown sugar**
1 **tsp. soy sauce**
½ **tsp. garlic, crushed**
¼ **cup cooked rice**
1 **cup combined currants**
and chopped dates
Pistachios, toasted as
garnish
Scallions, diced as
garnish

 lace spring roll wrappers over 4 lightly oiled cups and bake 4–5 minutes until golden. Set aside.

In a large mixing bowl, combine the cabbage, lettuces, bell pepper, green onions. Prepare a light vinaigrette by combining the sugar, wine vinegar, lime juice and oil. Toss with the greens and set aside.

Prepare the jicama mango salsa by combining the jicama, onion, mango, chiles, pineapple juice and ⅛ cup rice wine vinegar. Set aside.

Combine duck or chicken with the coconut milk, brown sugar, soy sauce and garlic. Set aside.

Combine the cooked rice with currants and dates.

To assemble, place the spring roll wrappers on a small amount of lettuce to prevent slippage. Add tossed greens, then rice mixture, then duck and top with salsa. Garnish with pistachios and scallions.

William Donnelly
Chez Melange
Redondo Beach

Chicken Quesadilla with Avocado and Cilantro Salsa

Prepare the salsa by peeling 3 tomatoes and dicing them with the avocados. Add the onions, cilantro, garlic and jalapeño. Add tomato juice, cayenne, Tabasco and lemon juice. Set aside.

Cut flour tortillas in 3" circles. Blanch and peel 3 tomatoes then slice.

Charbroil peppers on open flame, then peel, remove seeds and slice.

Charbroil or sauté chicken until well done and crisp, then slice.

Between 2 tortilla circles, layer the sliced tomato, chicken, pepper, and grated cheese.

Serve with salsa on the side or on top.

Serves 4
Preparation Time:
  30 Minutes

6 **Roma tomatoes**
2 **avocados**
4 **Tbsps. red onion, diced**
1 **bunch cilantro leaves, chopped**
  Garlic to taste, chopped
  Jalapeño peppers to taste, chopped
1 **Tbsp. tomato juice**
  Cayenne pepper
  Tabasco
  Juice of 1 small lemon
4 **large flour tortillas**
2 **Anaheim chiles**
½ **cup Monterey jack cheese**
1 **cup chicken white meat**
2 **Tbsps. corn oil**

Joachim Splichal
Patina
Los Angeles

⭐

Crab cakes, mustard sauce
Crayfish, honey-mustard sauce
Lobster tacos
Grilled marinated prawns
Prawns with walnuts
Grilled salmon with saffron sauce
Evil jungle salmon
Salmon in parchment
Roast salmon, niçoise vegetables
Scallops with artichokes
Scallop ragout
Tequila sea bass
Sautéed red snapper
Swordfish, spicy papaya vinaigrette
Tilapia, green cashew sauce

Fish
and
Shellfish

Crab Cakes with Mustard Sauce

Prepare the mustard sauce by lightly sautéing the shallots in a sauce pot until soft. Add white wine and bring to a full boil then reduce by 75%. Add the mustard and stir it through. Add the cream and bring to a gentle boil. Simmer and reduce until thick enough to cling to the back of a spoon. Strain and set aside.

Combine the egg, mayonnaise, garlic, Tabasco, Worcestershire, salt and pepper, mixing together well. Add all the minced vegetables and mix thoroughly.

Pour the vegetable sauce over the crab meat and mix together gently. Sprinkle the bread crumbs over this mixture and combine.

Pre-heat a skillet with a small amount of butter/oil mix. Place the crabcakes in the pan and cook to golden brown. Turn them and place in 450° oven for about 3 minutes.

Serve warm with the mustard sauce.

Serves 6
Preparation Time:
  30 Minutes
Pre-heat oven to 450°

- 2 Tbsps. shallots, minced
- 1½ cups dry white wine
- 2 Tbsps. Dijon mustard
- 1½ cups heavy cream
- 1 egg, beaten
- ½ cup mayonnaise
- ½ tsp. garlic, minced
- ½ tsp. Tabasco
- 2 tsps. Worcestershire
  Salt and pepper to taste
- ½ cup red bell pepper, minced
- ½ cup gold pepper, minced
- 2 stalks celery, minced
- ¼ cup red onion, minced
- 1 Tbsp. jalapeño pepper, minced
- 2 lbs. crab meat, squeezed dry
- ½ cup bread crumbs
  Butter/oil mixture

Russell Armstrong
Trees
Corona del Mar

Crayfish with Honey-Mustard Dipping Sauce

Serves 6
Preparation Time:
20 Minutes
(note marinating time)

6 Tbsps. honey
½ cup Dijon mustard
15–30 dashes of Tabasco
1 cup all-purpose flour
2 tsps. cayenne
2 tsps. salt
½ tsp. baking powder
1 tsp. sugar
8 oz. of beer, room
temperature
4 cups peanut oil for
frying
1½ lbs. crayfish, sliced
Lemon wedges for
garnish

repare the honey-mustard dipping sauce by mixing together the honey, mustard and Tabasco to taste, in a small bowl. Set aside.

Combine the flour, cayenne, salt, baking powder and sugar in a medium bowl. Add beer, all at once, and whisk until smooth. Set aside, uncovered, at least 1 hour.

Heat oil to deep-fry temperature (350°) in a large saucepan. Test oil by sprinkling in a few drops of batter. If they immediately rise to the surface, the oil is ready. Thoroughly coat crayfish strips by dipping one at a time in batter. Fry 4 or 5 pieces at a time until crisp and golden, about 2 minutes. Remove with a slotted spoon and drain on paper towels.

Serve immediately with lemon wedges and honey-mustard dipping sauce.

Susan Feniger & Mary Sue Milliken
Border Grill, City
Santa Monica, Los Angeles

Lobster Tacos

Fry tortillas quickly in hot oil until soft and pliable. Lay out tortillas and build each taco by layering the ingredients in this order: a piece of lettuce, 4 Tbsps. lobster, 2 Tbsps. cucumber relish, a dab of mashed avocado, 1 Tbsp. sweet peas, a few slices of radish and a pinch of chopped cilantro. Finish each taco by squeezing with fresh lime juice, then drizzle with 1 Tsp. of olive oil.

Fold tortillas in half and serve immediately.

Serves 6
Preparation Time:
   15 Minutes

12 yellow corn tortillas,
     6" diameter
     Oil for frying
 6 leaves of green leaf
     lettuce
 2 lbs. fresh lobster,
     cooked
 3 cups cucumber relishes,
     see recipe page 213
 2 cups sweet peas,
     blanched
 2 fresh limes
 6 Tbsps. extra virgin olive
     oil
 1 bunch red radishes,
     sliced thin
 1 avocado, skinned,
     seeded, mashed
 1 bunch cilantro, stems
     removed, chopped
     roughly

Susan Feniger & Mary Sue Milliken
Border Grill, City
Santa Monica, Los Angeles

Grilled Marinated Prawns with Melon Salsa

Serves 4
Preparation Time:
  30 Minutes
(note refrigeration time)

1½ cups melon, diced
 ½ cup fresh pineapple, diced
 1 tsp. serrano chile, seeded, minced
 ¼ cup sweet red onion, diced
 ⅓ cup + 2 Tbsps. light olive oil
1½ tsps. garlic, minced fine
 1 Tbsp. raspberry or other fruit vinegar
 1 Tbsp. fresh lemon or lime juice
 ½ tsp. honey
   Salt and fresh ground pepper to taste
 1 lb. large prawns (16–20)
 1 Tbsp. scallions, minced
 ½ tsp. fresh oregano, chopped, or ¼ tsp. dried
 ¼ tsp. red chile flakes
 2 Tbsps. dry white wine
 2 Tbsps. cilantro leaves, finely chopped
   Avocado slices, garnish, optional

Prepare the salsa by carefully combining the melon, pineapple, chile and onion in a bowl. Separately, whisk 2 Tbsps. oil, ½ tsp. garlic, vinegar, lemon juice and honey together. Add to melon mixture, taste and correct seasoning. Makes approximately 2½ cups salsa.

Peel and devein the prawns, leaving the tails on.

Prepare the marinade by whisking together ⅓ cup olive oil, 1 tsp. garlic, the scallions, oregano, red chile flakes, wine and ½ tsp. salt. Marinate prawns for 2 hours, refrigerated. Be careful not to over-marinate. Skewer if desired to facilitate grilling.

Grill or broil the prawns quickly, 1 to 2 minutes per side, until they just begin to turn pink. Be careful not to overcook. Prawns should remain slightly transparent in the middle.

Divide the salsa among plates and place the prawns attractively on top and garnish with cilantro sprigs and avocado slices if desired.

Trade Secret: For additional flavor, lightly oil and grill the pineapple before cutting it up.

John Ash
John Ash & Co.
Santa Rosa

Prawns with Walnuts

Shell, devein and rinse prawns. Pat dry with paper towels. Combine egg yolk, ¼ tsp. salt and pepper. Mix with cornstarch. Dip prawns in this batter.

Heat oil in a deep skillet to 350.° Add prawns one by one, and deep fry a few at a time for 3 minutes. Remove with a strainer and drain on paper towels. Pour oil out of pan. Add mayonnaise, ¼ tsp. salt, sugar and water. Stir well. Add prawns and stir-fry for a few seconds.

To serve, place prawns in enter of platter and surround with sweet walnuts.

Serves 4
Preparation Time:
 35 Minutes

¾ **lb. fresh prawns in the**
   shell (approximately 32)
1 **egg yolk**
   Salt and fresh pepper to
   taste
1 **cup cornstarch**
3 **cups vegetable oil**
½ **cup mayonnaise**
½ **tsp. sugar**
3 **tsps. water**
½ **cup sweet walnuts**
   (glazed walnuts,
   available in Chinese
   markets)

Philip Lo
Hong Kong Flower Lounge
Millbrae
☆

Grilled Salmon with Saffron Sauce

Serves 6
Preparation Time:
30 Minutes

    Salmon
2 **large shallots, diced**
1 **cup white wine**
6 **small white**
    peppercorns
1 **bay leaf**
    Cream
2 **sticks butter**
½ **tsp. saffron threads**
    Salt and ground white
    pepper
    Sprig of chervil, garnish

 cale the salmon, separate into 2 filets and remove the bones. Cut to the size you want.

In a saucepan, put the shallots and ¾ cup white wine, peppercorns and bay leaf and reduce until the wine is almost gone. Add a little cream to taste and then slowly add the butter. Set the beurre blanc aside.

Put the saffron in a saucepan and pound with a wooden handle. Add ¼ cup wine and cook for 1 minute. Then, strain the saffron liquid and add to the beurre blanc. Salt and pepper to taste.

Salt and pepper salmon steaks and cook on the grill with the skin down until the skin is very crispy. Put steaks in a pan with a little oil and put in a 450° oven for 3 minutes.

To serve, place a dollop of sauce in the center of the plate. Put salmon on the sauce with skin side up. Garnish with sprigs of chervil.

Julian Serrano
Masa's
San Francisco

Evil Jungle Salmon

Lightly salt and pepper each salmon filet. Let stand 15 minutes at room temperature.

Bring a wok or steamer to high boil. Steam salmon about 4–7 minutes, depending upon thickness of filets.

In another pot, blanch the cabbage about 30 seconds until wilted and bright green. Divide the cabbage and place in the center of four serving plates.

Simmer together coconut milk, sugar, red curry paste, vinegar, fish sauce and oyster sauce and bring to a boil.

Mix cornstarch and water together and add to the coconut milk mixture to thicken. The sauce should coat the back of a spoon.

Before serving, swirl in a little unsalted butter to make the sauce look glossy. Add some fresh mint leaves and/or fresh cilantro to sauce for color and taste.

To serve, cover the cabbage with the steamed salmon filets. Ladle Evil Jungle sauce over salmon filets. Garnish with a little mound of shredded coconut on top of the salmon. Serve immediately.

Trade Secret: If salmon is not fresh, add ¼ tsp. granulated sugar to each salmon filet and this will help the salmon taste young and fresh.

Serves 4
Preparation Time:
  25 Minutes

Four 6 oz. salmon filets
Salt and pepper to taste
1 head green cabbage, shredded
2 cans coconut milk, Chaockoh brand, 13.5 oz. each
1½ cups granulated sugar
4 Tbsps. Thai red curry paste, Mae Ploy brand
½ cup white vinegar
2 tsps. fish sauce
1 Tbsp. oyster sauce
2 Tbsps. cornstarch
3 Tbsps. cold water
Unsalted butter
Fresh mint leaves or fresh cilantro, chopped
Shredded coconut

David SooHoo
Chinois East West
Sacramento

Salmon in Parchment

Serves 4
Preparation Time:
  25 Minutes
Pre-heat oven to 400°

  Four 8 oz. salmon filets,
  skinned and deboned
4 sheets parchment paper
  Butter for parchment
  Salt and pepper to taste
8 Tbsps. crème fraîche
2 Tbsps. fresh dill,
  chopped
1 cup zucchini, julienne
1 cup mushrooms, sliced

 old parchment in half to form a crease. Spread butter liberally just below crease.

Place filet in buttered parchment and sprinkle with salt and pepper to taste. Top with crème fraîche. Sprinkle with dill, zucchini and mushrooms.

Fold parchment over, starting at right side of fish, making about 30° folds. Be sure that each previous fold is thoroughly covered by each succeeding fold. This ensures the parchment "bag" will be airtight and will steam the fish and vegetables as it bakes in the oven.

Place bag on hot platter in 400° oven for about 10–15 minutes until bag turns gold brown and puffs up fully. Remove from oven, open bag and transfer salmon to warmed plates with the vegetable garnish.

Jay Trubee
Dolly Cunard's
La Quinta

Roast Salmon on Warm Niçoise Vegetables with Basil Pesto

Prepare the basil pesto by combining the basil, 2 garlic cloves and pine nuts in a food processor and purée. Add ⅓ cup olive oil to form a paste. Add cheese, 1 Tbsp. lemon juice, salt and pepper. Set aside.

In a hot saucepan, add 3 Tbsps. olive oil. Season salmon steaks with salt and pepper and sear on both sides until golden brown. Then place salmon in 350° oven until cooked to desired doneness.

Add 2 Tbsps. olive oil to saucepan and sauté one minced garlic clove for 30 seconds. Add beans and potatoes and cook for 2 minutes. Add tomatoes, olives, capers, salt, pepper, and 1 Tbsp. lemon juice, cooking for 1 minute.

Divide vegetables evenly among warmed plates. Remove salmon from oven and place in center atop vegetables. Top with basil pesto and grated Parmesan.

Serves 4
Preparation Time:
  30 Minutes

  2 **bunches basil**
  3 **garlic cloves**
  1 **tsp. pine nuts**
  ⅔ **cup olive oil**
  1 **Tbsp. Parmesan cheese,**
    grated
  2 **Tbsps. lemon juice**
    Salt and pepper to taste
  4 **salmon steaks**
  ½ **lb. green beans,**
    blanched, sliced
  2 **russet potatoes, peeled,**
    diced, blanched
  2 **tomatoes, peeled,**
    seeded, diced
  ¼ **cup Niçoise olives,**
    pitted
  2 **Tbsps. capers**

Michael Flynn
Grille at Sonoma Mission Inn
Boyes Hot Springs

Seared Scallops with Artichokes and Fava Beans

Serves 4
Preparation Time:
  30 Minutes

12 baby artichokes
 4 Tbsps. lemon juice
   Salt and fresh ground
   pepper
⅛ cup olive oil
   Mint sprigs
 1 cup blanched fresh fava
   beans
½ cup white wine
 2 Tbsps. shallots, minced
¼ cup heavy cream
 2 sticks cold, unsalted
   butter
24 jumbo sea scallops,
   small muscles removed
 1 tsp. garlic, chopped
½ cup basil pesto
   Chopped chives as
   garnish

Prepare the artichokes by peeling away the tough outer leaves, cutting off the tips and trimming the stems. Drop artichokes into a bowl of cold water with 2 Tbsps. lemon juice. Transfer to a heavy-bottomed saucepan. Add salt, pepper, 2 Tbsps. olive oil and mint sprigs. Bring to a boil and cook 2–3 minutes. Allow artichokes to cool in the cooking liquid. Be careful not to overcook. Cut into quarters and set aside.

To prepare fava beans, blanch in boiling salted water for 2–3 minutes until outer membrane is loosened and the fava bean can be easily extracted. Put blanched beans into ice water, drain and peel. Set aside.

Reduce ½ cup white wine with 1 Tbsp. chopped shallots, 2 Tbsps. lemon juice and cream. When sauce is thick, whisk in the cold butter, cut into bits, a few at a time until all the butter is incorporated. Strain sauce and keep warm.

Wash and pat dry scallops and season with salt and pepper. Heat a large Teflon skillet, add a scant amount of olive oil and heat until very hot. Add scallops and sear until golden. Cook on other side and remove to a plate covered with a towel.

Lightly oil a sauté pan over high heat and add the artichokes, fava beans, shallots and garlic. Cook until warmed through. Salt and pepper to taste.

Divide vegetables and scallops among individual plates. Drizzle with the basil pesto and the wine butter sauce. Garnish with chopped chives.

Wendy Little
Post Ranch Inn
Big Sur

Sautéed Scallops with a Ragout of Chanterelle Mushrooms & Glazed Onions

Put onions in sauté pan and cover with water, add honey. Simmer until all liquid evaporates. Add chanterelle mushrooms and 1 Tbsp. butter and sauté for 2 minutes. Add red wine and 2 Tbsps. vinegar and reduce by half. Add veal stock and simmer for 5 minutes.

Slice fennel thin and toss in 1 Tbsp. olive oil and 1 Tbsp. balsamic vinegar. Season with salt and pepper. Set aside.

Season scallops with salt and pepper and place in hot pan with 2 Tbsps. olive oil. Cook until lightly browned on each side. Remove and place in center of serving plate.

Finish ragout with 1 Tbsp. butter, thyme and parsley. Salt and pepper to taste.

Spoon ragout over scallops and garnish with fennel on top.

Serves 4
Preparation Time:
 60 Minutes

 1 **cup red pearl onions**
 1 **cup white pearl onions**
 1 **Tbsp. honey**
 1 **cup chanterelle**
  mushrooms
 2 **Tbsps. butter**
 ½ **cup red wine**
 3 **Tbsps. balsamic vinegar**
 1 **cup veal or chicken**
  stock
 1 **head fennel**
 ¼ **cup olive oil**
 16 **large sea scallops**
 2 **Tbsps. thyme, chopped**

Cory Schreiber
Cypress Club
San Francisco

Tequila Sunrise Marinated Sea Bass

Serves 4
Preparation Time:
 5 Minutes
(note marinating time)

 Four 7 oz. seabass filets
 4 oz. tequila
1½ cups orange juice
 8 dashes grenadine

repare the marinade by combining the tequila, orange juice and grenadine. Marinate seabass filets for 2 hours.

Grill over a hot flame 5 minutes on each side.

Trade Secret: For a unique entree, serve the sea bass over hot tortillas with melted cheddar and jack cheeses. Accompany with guacamole, fiery salsa and chips.

William Donnelly
Chez Melange
Redondo Beach

Sautéed Red Snapper with Tomato Ginger Mint Vinaigrette and Angel Hair "Net"

In a salad bowl, combine the tomatoes, mint, ginger, shallots, garlic, ½ cup olive oil and vinegar. Season to taste.

In a heated skillet, sauté the filets in 1 tsp. olive oil. Sauté for 2 minutes and add butter before turning over, to get the golden color.

Blanch the angel hair for 1 minute and place in deep fryer until hard in 2 oz. portions. The angel hair should form a net. Place on a paper towel.

For presentation, serve the fish with vinaigrette and stand 2 nets upright as a "roof" about the fish. This makes a very visual dish at least 6″ to 8″ tall.

Garnish the plate with borders of finely diced red bell pepper skin. Use a vegetable peeler to remove the skin.

Serves 4
Preparation Time:
  20 Minutes

  4 **red snapper filets,**
    6–8 oz. each
  8 **Roma tomatoes,**
    seeded, peeled, diced
  1 **bunch mint, diced**
1½ **tsps. ginger, minced**
1½ **tsps. shallots, minced**
  ¼ **tsp. garlic, minced**
  ½ **cup + 1 tsp. extra virgin**
    olive oil
  3 **Tbsps. rice wine**
    vinegar
  2 **tsps. unsalted butter**
    Angel hair pasta
    Diced red bell pepper
    skin, garnish

Serge Falesitch
Delicias
Rancho Santa Fe

Grilled Swordfish with Spicy Papaya Vinaigrette

Serves 6
Preparation Time:
  1 Hour

1 cup unseasoned rice
  vinegar
  Juice and zest of 2 limes
1 Tbsp. honey
1 cup olive oil
½ jalapeño, minced
  **Pinch of salt and freshly
  ground pepper**
2 papayas, peeled, seeded,
  diced small
1 red bell pepper, peeled,
  diced
3 green onions, sliced
  thin
½ red onion, diced fine
6 swordfish steaks
  Cilantro as garnish

repare the vinaigrette by combining the rice vinegar, juice and zest of 2 limes and honey together over high heat. Bring to a boil and simmer for 5 minutes or until reduced to about ⅔ cup. Remove from heat and cool, then add the olive oil, jalapeño, salt and pepper.

Just before serving the vinaigrette, warm through gently again and add the papayas, red bell pepper, green onion, red onion and a few of the seeds from the papaya. Set aside.

Season swordfish steaks with a little salt and pepper. Brush lightly with olive oil and sear quickly on the hot grill. Turn once to form a cross pattern, then flip over until just cooked through. Cooking time will vary greatly depending on thickness of fish and grill temperature. To test, push the fish gently—it should be firm to the touch (like a tense muscle.) Don't overcook.

To serve, spoon the vinaigrette generously over a warm plate and place the fish on top. Garnish with cilantro.

Trade Secret: This recipe will dazzle your barbecue friends. The vinaigrette may be prepared well in advance, but don't mix it all together until you need it.

John Downey
Downey's
Santa Barbara

★

Tilapia Cancun with Green Cashew Sauce

In a food processor, purée the cashews, garlic, shallots and chiles. When the mixture has become a paste, add the oil and continue to purée. Add the vinegar and cilantro and purée until smooth. Season with salt and pepper. Set cashew sauce aside.

Rinse and dry the filets with a towel. Rub each side with a lime half and coat with paprika and cayenne. Sauté or flat grill the filets.

On individual plates, place each cooked filet on a small pool of green cashew sauce. Serve immediately.

Trade Secret: If fresh tilapia is not available, rock cod, snapper or any light fish is suitable.

Serves 8
Preparation Time:
  20 Minutes

1 **cup cashews, roasted**
2 **garlic cloves**
1 **tsp. shallots**
2 **serrano chiles**
¼ **cup peanut oil**
3 **Tbsps. rice vinegar**
½ **bunch fresh cilantro**
  Salt and pepper to taste
8 **tilapia filets, ¼ lb. each**
2 **Tbsps. paprika**
1 **tsp. cayenne**
1 **lime, cut in half**

Julio Ramirez
The Fishwife, El Cocodrilo
Pacific Grove

Lentils with lamb, sausage, pork
Lamb with anchovy black olive sauce
Lamb with black currants
Lamb in blackberry pinot noir sauce
Mongolian lamb chops
Lamb in green peppercorn, brandy
Rack of lamb
Braised lamb shanks
Liver with onions, pancetta & sherry
Pork carnitas
Pork loin, cider/sage sauce
Grilled pork loin
Veal carpaccio
Veal on rosemary brochette,
blueberry sauce
Veal tenderloin in white wine, sage
Veal loin, baby vegetable ragout

Meats

Cassoulet of Lentils with Lamb, Sausage & Pork

Sauté carrots, onion and celery with olive oil over medium heat. Add lentils, bay leaf and thyme and sauté 1 minute more. Add chicken stock and bring to a boil. Cover and cook for 15 minutes on medium heat or until lentils are al dente, stirring occasionally. Remove from heat.

Cut the pork loin and lamb in half. Season with salt and pepper. Sear until rare. Remove from pan and quarter lamb and pork pieces.

Cut sausages in half and sear over high heat. Remove from heat and set aside.

Sauté mushrooms separately with butter.

Return lentils to heat. Add all ingredients to lentils and cook until meats reach desired doneness. (2 minutes rare, 4 minutes medium, 6 minutes well-done). Season to taste.

Portion into 8 individual serving bowls and garnish with chives.

Trade Secret: Try duck, venison or specialty game sausages for variation.

Serves 8
Preparation Time:
  45 Minutes

1 carrot, diced
1 medium onion, diced
2 celery stalks, diced
¼ cup olive oil
2 cups lentils
1 bay leaf
2 thyme sprigs
1¼ cups chicken stock
1 lb. pork loin
1 lb. leg of lamb, trimmed
  Salt and white pepper to taste
1 lb. link sausages
1 lb. mushrooms, quartered
2 Tbsps. unsalted butter
1 bunch chives, chopped

Fred Halpert
Brava Terrace
St. Helena

Medallions of Lamb with Black Olive Anchovy Sauce

Serves 6
Preparation Time:
   45 Minutes
(note marinating time)

   6 lamb loins, ½ lb. each
   2 Tbsps. olive oil
   2 tsps. thyme, chopped
   1 tsp. rosemary, chopped
   1 tsp. garlic, chopped
   1 Tbsp. butter
   ½ cup white wine
   1 cup lamb stock
   ¼ cup tomato purée
   2 Tbsps. black olives,
      chopped
   1 Tbsp. anchovies,
      chopped
      Salt and pepper to taste

ub the lamb loins with olive oil. Season with thyme and rosemary. Allow to marinate for at least one hour prior to grilling.

Prepare the sauce by sautéing the garlic in butter until lightly brown. Add the white wine and reduce to 1 Tbsp. Add lamb stock and tomato purée and reduce to 1 cup. Add olives, anchovies, salt and pepper. Set aside.

Grill the lamb loins.

To serve, place warm sauce on plates with sliced lamb on top.

Hiroyoshi Sone
Terra Restaurant
St. Helena

Grilled Saddle of Lamb with Black Currants in Cabernet Cassis Sauce

Brush the lamb liberally with the red currant jelly and leave it to marinate for about 30 minutes at room temperature.

Prepare the sauce in a small, heavy non-aluminum saucepan. Boil the Cabernet with ¼ cup black currants and cassis syrup over high heat until the liquid has reduced by ¾ to a thick syrup, 5 to 7 minutes.

Add the stock and simmer over medium heat, skimming the surface frequently, until the sauce is thick enough to coat the back of a spoon and has reduced to about 1½ cups, about 10 to 15 minutes. Add the garlic and basil and swirl in the butter until thoroughly incorporated.

Strain the sauce through a fine-mesh sieve and return it to the pan to warm through gently. Season to taste with salt and pepper. To keep the sauce warm, set the saucepan inside a bowl or larger pan of hot but not boiling water.

Grill the lamb, about 3 minutes per side for medium-rare on the tenderloins, 5 minutes per side on the loins; halfway through the cooking on each side, rotate the meat 90° to give it cross-hatched grill marks.

Carve the lamb into ¼″ slices and arrange on heated serving plates. Spoon the sauce on top and garnish with ¾ cup black currants and a sprinkling of fresh tarragon and thyme.

© *Michael's Cookbook*

Serves 6
Preparation Time:
 30 Minutes
(note marinating time)

 1 **whole saddle of lamb, about 10 lbs., boned**
 ½ **cup red currant jelly, melted**
 ¾ **cup Cabernet Sauvignon**
 1 **cup fresh or frozen black currants**
 2 **Tbsps. cassis syrup**
 2 **cups chicken or lamb stock**
 1 **clove garlic**
 2 **basil leaves**
 1 **tsp. unsalted butter, chilled**
  Salt and freshly ground white pepper
 1 **Tbsp. fresh tarragon leaves**
 1 **tsp. fresh thyme leaves**

Martin Garcia
Michael's
Santa Monica

Lamb in Blackberry Pinot Noir Sauce

Serves 4
Preparation Time:
  1½ Hours
Pre-heat oven to 350°

  4 Tbsps. shallots, chopped
    fine
  2 baskets of blackberries
  ½ bottle Pinot Noir,
    750 ml.
  2 cups chicken stock
  2 Tbsps. butter
  1 Tbsp. basil, chopped
    fine
  2 Tbsps. garlic, chopped
    fine
    Salt and pepper to taste
  ⅓ cup honey
  2 Tbsps. pure maple syrup
  1 Tbsp. fresh thyme,
    chopped fine
  1 Tbsp. soy sauce
  1 Tbsp. fresh ginger,
    chopped
  ¾ cup pecans, puréed
  ½ saddle of lamb, about
    5 lbs., boned
  ¼ cup walnut oil

Prepare the blackberry Pinot Noir sauce in a heavy-bottomed sauce pan by combining the shallots, blackberries (reserve some for garnish) and wine over medium heat. Reduce liquid until it barely coats the bottom of the pan. Add the stock and reduce by half.

Remove from heat and add butter, basil and 1 Tbsp. garlic. Let butter melt while swirling into sauce. Pass sauce through a strainer. Salt and pepper to taste. Set aside.

Prepare the honey-maple glaze in a large mixing bowl by combining the honey, maple syrup, thyme, soy sauce, ginger, 1 Tbsp. garlic and 1 tsp. black pepper. Set aside.

Sear the lamb over high heat on all sides. Let cool. Then dredge the lamb in the honey-glaze and cover with pecans. Place lamb in a roasting pan and cook in a 350° oven for 20 to 25 minutes, until medium-rare.

To serve, slice lamb and drape with sauce. Garnish lightly with whole fresh blackberries.

Trade Secret: This recipe won the statewide game cookoff using saddle of caribou. Other game substitutes are elk or venison.

Scott Kirkwood
Pacifica del Mar
Del Mar

Mongolian Lamb Chops

Mix together the hoisin sauce, wine, Tabasco, vinegar, sugar, Worcestershire sauce, garlic, and sesame oil. Set aside.

Before grilling, lightly oil and sprinkle a pinch of salt and pepper on each lamb chop. Let rest for 10 minutes.

Grill lamb over a hot fire and baste with the flavored hoisin mixture. Cook until medium-rare, about 6 minutes total or as desired.

Garnish with toasted sesame seeds and/or mint leaves.

Trade Secret: I suggest serving with bread or rice and a big bowl of salad.

Serves 4
Preparation Time:
  25 Minutes

½ cup hoisin sauce
2 tsps. white wine
2 tsps. Tabasco or red chile sauce
2 tsps. cider vinegar
1 Tbsp. brown sugar
1 tsp. Worcestershire sauce
2 tsps. garlic, minced
1 tsp. sesame oil
8 lamb chops, each 1½" thick
Vegetable oil
Salt and pepper to taste
Toasted sesame seeds as garnish
1 Tbsp. fresh mint leaves, minced, as garnish

David SooHoo
Chinois East West
Sacramento

Baked Rack of Lamb with Green Peppercorn and Brandy Sauce

Serves 4
Preparation Time:
  25 Minutes

1 Tbsp. garlic, minced
2 Tbsps. olive oil
4 Tbsps. brandy
4 Tbsps. port
1½ cups rich lamb stock
1 Tbsp. green
   peppercorns in brine
6 Tbsps. sweet butter
   Salt and pepper to
   taste
2 Tbsps. red bell pepper,
   chopped
1 Tbsp. chives, chopped
2 whole racks of lamb,
   trimmed
   Olive oil
   Dijon mustard
   Dry herbs such as
   thyme and basil

 Sauté garlic in olive oil until translucent. Add brandy and port, cooking for about 1 minute. Add lamb stock and peppercorns. Cook for 2 minutes more, then add butter. Remove from heat and add salt and pepper, red bell pepper and chives. Set aside.

Coat lamb with salt, pepper, olive oil and Dijon mustard in dry herbs. Roast in oven at 350–400° for about 10 minutes or until desired doneness is reached.

To serve, cut lamb into individual portions on center of plate. Pour sauce over lamb and serve.

Hugo Molina
Parkway Grill
Pasadena

☆

Rack of Lamb with Goat Cheese Wontons and Ratatouille Vegetables

Prepare the lamb juice in a heavy roasting pan by placing the lamb and beef bones in oven for 15 minutes (they should be just starting to brown.) Turn oven down to 400.° Stir bones with a spoon to allow even roasting. Add onions, garlic and tomato paste. Roast for 20 minutes more. Remove pan from oven and pour 2 cups water over bones.

Scrape all food particles and juices into a heavy-bottomed saucepan and add remaining 4½ cups water. Add celery, carrots, bay leaf and thyme. Bring to a boil over high heat then reduce heat to a slow boil, skimming the impurities off the top. Cook the stock for 4 hours, then strain through a colander. Season with salt and pepper. Set aside in a small pot ready to reheat.

Heat two 10″ heavy-bottom skillets with 2 Tbsps. olive oil in each, just to the point of smoking. Season racks with salt and pepper. Place in skillets fat-side down and brown well 2 to 4 minutes on each side. Carefully pour off excess oil and turn rack fat-side up and place skillets in 425° oven. For medium to medium rare, roast 15 minutes. Remove from oven and skillets, placing on wire rack and allow meat to rest a minimum of 5 to 10 minutes before slicing.

To serve, ladle hot lamb juice over the sliced lamb and goat cheese wontons.

Serves 8
Preparation Time:
 3½ Hours
Pre-heat oven to 450°

1½ lbs. lamb bones, split
1½ lbs. beef bones, split
 1 **large yellow onion,**
    quartered, skin on
 2 **bulbs garlic, cut in half**
 3 **Tbsps. tomato paste**
6½ **cups water**
 2 **ribs celery washed, cut**
    in 1″ pieces
 1 **large carrot, cut in**
    1″ pieces
 1 **bay leaf**
 3 **sprigs fresh thyme or**
    1 Tbsp. dried thyme
 1 **tsp. salt**
    Fresh black pepper to
    taste
    Eight 4-rib lamb racks,
    trimmed
 4 **Tbsps. olive oil**
    Wonton recipe,
    page 197

Brian Whitmer
Pacific's Edge, Highlands Inn
Carmel
★

Braised Lamb Shanks

Serves 4
Preparation Time:
  2½ Hours
Pre-heat oven to 300°

  4 **lamb shanks**
    Salt and freshly ground
    pepper
 12 **garlic cloves, unpeeled**
  6 **bay leaves**
  6 **sprigs fresh thyme**
  1 **cup fresh mint leaves**
  ½ **Tbsp. fresh rosemary**
    leaves
  1 **Qt. chicken, lamb, veal**
    or beef stock
  1 **cup aioli**
 24 **cloves garlic, peeled**
  1 **each large red and**
    yellow bell pepper,
    julienne
  1 **Tbsp. fresh thyme or**
    marjoram leaves
  1 **Tbsp. butter**

eason the lamb shanks heavily with salt and pepper and put them in a casserole or heavy pot with the unpeeled garlic, bay leaves and thyme sprigs. Brown over medium heat for 15 minutes, turn shanks every 3 minutes. Cover pot, and cook at 300° until shanks are very tender, about 2 hours.

While the lamb is cooking, blanch the mint leaves in boiling water for 1 minute. Drain, squeeze dry and purée with the rosemary and 2 Tbsps. stock in a blender. There should be a slight texture of the leaves in the purée. Mix into the aioli and let sit to develop the flavors.

Remove the shanks when they are done and keep warm and covered. Pour the remaining stock into the cooking pot and bring to a boil, scraping loose any meat juices. The moment the stock boils, turn off the heat and skim off all the fat. Bring the stock back to a boil and reduce the liquid to 2 cups. Skim off any fat and strain. Put the peeled garlic cloves in the stock and simmer until tender, about 15 minutes. Strain and reserve the garlic and stock separately.

Put the shanks, peeled garlic, peppers, stock, marjoram and a pinch of salt in a sauté pan. Cook over medium heat, turning the shanks a couple of times, until the peppers are tender, about 10 minutes.

Place the shanks on warm plates. Stir the butter into the peppers and season. Spoon the peppers and garlic cloves around the shanks. Spoon some aioli over the shanks and serve the rest separately.

©*New American Classics*

Jeremiah Tower
Stars
San Francisco

Liver with Onions, Pancetta and Sherry

Soak liver in milk to cover at least 4 hours or overnight.

In a skillet, sauté pancetta over high heat, allowing it to caramelize slightly. Add onions and sauté, add bay leaves and half the sherry, then reduce the heat and simmer until onions are soft. Keep onions moist by alternating chicken stock and sherry to the skillet. When onions have softened, allow them to cook almost dry, then set aside.

In a mixing bowl, combine eggs, cream, parsley, Parmesan, salt and pepper. Drain liver and flour it lightly. Dip in egg mixture, then in bread crumbs, patting them on to make them adhere. Heat a sauté pan over moderately high heat. Add oil and swirl to coat bottom of pan. Add butter and liver and sauté gently until golden, then turn with spatula and continue cooking until liver is medium-rare.

Serve with sautéed onions and lemon wedges.

Serves 4
Preparation Time:
   30 Minutes
(note marinating time)

- 1 lb. well-trimmed calf's liver
  Milk
- ¼ lb. pancetta, cut crosswise into ¼" widths
- 2 medium onions, sliced
- 2 bay leaves
- 1 cup dry sherry
- ½ cup chicken stock
- 2 eggs
- ½ cup heavy cream
- 2 Tbsps. fresh parsley, chopped
- 1½ Tbsps. Parmesan cheese, grated
  Pinch salt and black pepper
  Flour
- 1½ cups soft fresh white bread crumbs
- 1 Tbsp. olive oil
- 1 Tbsp. butter
  Lemon wedges, garnish

Suzette Gresham-Tognetti
Acquerello
San Francisco

Pork Carnitas

Serves 8
Preparation Time:
  2 Hours

  ½ **Tbsp. achiote seeds**
 1½ **cups orange juice**
 1½ **cups white wine**
    vinegar
  1 **Tbsp. dry Mexican**
    oregano
  1 **Tbsp. ground toasted**
    cumin seeds
  8 **garlic cloves**
 10 **lbs. pork butt or**
    shoulder
    Salt, pepper and garlic
    powder to taste
  3 **cups dark Mexican**
    beer
  2 **white onions, sliced**
    Peanut oil

 lend achiote seeds with orange juice, vinegar, oregano, cumin and garlic cloves. Set aside.

Cut pork into ¾″ pieces. Season with salt, pepper and garlic powder.

Heat 1″ peanut oil in a heavy saucepan. Brown pork on all sides, then remove. Clean oil from pan and add pork, achiote mixture, beer and onions. Season with salt and pepper. Bring to a boil and pack in 350° oven, covered for 1½ hours.

Remove meat and trim excess fat while meat is still warm. Reduce cooking liquid over a high flame by half.

Serve the pork drizzled with the cooking juices.

Trade Secret: A great accompaniment to pork carnitas is black beans, hot salsa, guacamole and warm tortillas.

Tim Sullivan
Cilantro's
Del Mar

Braised Pork Loin with Cider/Sage Sauce

Have your butcher remove the bone from the pork loin and chop it into small pieces. Sauté the bones in a little oil in a large, deep skillet until golden brown. Pour off the excess grease and add the chopped vegetables. Sauté for another 10 minutes, stirring occasionally. Add the herbs, apple and ¾ cup of the cider. Add the veal stock and simmer for 1 hour with the cover on.

Meanwhile, trim the excess fat from the pork loin. Season well with salt and pepper. In a clean skillet, sauté the meat quickly until brown on all sides. Place the meat in with the stock. It should be half covered with liquid. Braise in a 350° oven for about 30 minutes. Turn the meat once after 15 minutes.

Remove the meat and keep in a warm place. Strain the sauce and adjust the seasonings. Finish with the remaining ¼ cup of cider.

To serve, slice the pork thinly and arrange on top of the sauce on hot plates.

Trade Secret: The pork, if cooked slowly and carefully, will be moist and tender. It will truly live up to the reputation as "the other white meat."

Serves 6
Preparation Time:
   1½ Hours

6 lb. center cut pork loin, including the bone
1 medium onion, chopped
1 medium carrot, chopped
1 leek, chopped
2 stalks celery, chopped
6 bay leaves
2 tsps. thyme
2 tsps. sage
1 apple, sliced
1 cup hard cider
2 qts. chicken or veal stock
   Oil
   Salt and pepper

John Downey
Downey's
Santa Barbara

Grilled Pork Loin with Black Beans

Serve 6
Preparation Time:
  1½ Hours
(note soaking time)

  1 lb. black beans,
4½ cups water
  ¼ lb. bacon, chopped
  5 medium garlic cloves,
    peeled, minced
  2 stalks celery, minced
  1 carrot, peeled, diced
  1 onion, peeled, diced
  1 jalapeño chile, seeded,
    minced
  1 bay leaf
  1 Tbsp. chile powder
  1 tsp. ground cumin
  1 tsp. cayenne
  ¾ tsp. white pepper
  2 qts. chicken stock or
    canned chicken broth
  1 cup mesquite chips
    One 4 lb. pork loin,
    boned, cut into
    ¾" slices

oak beans in water for 24 hours. Drain. Transfer to a large saucepan and cover with a generous amount of cold water. Boil for 20 minutes. Drain. Rinse beans and drain again.

In a large, heavy saucepan, cook bacon until golden brown and crisp, stirring frequently, about 5 minutes. Add garlic, celery, carrot, onion, jalapeño and bay leaf. Cook until vegetables are tender, stirring occasionally, about 10 minutes. Add chile powder, cumin, cayenne and white pepper. Add beans and stock. Simmer, stirring occasionally, until beans are tender and most of the liquid is absorbed, about 1½ hours. Season to taste with salt.

Build a wood or charcoal fire. Soak mesquite chips in water for 30 minutes and drain. Place pork slices between sheets of waxed paper. Using a mallet or the flat side of a cleaver, pound to a thickness of ½." Sprinkle pork with salt and pepper to taste. Grease grill rack. Sprinkle coals with mesquite chips. Arrange pork on grill rack and cook until springy to touch, about 3 minutes per side. Serve warm with the black beans.

Cindy Pawlcyn
Bistro Roti, Bix, Buckeye Roadhouse, Fog City Diner,
Mustards Grill, Tra Vigne
San Francisco, Marin, Napa

Veal Carpaccio
with Marinated Wild Mushrooms

C lean mushrooms and boil in water and vinegar with salt for 2 minutes. Drain and let dry in cheesecloth for 10 minutes.

Place mushrooms in a plastic container and add ¼ cup olive oil, 1 Tbsp. lemon juice, garlic, salt and pepper. Let marinate for 2 hours before serving.

To serve, lay the slices of veal, warm or cold, on individual serving plates. Sprinkle with lemon juice, salt, pepper and ¼ cup olive oil. Place the marinated mushrooms in middle of the plate and garnish with shaved Parmesan cheese.

Serves 6
Preparation Time:
  45 Minutes
(note marinating time)

¾ cup chanterelle
  mushrooms
¾ cup oyster mushrooms
¾ cup shiitake
  mushrooms
 2 qts. water
 1 qt. white vinegar
½ cup extra virgin olive oil
 2 Tbsps. lemon juice
 2 garlic cloves, blanched,
  chopped
  Salt and fresh ground
  pepper
½ lb. cooked veal, cooked,
  sliced paper thin
  Parmesan cheese

Gianpaolo Putzu
Il Fornaio Cucina Italiana
Del Mar

Veal on Rosemary Brochette with Blueberry Sauce

Serves 8
Preparation Time:
 20 Minutes
(note marinating time)

2 lbs. range veal leg
6 rosemary branches
1 Tbsp. rosemary,
  chopped
½ cup olive oil
½ cup white wine
  Cracked pepper
½ bottle blueberry wine
  or other berry wine
1 cup demi-glace
½ cup blueberries
  Juice of 1 lemon
  Sugar to taste

 ut veal meat into 1″ cubes and rub the meat with the rosemary branches. Set aside.

Prepare the marinade by combining the chopped rosemary with the olive oil, white wine and pepper. Marinate the veal for 2 hours.

Prepare the blueberry sauce by combining the blueberry wine, demi-glace, blueberries, lemon juice and sugar over low heat. Keep warm.

Mesquite grill the veal for 10 minutes or until done. Serve with the blueberry sauce.

Todd Muir
Madrona Manor
Healdsburg

★

Veal Tenderloin with White Wine and Sage Sauce

C lean potatoes and artichokes. Cut potatoes into small cubes and slice the artichokes. Drop both into boiling water and cook until the water boils again, approximately 4 minutes. Drain the vegetables and place them in a frying pan with a little oil. Sauté until potatoes become crispy.

Clean veal and remove fat. Roll veal in flour and sauté in a little oil for about 10 minutes over medium heat until both sides are crisp. Remove and empty oil out of pan. In the same pan, add wine and simmer until half of the wine has evaporated. Add the broth and sage leaves and boil for 5 minutes over high heat. Roll the butter in the flour and add it to the sauce, mixing until liquid thickens. Season to taste with salt and pepper.

Place vegetables on 4 serving plates and slice each tenderloin on top of the vegetables. Cover with sauce and serve.

Serves 4
Preparation Time:
   20 Minutes

4 **medium potatoes**
4 **medium artichokes**
1 **cup oil**
4 **veal tenderloins, cut**
   short
1 **cup flour**
2 **cups white wine**
3 **cups chicken broth**
4 **sage leaves**
2 **Tbsps. butter**
   Salt and pepper to taste

Enrico Glaudo
Primi
Los Angeles

Mesquite Grilled Veal Loin with Baby Vegetable Ragout

Serves 4
Preparation Time:
  20 Minutes
(note marinating time)

  4 **veal loin steaks,**
    5 oz. each
 ½ **cup white wine**
  1 **Tbsp. coriander seeds,**
    crushed
  4 **sprigs thyme**
  4 **sprigs parsley**
    Juice and diced flesh
    of 1 lemon
    Cracked white pepper
    to taste
 16 **garlic cloves, peeled**
 12 **baby carrots, peeled,**
    blanched
 12 **baby yellow squash,**
    blanched
 12 **baby turnips, blanched**
 12 **creamer or boiling**
    onions, cooked, peeled
 ½ **cup veal stock**
  1 **cup heavy cream,**
    reduced by half
 ¼ **cup cooked black beans**
  1 **tsp. oregano**
    Butter to sauté
    Cilantro garnish

 Marinate the veal steaks in white wine, coriander, thyme, parsley, lemon and pepper for 4 hours. Grill medium-rare.

Sauté the garlic, carrots, squash, turnips and onion in butter until heated. Add the veal stock and cream to the desired thickness. The sauce should coat the back of a spoon. Add the cooked beans, the cumin and oregano to the sauce. Season to taste with salt and pepper.

To serve, place ¼ of the sauce and vegetables in the center of each plate. Tilt the plate so that the sauce runs toward the edge and then rotate the plate to form a 6" circle. Scatter the vegetables toward the outside edge of the sauce. Place the grilled veal steak in the center of the vegetables and garnish with cilantro.

Todd Muir
Madrona Manor
Healdsburg

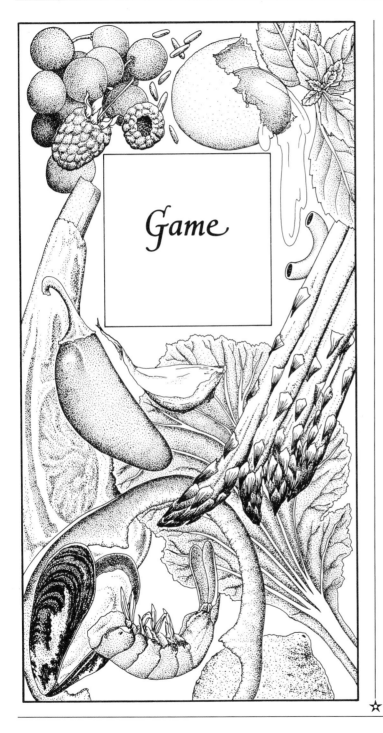

Game

Roasted wild boar
Five-spice duck breasts
Duck sausage
Duckling with a curry glaze
Grilled quail with mustard glaze
Grilled squab marinated in berry purée
Squab marinated in beer
Venison chile verde
Venison in juniper berry sauce
Venison, caramelized green apples
Venison with white raisins

Roasted Wild Boar

Serves 4
Preparation Time:
  30 Minutes
Pre-heat oven to 500°

1¼ **lb. loin of wild boar,**
    trimmed
    Clarified butter
1 **shallot, finely diced**
1 **Tbsp. honey**
3 **Tbsps. sherry vinegar**
1 **cup reduced veal stock**
¾ **stick sweet butter**
2 **Tbsps. sage leaves,**
    chopped
    Salt to taste

 ut boar in four equal pieces and sauté in a little clarified butter. Cook until medium to medium-well in a hot oven for about 5 minutes. Keep boar in a warm place.

In a saucepan, add shallots, honey and sherry vinegar. Caramelize lightly. Add veal stock and butter. Whisk to emulsify and reduce until thickened slightly. Add sage leaves and salt to taste.

Slice each portion of boar in thin slices. Serve with sauce.

John McLaughlin
J.W's Restaurant
Anaheim

Five-Spice Duck Breasts

Cut the whole joined breasts in half along the keep line, trimming the individual breast pieces neatly at the borders. Remove any excess fat or cartilage.

Combine the five-spice, mustard and salt. Sprinkle evenly on both sides of the breasts, then rub well into the skin. Seal and set aside to marinate for several hours at room temperature or overnight in the refrigerator. Bring to room temperature before cooking.

In a large heavy skillet over high heat, add enough duck fat or oil to glaze the pan. Reduce to medium heat and add the breasts, skin-side down in a single layer. Cook until the skin browns, about 3 minutes, then turn and brown the meat side 4 minutes more. The duck should be browned and the skin crispy on the outside, the meat medium-rare within. The fat will smoke during browning.

To serve, slice the breasts thinly, crosswise against the grain, and fan the slices.

Trade Secret: This recipes serves 4 as a light entree or 6 as an appetizer. At China Moon Cafe, this dish is served with a citrus-dressed salad of baby greens and/or slices of sweet orange and persimmon.

©*China Moon Cookbook*

Serves 6
Preparation Time:
 1 Hour
(note refrigeration time)

2 fresh whole duck
  breasts, skin left on
1 Tbsp. five-spice powder
1 tsp. dry mustard
1 Tbsp. kosher salt
¼ cup rendered duck fat,
  corn or peanut oil
  Garnish of scallion
  threads, finely julienne

Barbara Tropp
China Moon Cafe
San Francisco

Duck Sausage

Yield: 5 lbs.
Preparation Time:
  30 Minutes

3½ lb. roasted duckling,
  meat and skin only,
  coarsely ground
1 lb. ground chicken
  meat, both dark and
  white, coarsely ground
½ lb. bacon, coarsely
  ground
¼ cup water chestnuts,
  chopped
¼ cup raisins, chopped
¼ cup almonds, sliced
2 Tbsps. garlic, chopped
2 Tbsps. hoisin sauce
1 Tbsp. sugar
1 Tbsp. oyster sauce
¼ tsp. red chile pepper
¼ tsp. salt
2 stalks green onion,
  chopped
½ bunch cilantro or mint
  leaves, chopped
  Sausage casing, sold in
  butcher shops
  Cotton string

nead all food ingredients together in a large bowl. Follow grinder instructions for using sausage attachment. Stuff into casing and tie with cotton string.

Prick holes into sausage casing using a toothpick. This will help prevent bursting of casing during cooking.

Bring a large pot of water to a simmer boil. Simmer sausages in hot water until just cooked, about 5 minutes.

Chill with cold running water and refrigerate.

Finish cooking before serving, by browning over charcoal grill or oiled griddle top until thoroughly hot inside.

Trade Secret: Customers thoroughly enjoy this sausage. The raisins and almonds add an interesting taste and texture to the traditional Chinese duck flavor.

David SooHoo
Chinois East West
Sacramento

Duckling with a Curry Glaze

Bone the duck into 4 pieces, leg and thigh (2) and the breast with wing connections (2). Use bones and giblets, excluding liver, to make a stock.

Cover the bones and giblets with at least 2 qts. water and add 1 onion, 1 Tbsp. ginger, parsley sprigs and black peppercorns. Simmer at least 2 hours. Strain and skim fat. This should yield at least 1 qt. of stock.

Place duck, skin side up, on a baking sheet with sides, and bake uncovered at 400° for 1 to 1½ hours, basting with the fat that accumulates, until very brown. Remove from oven and pour off fat.

Sauté the remaining onion, garlic and ginger in a little of the duck fat. Add curry powder and cook for a few minutes. Add the duck stock and let simmer until needed. Salt to taste.

Drizzle 1 cup of the curry stock over the duck pieces. Cover loosely with foil and return to the oven at 250° for another 1½ hours. This will return moisture to the duck and will tenderize it. Remove foil from top of duck and let crisp for 30 minutes.

Finish the curry glaze by skimming off any fat. Whirl in blender until smooth. Reheat and add a squeeze of lime to sharpen the flavor.

To serve, spoon glaze over each duck piece. May be served with apricot chutney.

Trade Secret: Accompany with Basmati rice and baby bok choy sautéed with sliced shiitake mushrooms.

Serves 4
Preparation Time:
   3½ Hours
Pre-heat oven to 400°

   Two 5 lb. ducks
2 onions, minced
2 Tbsps. fresh ginger,
   minced
   Parsley sprigs
   Black peppercorns
4 cloves garlic, sliced
2 Tbsps. curry powder
4 cups duck stock
   Salt to taste
   Squeeze of lime

Sally Schmitt
The French Laundry
Yountville

Grilled Quail with Mustard Glaze

Serves 4
Preparation Time:
  45 Minutes
(note marinating time)

  8 **quail, whole**
  5 **Tbsps. Dijon mustard**
  2 **tsps. cracked black**
    pepper
  3 **Tbsps. olive oil**
  ¼ **cup Madeira**
  ½ **tsp. kosher salt**
 12 **sage leaves**
  8 **rosemary sprigs**
 12 **thyme sprigs**
  8 **savory sprigs**
  1 **cup dry vermouth**
  ½ **cup white wine vinegar**
  2 **Tbsps. lemon juice**
  ½ **bay leaf**
  1 **tsp. mustard seeds**
  1 **Tbsp. whole black**
    peppercorns
  ½ **tsp. coriander seeds**
  6 **stems of parsley**
  1 **cup quail stock**
  4 **Tbsps. unsalted butter**

 Bone the quail with small, sharp paring knife by cutting down the breastbone and carefully cutting away the carcass, keeping the blade of the knife toward the carcass so that it does not puncture the meat. Cut through the wing and leg joints and free the carcass. Lay the quail out flat, rub with 4 Tbsps. mustard and marinate with the black pepper, olive oil, Madeira, salt, and herbs. Place the quail in the refrigerator, covered with plastic wrap, for 24 to 48 hours, turning occasionally.

For the mustard glaze, combine vermouth, vinegar, lemon juice, bay leaf, mustard seeds, peppercorns, coriander seeds, parsley and stock. Over high heat, reduce mixture to ¼ cup. Strain and blend with softened butter and 1 Tbsp. Dijon mustard.

Light a charcoal or gas grill. While the grill is heating, remove quail from marinade, brush off the herbs, rub with olive oil and season lightly. Grill for 3 minutes, basting occasionally with the mustard glaze. Turn the quail over and grill for another 3 minutes, but still keeping the quail pink.

To serve, drizzle the mustard glaze over the quail.

Bradley Ogden
Lark Creek Inn
Larkspur

Grilled Squab Marinated in Berry Purée

C ut the backbones from the squabs. Flatten the birds and fold the wings under. Select 24 raspberries for garnish and purée the rest through a sieve. Divide the purée in half. Mix half with the butter, salt and pepper in a food processor and set aside. Stir 2 Tbsps. of the olive oil into the other half of the raspberry purée. Season the birds and cover with the raspberry-oil marinade. Marinate for 1 hour.

Meanwhile, blanch the salt pork, rinse, and drain. Trim the squab liver. Mix the remaining olive oil and the thyme and marinate the salt pork, livers, hearts and mushrooms in the oil for 45 minutes; then put them on skewers.

Start a charcoal fire or heat the broiler. Grill the squabs, breast side down, for 5 minutes, moving them to a cooler part of the grill if they begin to brown too fast. Turn the squabs and grill cavity side down until the breast meat feels firm to the touch, about 8 minutes. Don't overcook them; they are best still a little pink. Put them aside to rest for 5 minutes while you grill the skewers for 5 minutes, turning them often.

Mix salt and pepper with the lemon juice and whisk in the walnut oil. Dress the watercress and put it on warm plates. Put the squabs in the center of each plate and the skewers around. Dress the whole raspberries in the vinaigrette dressing remaining in the bowl and scatter them around the plate. Put some of the raspberry butter on top of each bird and serve.

©*New American Classics*

Serves 4
Preparation Time:
   30 Minutes
(note marinating time)

   4 **squabs, with livers and hearts**
2½ **cups fresh raspberries**
   ½ **lb. butter**
      Salt and freshly ground pepper
   4 **Tbsp. olive oil**
   ½ **lb. salt pork, cut into 1" pieces**
   1 **Tbsps. fresh thyme leaves, chopped**
16 **mushrooms**
   2 **Tbsps. lemon juice**
   ½ **cup walnut oil**
   3 **bunches watercress**

Jeremiah Tower
Stars
San Francisco
★

Squab Marinated in Beer

Serves 4
Preparation Time:
  25 Minutes
(note marinating time)

  4 squabs
  8 whole star anise
  3 bay leaves
2″ piece ginger root,
    peeled, sliced
  4 scallions, sliced
  2 tsps. salt
  2 cups white wine
  2 bottles beer
  1 cup fish sauce

Place squab, star anise, bay leaves, ginger root, scallions, salt and wine in a small saucepan with barely enough water to cover the squab. Bring liquid to a boil. Reduce heat to medium and boil for 15 minutes. Drain squab and chill in cold water. Drain again.

In a separate bowl, combine beer and fish sauce. Add squab and marinate, covered, overnight. Chop into small pieces and serve cold.

Philip Lo
Hong Kong Flower Lounge
Millbrae

☆

Venison Chile Verde

Season the venison liberally with salt and pepper. Add 2 Tbsps of the olive oil to a heavy-bottomed 8 qt. casserole and brown the meat thoroughly. Remove the meat, add remaining oil, onions, garlic, optional sausage and brown lightly. Add the browned venison, tomatillos, chiles, herbs and spices, stock and wine. Simmer partially covered for 1½ hours or until meat is tender.

Stir in the Swiss chard and cilantro and simmer for 5 minutes longer. Correct seasoning and add more stock if desired.

Serves 8
Preparation Time:
  2 Hours

  4 **lbs. lean venison stew meat, cut into 1″ cubes**
  2 **cups yellow onions, peeled, chopped**
  2 **Tbsps. garlic, slivered**
  1 **lb. chorizo sausage, cut into ½″ dice, optional**
  4 **Tbsps. olive oil**
  2 **lbs. tomatillos, husks removed, quartered, or two 16 oz. cans tomatillos**
  1 **Tbsp. serrano chile, seeded, diced**
  2 **tsps. fennel seed**
  1 **tsp. cumin seed, toasted, crushed**
  ½ **tsp. cinnamon**
  ½ **tsp. clove**
  2 **large bay leaves**
  4 **cups venison stock or beef consommé**
  1 **cup dry white wine**
  ⅓ **cup Swiss chard, finely shredded**
    Salt and freshly ground black pepper

John Ash
John Ash & Co.
Santa Rosa

Venison Topped with Black Chanterelles and Juniper Berry Sauce

Serves 6
Preparation Time:
  35 Minutes
(note marinating time)

  2 carrots, peeled,
     chopped
  1 large onion, chopped
  4 garlic cloves, chopped
  1 celery stalk, chopped
  ⅓ cup olive oil
  ½ cup wine vinegar
  1 bottle red wine
 10 peppercorns
 18 juniper berries
  1 bouquet garni (bay
     leaves, thyme, parsley)
2¼ lbs. venison filet,
     trimmed
  1 cup black chanterelle
     mushrooms
  ½ tsp. garlic, finely
     chopped
  ½ cup cream
  3 egg yolks
  2 Tbsp. chives, chopped
1½ tsps. tomato paste
  1 cup game stock
     Salt and pepper

Prepare the marinade by placing the carrots, onion, garlic and celery in a large skillet with 3 Tbsps. olive oil. Sauté until lightly brown. Add the vinegar, red wine, peppercorns, 12 juniper berries and bouquet garni. Bring to a boil, then simmer for 15 minutes. Cool and transfer to a large mixing bowl. Add the venison and marinate for 24 hours.

Place the mushrooms in a sauté pan with a little olive oil. Add the chopped garlic and cook for 3 minutes. Chop mushrooms roughly and set aside to cool.

In a small bowl, whisk cream until smooth and fold in the egg yolks. Add the chives and the mushrooms. Check the seasonings.

Remove the venison from the marinade and dry well with paper towels. Strain the marinade and pour into a sauce pot. Bring to a boil, add the tomato paste and 6 juniper berries and reduce. Add the stock and simmer over medium heat until reduced to 1 cup.

Cut the venison into 12 slices, season with salt and pepper. In a large pan, heat 3 Tbsps. olive oil and sauté the venison on both sides, about 3 minutes. Venison should be pink and juicy but not rare. Transfer the meat onto a sheet pan, and top each slice of venison with the mushrooms.

Broil for 1½ minutes until the topping turns a golden brown color. Meanwhile degrease the sauté pan and deglaze with 1 cup of liquid (from stock and marinade reduction). Check the seasoning.

Arrange the venison slices on a warmed serving platter. Pass the sauce separately in a sauce boat and serve immediately.

Hubert Keller
Fleur de Lys
San Francisco

☆

Medallions of Venison with Caramelized Green Apples

Debone and clean saddle. Reserve meat scraps and bone for sauce. Cut medallions to desired width. Cut the bones in small pieces.

In a large saucepan, use a small amount of oil to sauté the bones, until brown. Add the tomato paste, diced carrots, onions, celery and bouquet garni. Drain off the oil. Add water and cook for 1 hour.

In another saucepan, add shallots, wine and port and let the liquid reduce until it is almost gone. Add the stock from the venison bones and cook for 40 minutes. Strain and season with salt and pepper to taste.

Sauté the medallions, 3 per person, as you would any red meat. Heat the butter, add apples and powdered sugar and sauté for 30 seconds on each side. Blanch the asparagus and carrots.

To serve, place the medallions like 3 petals pointing out from the center of the plate. Between the outer tips of medallions place two pieces of apple curving outward like wings. Between the arch of the apples, place 1 baby carrot inside of 2 asparagus tips.

Serves 6
Preparation Time:
 1 Hour

  1 **saddle of venison**
    Extra virgin olive oil
  1 **Tbsp. tomato paste**
 ⅓ **cup carrots, diced**
 ⅓ **cup onions, diced**
 ⅓ **cup celery, diced**
    Bouquet garni
2½ **qts. water**
  2 **shallots**
  2 **cups red wine**
 ½ **cup port**
 ½ **cup clarified butter**
  5 **Granny Smith apples, sliced**
  2 **Tbsps. powdered sugar**
 36 **asparagus tips**
 18 **baby carrots**

Julian Serrano
Masa's
San Francisco

Roast Rack of Venison with Currants and White Raisins

Serves 4
Preparation Time:
   1½ Hours
(note marinating time)

1 rack of venison
1 bottle red wine
3 Tbsps. juniper berries, crushed
2 Tbsps. black pepper, cracked
1 onion, chopped
1 Tbsp. garlic, chopped
1 bunch parsley, chopped
2 bay leaves
2 cups port wine
2 cups venison marinade
1 qt. veal stock
1 Tbsp. peppercorns
10 mushrooms, chopped
¼ cup mixed currants and white raisins

arinate the venison overnight in red wine, 2 Tbsps. juniper berries, black pepper, onion, garlic, parsley and 1 bay leaf.

Two hours before serving time, make the sauce using port wine with the venison marinade. Reduce this to 1 cup, then add the veal stock, peppercorns, 1 Tbsp. juniper berries, mushrooms, 1 bay leaf, currants and raisins. Strain through a fine strainer, reserve currants and raisins and set aside.

45 minutes before serving time, pre-heat oven to 350°. Remove venison rack from marinade and pat dry. Season with salt and pepper.

Film a large sauté pan with olive oil and heat to high. Sear the venison rack all over until browned. Place on a roasting rack in oven and cook until rare, about 20–25 minutes or thermometer registers 120°. Remove to a warm place and allow to rest for 15–20 minutes.

Slice into portions and nap with sauce, sprinkled with currants and raisins.

Wendy Little
Post Ranch Inn
Big Sur

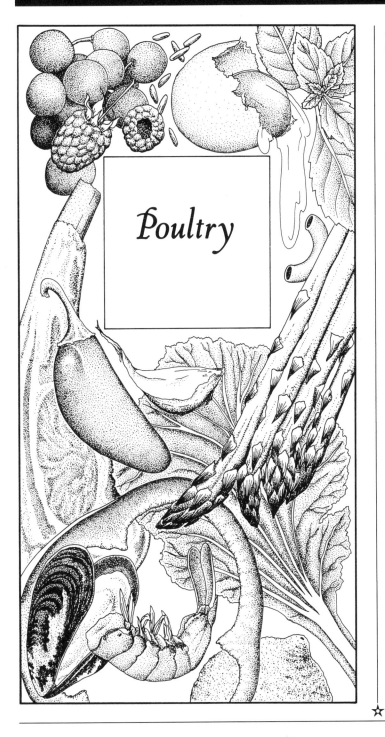

Poultry

Belize BBQ Chicken

Serves 4
Preparation Time:
  2 Hours

¾ cup chile sauce
⅔ cup chicken stock
  Juice of 1 lemon
  Juice of 1 lime
⅓ cup brown sugar
3 Tbsps. soy sauce
1 garlic clove
2 jalapeños or 1 Habanero
  chile, minced
2 Tbsps. coarse ground
  mustard
1 Tbsp. Worcestershire
  sauce
1 chipotle chile, minced
  Zest of 2 oranges
1 chicken fryer, 3 lbs.
  Sea salt and freshly
  ground pepper

lace all ingredients except the chicken, salt and pepper into a stock kettle and simmer for 20 minutes. Let cool.

Cut the backbone out of the chicken, then butterfly. Lightly season with sea salt and freshly ground pepper.

Apply sauce to both sides of chicken lavishly and cook slowly at 275° for 1½ hours. Raise heat to 400° for 15 minutes and serve immediately with natural juices.

Alan Greeley
The Golden Truffle
Costa Mesa

☆

Chicken Breasts Stuffed with Mushrooms and Spinach in a Hazelnut Sauce

Stem the spinach completely. Carefully wash the leaves to remove all sand and grit. Place the washed leaves in a pre-heated sauté pan with butter, stirring occasionally until the leaves are wilted, about 3 minutes. Drain in a colander and squeeze out excess moisture.

Sauté the mushrooms in olive oil for 5 minutes. Add salt and pepper. Set aside.

Remove the skin and tendons from the chicken breasts and discard. Flatten each breast lightly with a large knife. Season the filets on both sides with salt and pepper. Top them with 1 Tbsp. of wild mushrooms and an equal amount of wilted spinach. Roll each breast in 10″ plastic wrap. Set aside.

Poach the chicken in the hazelnut sauce on the following page.

Serves 4
Preparation Time:
  15 Minutes

  4 **large chicken breasts**
  2 **bunches spinach leaves**
  2 **Tbsps. butter**
  ¾ **cup wild mushrooms**
     (chanterelle, shiitake,
     morels)
  2 **Tbsps. olive oil**
     Salt and pepper

Hubert Keller
Fleur de Lys
San Francisco

175

Hazelnut Sauce

Preparation Time:
1½ Hours

Chicken bones,
   chopped
3 Tbsps. oil
1 carrot, chopped
1 onion, chopped
1 celery stalk, chopped
1 garlic clove, chopped
1½ cups white wine
1 Tbsp. tomato paste
1 bouquet garni (bay
   leaf, thyme, parsley)
4 cups water
2 Tbsps. port wine
4 Tbsps. butter
   Salt and pepper
4 Tbsps. hazelnut oil

 oast the chopped chicken bones in the oven or sauté bones in a stock pot in oil. When bones are browned to a golden color, add the carrots, onions, celery and garlic. When the vegetables brown, remove any grease with a spoon and pour in the white wine. Add the tomato paste and the bouquet garni and reduce by half.

Add water and bring to a boil, skimming off any film that rises to the top. Lower the heat to a simmer and cook for 1 hour. Pour the stock through a sieve. Discard the solids and skim off any fat.

Poach the chicken breasts in the plastic wrap for 12 minutes in the stock or until cooked. Remove the cooked chicken from the stock and keep warm.

Reduce the stock to ½ cup. Add the port wine and whisk in butter, a few pieces at a time. Stir in the salt and pepper to taste and add the hazelnut oil.

Remove the chicken breasts from the plastic wrap and slice the breasts on the bias. Serve with the hazelnut sauce.

Hubert Keller
Fleur de Lys
San Francisco

Grilled Chicken in Five-Spice Marinade

Heat the olive oil in a medium saucepan. Add the red pepper flakes, orange zest, garlic and ginger. After 10 minutes, add the remaining ingredients. Cool completely.

Pour the marinade over the chicken. Cover and refrigerate overnight. Bring to room temperature before broiling or grilling. Broil 4 minutes on each side.

Five-Spice Powder

Equal parts in weight of cinnamon sticks, star anise, cloves, fennel seed and black peppercorns. Grind in spice mill. Can be stored for a few months at room temperature in a tightly sealed jar.

Serves 4
Preparation Time:
   30 Minutes
(note refrigeration time)

  6 lbs. chicken, butterflied
     or half broilers
  2 cups olive oil
  3 Tbsps. red pepper flakes
     Zest of 3 oranges
  6 garlic cloves, smashed
     Six 2″ thick pieces
     ginger root, peeled and
     mashed
  2 Tbsps. five-spice
     powder, recipe follows
  1/8 cup sesame oil
  1/4 cup fresh lemon juice
     Salt

Joyce Goldstein
Square One Restaurant
San Francisco

Chicken Napolitana

Serves 4
Preparation Time:
 45 Minutes

 4 **chicken breasts,**
   skinless
   Olive oil
 1 **red bell pepper, sliced**
 1 **green bell pepper, sliced**
 1 **onion, sliced**
12 **baby artichokes, halved**
 3 **tsps. garlic, minced**
 4 **Roma tomatoes,**
   chopped
½ **bulb fennel, sliced thin**
⅓ **cup basil, chopped**
⅓ **cup oregano, chopped**
 1 **tsp. red chiles, crushed**
 1 **cup red wine**
 1 **cup chicken stock**
 1 **Tbsp. tomato paste**

 auté chicken breast in olive oil. Add bell peppers, onion, artichokes, garlic, tomatoes and fennel, cooking for 10 minutes over low heat.

Add basil, oregano and chiles and cook for 2 minutes. Add red wine and reduce by half.

Add chicken stock and reduce by half. Add tomato paste to thicken slightly.

To serve, place chicken breasts on individual plates and drape with sauce.

William Donnelly
Chez Melange
Redondo Beach

Taipei Grilled Chicken Breasts

Combine all ingredients in a medium mixing bowl except for the peanut oil and chicken.

Briskly whip in the peanut oil and baste over the chicken breasts. Marinate for 2 hours prior to grilling or baking chicken.

Allow 15 minutes if chicken is to be grilled and 30 minutes to cook chicken in the oven.

Trade Secret: This sauce is an excellent dipping sauce on the side for chicken, pork, veal or rabbit and will store up to 2 weeks in the refrigerator.

Serves 6
Preparation Time:
   20 Minutes
(note marinating time)

 1 **cup Hoisin sauce**
 ¼ **cup red wine vinegar**
 2 **Tbsps. black bean paste**
 4 **garlic cloves, diced**
 1 **two-inch piece fresh ginger, peeled, grated**
 4 **scallions, chopped**
 1 **Tbsp. soy sauce**
 1 **Tbsp. dry mustard**
 1 **Tbsp. Tabasco**
 ¼ **cup peanut oil**
 6 **chicken breasts**

David Beckwith
Central 159 Restaurant and Catering
Pacific Grove
☆

179

Chicken Breast Criollo with Mango Salsa

Serves 4
Preparation Time:
 15 Minutes
(note marinating time)

 4 **chicken breasts,**
   boneless
 ½ **cup soy sauce**
 ½ **cup peanut oil**
 1 **tsp. Cajun spices**
 1 **tsp. black pepper**
 1 **Tbsp. achiote paste**
 1 **tsp. garlic, puréed**
 ½ **cup jicama, diced**
 1½ **cups fresh mango (ripe**
   but not firm), diced
 2 **Tbsps. fresh dill,**
   chopped
 ½ **red bell pepper, diced**
   Juice of half lime
 2 **serrano chiles,**
   diced fine
   Salt and pepper
   to taste

Pound the chicken breasts to ¼-inch thick. Set aside.
Prepare the marinade by mixing the soy sauce, peanut oil, Cajun spices, pepper, achiote paste and garlic. Allow the chicken to marinate for 2 hours before cooking.

Prepare the mango salsa by mixing together the jicama, mango, dill, bell pepper, lime juice, chiles and salt and pepper. Set aside.

Grill the chicken breasts or sauté them for 3 minutes on each side. When cooked, serve each breast garnished with 4 Tbsps. mango salsa.

Trade Secret: Achiote is a spice blend of ground annatto seeds, cumin, vinegar, garlic and other spices. Achiote paste is available in the gourmet section of many food and specialty stores.

Julio Ramirez
The Fishwife, El Cocodrilo
Pacific Grove

Tarragon Chicken Breasts with Crab and Asparagus

T rim and discard bottom 1½-inch of asparagus stalks. Peel larger asparagus.

Combine broth, Pernod, salt, pepper, onion, garlic, celery seed and anise seed in a large non-reactive skillet. Cover and place skillet over high heat, bringing the mixture to a boil. Add the asparagus and cook until tender, about 2 minutes for pencil-thick asparagus and up to 4 minutes for thicker spears. Remove the asparagus when done and place covered in a 250° oven to keep warm.

Reduce heat to low and add the chicken breasts. If using dried tarragon, add it now. Cover and simmer 7 minutes or until breasts are done. Remove breasts and keep warm with the asparagus in the oven.

Increase heat to high and boil the liquid until it becomes sauce-like and is thick enough to coat the back of a spoon. Add the crab meat and cook another minute to heat through. Remove from the heat, whisk in the butter and cream and add the fresh tarragon.

To serve, arrange the asparagus on a plate and place a chicken breast on top. Place a piece of crab on the chicken and spoon the sauce around the plate. Serve immediately.

© *What's for Dinner*

Serves 4
Preparation Time:
30 Minutes

1 **lb. asparagus**
1 **cup fresh or canned low-sodium chicken broth**
1 **Tbsp. Pernod**
½ **tsp. salt or as desired**
½ **tsp. ground white pepper**
2 **Tbsps. onions or shallots, minced**
1 **garlic clove, minced**
½ **tsp. celery seed**
½ **tsp. anise seed**
2 **boneless chicken breasts, halved, skin removed**
1 **Tbsp. fresh tarragon leaves, chopped or 1 tsp. dried**
½ **lb. crab leg meat**
1 **Tbsp. butter, unsalted**
¼ **cup cream**

Michael Roberts
Trumps
West Hollywood

⋆

Roasted Cornish Game Hens

Serves 6
Preparation Time:
  1 Hour
(note marinating time)

⅓ cup honey
 3 Tbsps. vinegar
 3 Tbsps. garlic, minced
    Fresh thyme
    Fresh marjoram
    Fresh sage
    Salt and pepper to taste
 3 Cornish game hens

repare the marinade by mixing together the honey, vinegar, garlic, herbs and salt and pepper. Marinate the hens for 4 hours.

Spit-roast the hens for 1 hour over a low fire.

Trade Secret: Arrange ½ game hen per person on a nest of cooked pasta surrounded by vegetables.

Todd Muir
Madrona Manor
Healdsburg

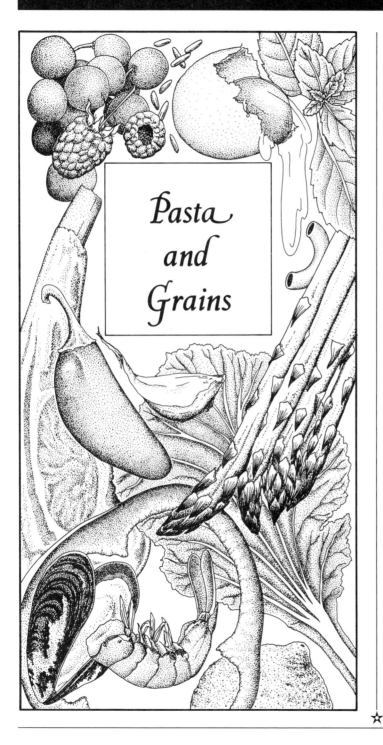

Pasta and Grains

Fettucine with grilled artichokes
Fettucine, olive, tomato & basil
Linguine, cherry tomato vinaigrette
Linguine with seafood
Pasta with grilled lobster
Pasta fantasia
Sun-dried tomato pasta
Penne with grilled swordfish
Creamy wild mushroom polenta
Grilled polenta with cheese
Risotto with asparagus, smoked ham
Risotto in puff pastry
Seafood ravioli
Goat cheese wontons

Fettucine with Grilled Artichokes

Serves 4
Preparation Time:
  20 Minutes

  4 **fresh artichoke hearts**
     Juice of 1 lemon
  4 **Tbsps. olive oil**
  1 **head garlic, peeled,**
     cloves crushed
  4 **cups chicken stock**
  ½ **cup corn kernels**
  2 **Tbsps. chervil, chopped**
  2 **tsps. marjoram,**
     chopped
  3 **Tbsps. butter**
     Salt and pepper to taste
     Fresh fettucine for 4

repare artichoke hearts by rubbing with lemon juice and 2 Tbsps. olive oil. Grill until tender. Slice thin.
In a large sauté pan, heat 2 Tbsps. olive oil to the point of smoking, then reduce heat to medium. Add garlic and sauté until golden brown. Add sliced artichokes and toss well. Add chicken stock and reduce until sauce begins to take on body. Add corn, chervil, marjoram and butter. Simmer until butter has been incorporated, then adjust seasonings with salt and pepper as needed.

Cook fresh pasta in rapidly boiling salted water until firm to the tooth (al dente). Drain and toss with the sauce. Serve immediately.

Cindy Pawlcyn
Bistro Roti, Bix, Buckeye Roadhouse, Fog City Diner, Mustards Grill, Tra Vigne
San Francisco, Marin, Napa

Fettucine Noodles with Olive, Tomato and Basil

Prepare the olive tapenade by puréeing the olives, ⅓ cup olive oil, 1 Tbsp. chopped garlic and white pepper in a blender or food processor. Set aside.

Prepare the tomato concasse by peeling the tomatoes, then seeding and chopping finely. Cook the tomatoes in a heavy-bottomed pan, stirring frequently, until all liquid has evaporated, leaving a thick tomato paste. Season with salt and pepper. Set aside.

Prepare the pesto by puréeing basil leaves with 6 garlic cloves, olive oil, lemon juice, salt and pepper. Purée well, add pinenuts and Parmesan cheese. Purée again and reserve.

Cook noodles in plenty of boiling salted water until al dente. Chill immediately in ice water. Drain well. Toss with a little olive oil to prevent noodles from sticking.

To assemble pasta, toss with olive tapenade, tomato concasse and pesto. Garnish with Parmesan cheese.

Serves 4
Preparation Time:
  30 Minutes

  ½ **lb. Kalamata olives,**
    pitted
1⅓ **cup olive oil**
  1 **Tbsp. garlic, chopped**
  1 **tsp. fresh ground**
    white pepper
  1 **lb. ripe tomatoes**
  2 **big bunches basil**
  6 **garlic cloves**
    Juice of 1 lemon
  2 **Tbsps. pinenuts,**
    toasted
  ¼ **cup Parmesan cheese,**
    grated
  1 **lb. good quality**
    fettucine noodles

Wendy Little
Post Ranch Inn
Big Sur
☆

Linguine with Cherry Tomato Vinaigrette

Serves 4
Preparation Time:
  25 Minutes

  5 **cups cherry tomatoes,**
    preferably Sweet 100
  1 **cup virgin olive oil**
    Red wine vinegar
    Salt and pepper
1½ **cups fresh bread**
    crumbs
  1 **handful fresh basil**
    leaves
    Linguine for 4

he quality of this simple pasta depends on the excellence of the tomatoes (Sweet 100 is a varietal name. They are very small and intensely sweet.)

Cut the tomatoes in half and marinate them in olive oil, red wine vinegar to taste, and salt and pepper. Toast the fresh bread crumbs in the oven until dry and lightly browned. Take them from the oven and toss with some olive oil while still warm.

Cook the pasta, and while it is boiling, put the tomatoes in a pan and warm them. Add the pasta to the pan, toss together with the tomatoes, and serve.

Garnish the dish with the bread crumbs and basil leaves cut into tiny ribbons.

Variations: Peel large ripe tomatoes and quarter them. Dress them with virgin olive oil, red wine vinegar, salt and pepper, minced garlic, and lots of dwarf basil leaves. Cook fresh noodles and toss the hot pasta with the cold tomatoes. Finely dice peeled and seeded tomatoes, a mixture of multicolored sweet peppers and red onion. Season with salt, pepper, vinegar and chopped parsley, basil and coriander.

Boil linguine, drain, toss in olive oil, then mix with the tomato mixture and chill.

©*Chez Panisse Pasta, Pizza and Calzone Cookbook*

Alice Waters
Chez Panisse Cafe & Restaurant
Berkeley

Linguine with Seafood and Steamed Tomatoes

Steam tomatoes or cook them whole until soft but not dry. Cool, then remove the skin and seeds. Chop coarsely and set aside.

In a 2 qt. saucepan add the garlic, shallots, olive oil and half the butter. Sauté until light brown. Add the seafood and sauté for 1 minute. Add the Pernod carefully as it may flame. Then add the tomatoes, basil, salt and pepper. Cook for about 3 minutes. Add the remaining butter.

Cook noodles in boiling water for 2 minutes or until desired doneness is reached. Mix noodles in sauce and serve hot.

Serves 4
Preparation Time:
  30 Minutes

1½ **lbs. tomatoes**
  4 **Tbsps. garlic, chopped fine**
  4 **Tbsps. shallots, chopped fine**
  ½ **cup olive oil**
  8 **Tbsps. butter, (1 stick) unsalted**
  ¼ **lb. scallops or chopped raw shrimp**
  ¼ **lb. whole clams**
  ¼ **cup Pernod liqueur, optional**
  4 **Tbsps. basil, julienne**
    Salt and pepper to taste
  1 **lb. fresh noodles: linguine, angel hair or fettucine**

Hugo Molina
Parkway Grill
Pasadena

Pasta with Grilled Lobster and Beluga Caviar in Chardonnay Cream Sauce

Serves 6
Preparation Time:
  30 Minutes

¾ cup California
  Chardonnay
1 medium-size shallot,
  chopped fine
2 cups heavy cream
  Salt and freshly ground
  white pepper
  Fresh lemon juice
2 lobsters, 1½ lb. each
3 Tbsps. extra-virgin
  olive oil
  Fresh angel hair pasta
  for 6
2 Tbsps. clarified butter
2 Tbsps. fresh basil,
  julienne
¼ cup beluga caviar

In a small heavy, nonaluminum saucepan, boil the Chardonnay with the shallots over high heat until only about 2 Tbsps. of liquid are left, 5 to 7 minutes. Then add the cream, reduce the heat slightly and simmer until the sauce is thick and reduced by about half, 7 to 10 minutes more. Season to taste with salt, pepper and a little lemon juice.

In a food processor, or with a hand-held blender, process the sauce until smooth, 1 to 2 minutes. Strain it through a fine-mesh sieve and return it to the pan to warm through gently. Adjust the seasonings to taste.

To keep the sauce warm, set the saucepan inside a bowl or larger pan of hot but not boiling water.

Blanch the lobsters in boiling water for 5 minutes, then remove and shell, leaving claws whole and tails cut into ¾-inch medallions.

In a large pot, bring 8 qts. of lightly salted water to a boil; add the olive oil. Add the pasta to the boiling water and cook until al dente, no more than 2 minutes. Drain well.

At the same time, brush the lobster medallions and claws with the butter and season lightly with salt and pepper. Grill them about 30 seconds per side.

Toss the pasta with the sauce and mound it in the middle of each of 6 heated large, shallow serving plates. Place 3 pieces of lobster on top of each serving and garnish with basil and a dollop of caviar.

©*Michael's Cookbook*

Martin Garcia
Michael's
Santa Monica

Pasta Fantasia

Bring a large pot of salted water to a boil.
In a large skillet, heat olive oil, adding the shrimp, garlic and chile flakes. Cook over medium heat for about 3 minutes.

Add pasta to boiling water. Fresh pasta will cook in about 3 to 4 minutes. If you use dry pasta, start boiling your pasta before you start cooking the shrimp.

Add parsley, salt and fresh ground pepper to the sautéed shrimp. Stir in lemon juice and butter.

Drain pasta and add to the shrimp. Toss in tomatoes and arugula. Check the seasoning and adjust if necessary. Serve immediately.

Serves 4
Preparation Time:
  15 Minutes

 4 Tbsps. olive oil
28 large shrimp, peeled, deveined
 3 cloves garlic, finely chopped
½ tsp. chile flakes
 1 lb. fresh papardelle or fettucine pasta
 2 Tbsps. Italian parsley, chopped
   Salt and fresh ground black pepper to taste
   Juice of 1 lemon
10 Tbsps. (1¼ sticks) butter
 4 large Roma tomatoes, seeded, diced
 2 bunches arugula, stems removed

Donna Scala
Piatti Ristorante
Sacramento, Napa, Sonoma, Carmel, Montecito, La Jolla

Sun-Dried Tomato Pasta

Yield: 2 pounds
Preparation Time:
 1 Hour

8 Tbsps. sun-dried tomato
   paste
4 cups flour (all-purpose
   or semolina)
6 eggs, beaten
¼ cup olive oil
¼ tsp. salt

lace all ingredients into a mixer bowl. Using the paddle attachment, with mixer on #2 speed, beat the ingredients for 3 to 5 minutes to form a dough, stopping the mixer to scrape the sides of the bowl as necessary.

Turn the dough onto a worktable and knead for 1 to 2 minutes. Allow the dough to rest for about 1 hour before making it into pasta, or refrigerating or freezing.

With a rolling pin, roll the pasta out on a large lightly floured surface, stretching it as you roll. Rotate the dough a quarter turn each time you roll. The finished dough should be less than ¹⁄₁₆″ thick. If using a pasta machine, pass the pieces of kneaded dough through the rollers, decreasing the distance between the rollers with each run through. Do not fold it during this process. Continue to stretch it until you have reached the desired thickness. Flour the dough as necessary to keep it from sticking.

Allow the pasta to dry slightly before cutting it. To do this, arrange it on a suitable drying rack or spread it out on lightly floured towels. Let it dry until it no longer feels cold and wet, but do not let it become brittle. This could take 5 minutes or much longer. The time varies considerably, so feel it frequently as it dries.

Cut as desired using a knife, pasta cutter or a machine.

Todd Muir
Madrona Manor
Healdsburg

Penne with Marinated Grilled Swordfish and Plum Tomatoes

I n a medium bowl, prepare the marinade by combining the olive oil, lemon juice, parsley, 4 chopped garlic cloves, salt and pepper. Set aside.

Prepare the broiler, the grill or the barbecue. Brush the swordfish lightly with oil and place on the hot grill. Cook 2 to 3 minutes on each side. Place the swordfish in a shallow dish, add the marinade and leave 1 to 2 hours, basting or turning the fish a few times.

Bring a large pot of water to a boil. Add 1 tsp. of salt. Remove 5 Tbsps. of the marinade and place in a large skillet. Add 1 minced garlic clove, anchovies, tomatoes and pepper flakes. Cook over medium heat, stirring 2 to 3 minutes. Raise the heat and add the wine.

Cook, stirring until the wine is almost all reduced, 4 to 5 minutes. Season lightly with salt. Remember that anchovies are already quite salty.

Remove the swordfish from the marinade and cut into 1-inch pieces. Add to the skillet together with the capers and the basil. Stir once or twice.

Add the penne pasta to the pot of boiling water and cook until tender but still firm to the bite. Drain and add to the skillet with the sauce. Toss gently over low heat until the pasta and sauce are well combined. Taste and adjust the seasonings. Serve immediately.

Serves 4
Preparation Time:
 30 Minutes
(note marinating time)

- 1 **cup olive oil**
  Juice of 1 lemon
- 2 **Tbsps. parsley, chopped**
- 5 **garlic cloves, peeled, chopped**
  Salt and freshly ground pepper
- 2 **swordfish steaks, 7 to 8 oz. each, 1-inch thick**
- 4 **anchovy filets, mashed**
- 4 **ripe juicy plum tomatoes, diced**
- ½ **tsp. red chile pepper flakes**
- 1 **cup dry white wine**
- 2 **Tbsps. capers, rinsed**
- 8 **to 10 large basil leaves, thinly sliced**
- 1 **lb. penne pasta**

Biba Caggiano
Biba Restaurant
Sacramento

Creamy Wild Mushroom Polenta

Serves 6
Pre-heat oven to 350°

2 cups water
2 cups chicken stock
1 3-inch sprig of rosemary
4 tsps. garlic, minced
1 cup polenta (cornmeal)
8 Tbsps. butter, (1 stick) unsalted
½ lb. wild mushrooms cleaned, trimmed, and sliced ¼″ thick
1 Tbsp. kosher salt
1 tsp. ground white pepper
3 Tbsps. each parley, sage and marjoram, chopped
1 cup sour cream or mascarpone

 ring the water and stock to a rolling boil in oven-proof pot. Add the rosemary sprig, 2 tsps. garlic and polenta, stirring with a wooden spoon continuously, to ensure there are no lumps, for 5 to 10 minutes.

Cover pot and place in preheated oven, baking for 45 minutes, stirring occasionally. Remove from oven and add half the butter. Hold on a double boiler to keep warm.

Melt the remaining half of the butter in a sauté pan. Put the mushrooms in the skillet, sautéing in the butter for 2 minutes. Add remaining 2 tsps. garlic and season with salt and pepper to taste. Sauté for another 2 to 3 minutes or until mushrooms are soft. Add mushrooms to the polenta with the herbs and sour cream. Season to taste if necessary and serve immediately.

Bradley Ogden
Lark Creek Inn
Larkspur

Grilled Polenta with Sonoma Jack Cheese

In a large saucepan, bring stock, salt to taste, white pepper and thyme to a boil. Slowly stir in polenta or cornmeal with a whisk to avoid lumps. Reduce heat to low and stir to prevent sticking. Cook slowly for 10 minutes.

In a separate skillet, heat 2 Tbsps. butter. Sauté minced mushrooms and scallions until brown, about 5 minutes. Season with salt and pepper. Add wine and reduce until most of the wine cooks away. Add to the polenta mixture with remaining butter and parsley.

Butter a large shallow dish or baking sheet. Spread polenta mixture in the dish to a depth of ½″ and smooth top. Cool, cover with plastic wrap and refrigerate.

Cut polenta into 4″ diamonds. Grill until surface is lightly toasted. Turn, cover with a slice of jack cheese and grill until cheese is just starting to melt.

Sauté the shiitake mushrooms in butter.

Serve the grilled polenta warm, garnished with the shiitake mushrooms and slivers of sun-dried tomatoes.

Serves 6
Preparation Time:
  45 Minutes
(note refrigeration time)

- 1 qt. chicken stock or chicken broth
  Salt and white pepper
- 2 tsps. ground white pepper
- 1 tsp. fresh thyme, minced
- 1 cup polenta or yellow cornmeal
- 8 Tbsps. (1 stick) butter
- ½ cup mushrooms, minced
- ½ cup scallions, minced
- ½ cup dry white wine
- 1 Tbsp. parsley, minced
- ½ lb. Sonoma jack cheese, sliced
- ⅓ lb. shiitake mushrooms, sliced
- 2 Tbsps. sun-dried tomatoes, sliced

John Ash
John Ash & Co.
Santa Rosa

Risotto with Asparagus, Peas and Smoked Ham

Serves 4
Preparation Time:
  30 Minutes

1 lb. thin asparagus
1 cup freshly shelled peas
2 qts. chicken broth, preferably homemade
5 Tbsps. unsalted butter
1 small onion, finely minced
2 cups Italian Arborio rice
1 cup dry white wine
1 cup smoked ham, diced
⅓ cup Parmesan cheese, freshly grated

Wash the asparagus and cut off the tops. Bring a medium saucepan of salted water to a boil and add the asparagus tips. Cook until tender but still firm to the bite. Remove from water and set aside.

Add the fresh peas to the boiling water and cook until tender but still firm to the bite. Drain and set aside.

Heat the broth in a medium saucepan and keep warm over low heat.

Melt 4 Tbsps. butter in a large skillet over medium heat. When the butter foams, add the onion. Cook, stirring until pale yellow, 4 to 5 minutes.

Add the rice and mix a few times. When the rice is coated with the butter, add the wine. Cook, stirring constantly, until the wine is almost all reduced, 2 to 3 minutes. Add one ladle of hot broth, or just enough to cover the rice. Cook over medium heat, stirring, until the broth has been absorbed. Add another ladle of broth. Continue cooking and stirring the rice, adding broth a bit at a time for about 15 minutes. Add the asparagus tips, the peas, the remaining butter, the smoked ham and the Parmesan cheese. Cook and stir until all the ingredients have been thoroughly incorporated. At this point the rice should be moist and creamy and should still be firm to the bite. If too dry, add a bit more broth. Serve at once.

Biba Caggiano
Biba Restaurant
Sacramento

Risotto in Puff Pastry
with Fresh Porcini Mushrooms

Place the dry porcini mushrooms in warm water for 10 minutes, remove and drain, chop fine and set aside.

Melt half the butter in a deep pan over moderate heat. Add the dry porcini mushrooms, onion and garlic. Sauté until soft. Add rice and stir for 2 minutes. Pour in wine and cook until liquid evaporates. Add boiling chicken broth ½ cup at a time, stirring constantly until each addition is absorbed before adding the next. The rice should always be covered by a veil of broth. When rice is cooked, about 15 minutes, add Parmesan cheese, remaining butter, salt and pepper to taste.

Sauté the fresh porcini mushrooms in olive oil. Spoon the rice into a 6" × 2" deep soufflé container, cover with sautéed fresh porcini mushrooms. Cover with pizza dough and bake until golden brown, about 4 minutes. Serve immediately.

Serves 6
Preparation Time:
 45 Minutes
Pre-heat oven to 450°

½ oz. dry porcini
  mushrooms
6 Tbsps. butter, unsalted
1 small onion, chopped
  fine
2 garlic cloves, chopped
2 cups Arborio rice
1 cup dry white wine
6 cups chicken broth
½ cup Parmesan cheese,
  freshly grated
  Salt and fresh ground
  pepper
1 lb. fresh porcini
  mushrooms
3 Tbsps. extra virgin
  olive oil
6 rounds of pizza dough,
  7" each

Gianpaolo Putzu
Il Fornaio Cucina Italiana
Del Mar
✩

Seafood Ravioli with Smoked Sturgeon

Yield: 3 Dozen
Preparation Time:
  30 Minutes
(note refrigeration time)

  2 Tbsps. unsalted butter
  1 lb. prawns, chopped
  1 Tbsp. shallots, chopped
  2 Tbsps. heavy cream
  ⅓ tsp. salt
  1 tsp. sugar
  ⅛ tsp. white pepper
  1 tsp. oyster sauce
  ¾ cup cream cheese
  2 Tbsps. parsley, chopped
 72 fresh wonton wrappers,
    3″ × 3″ square
    Egg wash: 2 beaten eggs
  ¼ lb. smoked sturgeon,
    chopped

Melt the butter in a Teflon sauté pan. Add the prawns and shallots and sauté over medium heat until lightly browned. Add the cream and continue to sauté until the water has evaporated and the seafood mix begins to bind together. Transfer to a large mixing bowl and let cool.

Add salt, sugar, pepper, oyster sauce, cream cheese and parsley to the seafood mix and knead with your fingers until mixed well. Chill in the refrigerator.

Lay out wonton wrappers and brush edges with egg wash of beaten eggs. Spoon a heaping teaspoon of the seafood filling. Top with a pinch of smoked sturgeon. Lay another sheet of wonton into the center of each wonton over the filling and press to seal the finished ravioli.

Boil the ravioli in simmering hot water until dough is translucent and cooked. A good rule to follow is to remember that cooked pasta will float to the top.

Trade Secret: I like to serve raviolis with a light sauce made by boiling rich fish stock with garlic and a touch of oyster sauce. Add a little cornstarch dissolved in water for body. Swirl in a touch of butter for richness. Adjust to taste and ladle over raviolis. Garnish with grated Parmesan cheese and a sprig of cilantro.

David SooHoo
Chinois East West
Sacramento

Goat Cheese Wontons

I n a 10-inch skillet, pour 2 Tbsps. olive oil and place over medium heat, allowing to come just under smoking temperature. Add diced zucchini, yellow squash, red pepper and eggplant, tossing quickly in the skillet for 2 minutes. Add chopped shallots and garlic and continue to sauté for 1 minute. Remove from skillet and pour into colander to allow any extra oil to run off. Vegetables should be still slightly firm. Place strained vegetables in a mixing bowl and add olives and parsley. Add salt and pepper to taste. Mix in the goat cheese until well combined.

On a flat surface, lay out 24 wonton wrappers. In a small bowl, whisk egg yolks with a fork. With a small pastry brush, rub the outer area of each of the wonton skins with the egg wash. In the middle of each wonton, place a small mound of the filling, approximately 2 Tbsps. Top with another wonton, pressing edges firmly together. Make sure that all of the air has been pressed out from inside and that the wontons have been sealed well.

In boiling water with 1 Tbsp. oil and a pinch of salt, cook wontons in batches of 4 or 5 at a time for approximately 1 minute. Remove and cool in water to stop the cooking process. Drain well and toss lightly in oil to avoid any sticking.

Trade Secret: The filling for wontons can be made 2–3 days prior. Goat cheese wontons are served by Brian with a rack of lamb and ratatouille vegetables. The wontons are drizzled with hot lamb juice.

Yield: 24
Preparation Time:
  45 Minutes

  3 Tbsps. olive oil
  ¼ cup zucchini, diced
  ¼ cup yellow squash, diced
  ¼ cup red pepper, diced
  ¼ cup eggplant, peeled, diced
  2 Tbsps. shallots, chopped
  2 garlic cloves, chopped
  ¼ cup black olives (pitted calamatas) chopped
  1 Tbsp. parsley, chopped
  ¼ lb. goat cheese, crumbled, room temperature
  48 wonton wrappers
  4 egg yolks

Brian Whitmer
Pacific's Edge
Highlands Inn
Carmel

★

Fruits and Vegetables

Roasted Baby Artichokes

Squeeze the juice from 1 lemon into 4 cups water. Cut the remaining lemon in half. Wash the artichokes and remove the tough or discolored outer leaves. Cut off the stem close to the base. Chop about ½-inch off the top center leaves; then snip the remaining thorny tips. Squeeze lemon juice immediately on each artichoke and place them in the water mixed with lemon juice. Drain before cooking.

Place the remaining ingredients in a baking dish with the artichokes. Bake uncovered for 20 minutes. Baste occasionally with the juices from the pan. Test for doneness by piercing the bottom of an artichoke with a paring knife. If it is tender, it is done. Let cool in dish. Cut in half and remove the thistles.

Sauté until lightly brown in olive oil and serve 4 halves per person as an appetizer.

Serves 4
Preparation Time:
30 Minutes
Pre-heat oven to 375°

2 lemons
8 baby artichokes
    Pinch of salt
2 garlic cloves
¼ tsp. kosher salt
⅛ tsp. cracked black
    pepper
½ cup fresh tomatoes,
    diced
⅓ cup Pinot Noir
5 fresh thyme sprigs
3 fresh rosemary sprigs
8 fresh parsley stems
2 Tbsps. balsamic vinegar
3 Tbsps. olive oil
⅓ cup chicken stock

Bradley Ogden
Lark Creek Inn
Larkspur

Eggplant with Ginger Butter

Serves 6
Preparation Time:
  15 Minutes

  6 **Japanese eggplants,**
    medium sized
    Virgin olive oil
  3 **red onions, peeled,**
    sliced into rounds
 10 **Tbsps. (1¼ sticks)**
    unsalted butter, sliced
    1-inch piece ginger root,
    peeled, grated
  1 **shallot, peeled, minced**
 ¼ **tsp. salt**
    Ground white pepper to
    taste

Slice eggplants lengthwise almost to the core several times, so they fan out. Brush with olive oil and grill over hot coals, 3 minutes per side. Brush onion slices with oil and grill at the same time. Set aside.

Prepare the ginger butter by combining the butter, ginger root, shallot, salt and white pepper in a food processor. Mix well.

To serve, fan out eggplants, on plates, inserting a slice of onion between each slice of eggplant. Top with ginger butter.

Cindy Pawlcyn
Bistro Roti, Bix, Buckeye Roadhouse, Fog City Diner, Mustards Grill, Tra Vigne
San Francisco, Mill Valley, Napa

☆

Eggplant Scapece

Slice eggplant with skin on diagonal into ¼-inch thick slices. Fry in oil, 375° to 400° in small batches until golden brown. Drain well on paper towels. Season with salt and pepper. Set aside.

In a sauce pot, combine the vinegar, sugar, onion and olive oil and simmer over low heat. Reserve 3 leaves of mint julienne and add the remainder to the sauce pot. Cook 20 minutes, or until onions are transparent and sauce is reduced.

In straight-sided pan, layer fried eggplant with sprinkling of mint and marinade, until it's all used. Allow to rest at least 2 hours before serving. Eggplant should be served tepid.

Serves 4
Preparation Time:
  30 Minutes
(note marinating time)

 4 **small Japanese eggplants or 1 large eggplant**
   Oil for frying
   Salt and pepper to taste
 2 **cups red wine vinegar**
 1 **cup granulated sugar**
 1 **medium red onion, peeled, sliced thin**
 1 **Tbsp. extra virgin olive oil**
10 **large mint leaves, cut in julienne**

Suzette Gresham-Tognetti
Acquerello
San Francisco
✫

Grilled Leeks with Caper Beurre Blanc

Serves 4
Preparation Time:
30 Minutes

20 small leeks, about ½"
    in diameter
 1 cup dry white wine
 2 shallots, thinly sliced
 6 whole black
    peppercorns
 1 cup cold unsalted
    butter, cut into ½"
    pieces
 2 Tbsps. capers, coarsely
    chopped
¼ cup olive oil
    Kosher salt and freshly
    ground black pepper
 1 hard-cooked egg,
    optional
 2 Tbsps. Italian parsley,
    chopped

emove all wilted or brown outer layers from the leeks. Trim off the roots close to the end of the stalk. Do not trim too closely or the leeks will fall apart when cooked. Cut the leeks to a uniform length, 5 to 6 inches, and split the tops to within 2 inches of the base. Soak in cold water for 5 minutes and then rinse carefully to remove all sand and dirt. Drain.

Blanch the leeks in a large pot of boiling, salted water until the white parts are just tender when squeezed, about 5 minutes. Cool in ice-water bath, drain and set aside. The leeks can be covered and refrigerated overnight.

Place the wine, shallots and peppercorns in a small saucepan over medium heat. When the liquid has reduced to about 2 Tbsps., lower the heat and begin whisking in the butter, adding one piece at a time. Remove from heat and strain through a fine strainer. The sauce can be kept over warm, (not hot) water for a few minutes while you grill the leeks. Stir in the capers, taste and add a pinch of salt if needed, just before serving.

To finish the leeks, brush them with olive oil and season with salt and pepper. Grill them until browned on both sides. Serve on a warm platter. Spoon the warm caper beurre blanc and top with egg and parsley.

Bradley Ogden
Lark Creek Inn
Larkspur

Mushroom & Winter Vegetable Ragout with Soft Polenta

Prepare a quick mushroom stock by combining the dried shiitake mushrooms, a few sprigs of fresh herbs, ½ yellow onion, 4 garlic cloves, cold water, soy sauce and a pinch of salt to a boil. Simmer over low heat while cooking the polenta. Cook for 30 minutes, strain stock and discard vegetables. Set aside for ragout.

Allow 20 minutes to cook the polenta. It can be easily done while cooking the stock. Whisk polenta into boiling salted water and whisk vigorously until polenta dissolves. Turn down the heat and continue to stir so polenta does not stick to bottom of the pan. Cook over medium heat until the grains dissolve completely and the polenta is smooth, about 20 minutes. Add ¼ cup butter, salt and pepper. When the polenta is done, leave over low flame and stir occasionally until ready to serve. Thin with hot water if it begins to thicken. Add half of the cheese just before serving and sprinkle the rest of the cheese over the polenta when it is served.

Sauté 1 medium yellow onion in 2 Tbsps. butter and olive oil with 4 minced garlic cloves and salt and pepper until soft. Add half of the wine and reduce. Add the mushrooms, turnips, fennel and peppers. Season with a few splashes of soy sauce. Add more butter and olive oil as necessary, the remaining wine and just enough mushroom stock to make a sauce. Cook the vegetables until tender and flavorful.

Finish seasoning with fresh herbs, salt and pepper. Add crème fraîche or sour cream to lightly bind the sauce. Serve with soft polenta.

Trade Secret: Mushrooms that work well in this dish are fresh shiitake, chanterelle or porcini mushrooms. If using fresh shiitake mushrooms, use only the caps for the ragout.

Annie Somerville
Greens
San Francisco

Serves 6
Preparation Time:
 1 Hour

 3 oz. dried shiitake
  mushrooms
  A few sprigs of fresh
  herbs
1½ medium yellow
  onions, diced large
 8 garlic cloves
 2 cups cold water
 ¼ cup soy sauce
 1 cup polenta
 4 cups boiling salted
  water
 ½ cup butter
  Salt and black pepper
  to taste
 ½ lb. Parmesan cheese,
  grated
 2 Tbsps. olive oil
 1 cup red wine
 1 lb. mushrooms, sliced
  thick
 1 large turnip, cut into
  ½" cubes
 2 fennel bulbs, sliced
  thick
 1 medium red pepper,
  sliced thick
 1 medium yellow
  pepper, sliced thick
1½ cups fresh herbs,
  (parsley, marjoram,
  oregano, chives)
 ¼ cup sour cream or
  crème fraîche

Gallette of Pears and Bleu Cheese with Walnuts

Serves 6
Preparation Time:
  1 Hour
(note refrigeration time)
Preheat oven to 425°

  3 **pears**
  1 **cup port wine**
  1 **cup zinfandel**
  1 **cup water**
  ½ **cup sugar**
  2 **whole cloves**
    Pinch of cardamon
  ¾ **cup chopped walnuts**
  ½ **cup powdered sugar**
    Peanut oil for frying
  6 **oz. puff pastry**
  1 **cup gorgonzola or bleu**
    cheese, crumbled

Peel and core the pears and split them in half lengthwise. In a shallow saucepan, add port, zinfandel, water, sugar, cloves and cardamon. Bring this liquid to a gentle boil. Add the pears, cover with parchment paper and simmer for 10 to 15 minutes. Remove the pan from the heat and leave the pears in the liquid for 30 to 60 minutes. Remove the pears and drain on paper towels. Cool in the refrigerator before slicing them.

Glaze the walnuts by quickly blanching them in boiling water. Remove and shake off excess water. Toss with powdered sugar. Place the walnuts in a wire basket and dip them into a pot of 350° peanut oil for about 15 seconds until they sizzle and are crisp on the outside. Drain on paper towels to remove excess oil. Set aside.

Roll puff pastry to ¹⁄₁₆″ thick and cut into six 6″ circles. Arrange puff pastry circles on a sheet pan lined with parchment paper and bake for 10 minutes. The pastry should be quite done and fully risen. Remove the pastry from the oven and immediately crush down the center of the pastry, leaving a ¼″ edge on each piece. Divide the cheese among the gallettes and sprinkle it over the (crushed down) center of the pastry. Arrange ½ of a thinly sliced poached pear in the center of the pastry on top of the bleu cheese.

Prior to serving, reheat the gallettes for 5 more minutes at 425° Sprinkle the tops of the pears with the glazed walnuts and serve warm.

Trade Secret: This recipe can be used as an appetizer with wine or side dish, or dessert.

Russell Armstrong
Trees
Corona del Mar

☆

Potato Lasagna of Wild Mushrooms with Herb Sauce

Cut the potatoes in rectangular shapes of 3″ × 1½″. Slice each potato into cubes in 5 slices. Place the slices on a buttered sheet pan and bake in the oven for a few minutes until soft.

Sauté the mushrooms in half the butter over low heat. Add the shallot and cook until soft. Set aside.

Warm the celery broth over medium heat until broth begins to reduce. Add remaining butter to the broth in a blender and finish with the parsley and tomatoes.

In 4 alternate layers, place the potato slices and the mushrooms in a loaf type pan. To serve, place the potato lasagna in a soup plate and cover with the warm herb sauce.

Serves 4
Preparation Time:
  30 Minutes
Preheat oven to 300°

4 large Idaho potatoes
1 stick butter
⅓ cup shiitake
  mushrooms, chopped
⅓ cup oyster mushrooms,
  chopped
⅓ cup white mushrooms,
  chopped
⅓ cup chanterelles,
  chopped, optional
1 large shallot, chopped
  fine
¾ cup celery broth
½ bunch parsley, chopped
1 Roma tomato, diced

Joachim Splichal
Patina
Los Angeles

★

205

Gratin of Turnips and Bleu Cheese

Serves 4
Preparation Time:
  1 Hour
Preheat oven to 375°

  4 medium turnips,
    peeled, sliced paper thin
  1 medium yellow onion,
    peeled, sliced fine
  4 Tbsps. butter, melted
  ½ cup whipping cream
  4 anchovy filets, chopped
    fine
  ¼ tsp. nutmeg, preferably
    freshly ground
  ¼ tsp. fresh ground
    pepper
  ½ cup Roquefort, stilton or
    other bleu cheese,
    crumbled

oss the turnips and onion with the melted butter and place in a 9″ square or round baking dish. Cover tightly and place in oven for 30 minutes.

In a small pot over medium heat, combine cream, anchovies, nutmeg and pepper. Bring to a boil and let cook 1 minute.

Remove turnips from oven and pour the cream mixture over them. Sprinkle with cheese and return to oven. Let bake, uncovered, another 20 to 25 minutes.

If the gratin is golden brown, it is ready to serve. If not, preheat broiler. Place gratin under hot broiler about 3 minutes to brown the top before serving.

©*Secret Ingredients*

Michael Roberts
Trumps
Hollywood

★

Grilled Vegetables with Port Beurre Rouge

Prepare the port beurre rouge by combining the vinegar, port and shallots in a saucepan. Cook over high heat until most of the liquid has reduced. Watch the pan closely, as it is easy to burn the reduction in the last minutes of cooking. Turn heat down to moderate and slowly whisk in the butter cubes. Add a few pieces at a time, whisking until all the butter is incorporated. Remove pan from heat and season with salt and pepper. Add a few splashes of balsamic vinegar if sauce needs more sharpness. Set aside.

Be sure to select a thin-skinned winter squash for this dish. Wash squash, trim off ends and cut into ¾" thick rounds. Scoop seeds out of each round. Place squash rounds on a lightly oiled baking sheet.

Combine oil and garlic and brush over squash. Sprinkle with salt and pepper.

Bake until just tender, about 15 minutes. Do not over-bake, as it needs to be firm enough to hold its shape on the grill.

Stem shiitakes and brush with garlic, oil, salt and pepper.

Trim root hairs off scallions. Pull away outer membrane on white end of scallions. Trim away most of the scallion greens, so it is about 6" in length. Brush with garlic oil, salt and pepper.

Grill or broil the squash rounds, shiitake and scallions. Allow 6 minutes to cook vegetables, turning them after 3 minutes.

Ladle the port beurre rouge sauce onto a serving platter and arrange grilled vegetables on it.

Trade Secret: Port beurre rouge is a favorite fall and winter sauce for grilled vegetables. The sweetness of the port and balsamic vinegar are very pleasing and the color of the sauce is dramatic. People tend to shy away from butter sauces, but we have found them to be quite easy. This sauce is definitely worth the effort. It can be made ahead of time, as long as it is kept in a warm, but not hot place.

Annie Somerville
Greens
San Francisco

Serves 6
Preparation Time:
45 Minutes
Pre-heat oven to 375°

¼ **cup balsamic vinegar**
¼ **cup port wine**
2 **shallots, diced**
½ **lb. cold butter, cut into**
  ½" cubes
  Salt and freshly ground
  black pepper
2 **lbs. delicata squash or**
  any edible-skin squash
1 **lb. shiitake mushrooms**
1 **bunch scallions**
¼ **cup olive oil**
1 **garlic clove, diced fine**
  Bamboo skewers for
  mushrooms

Sauces
and
Condiments

Aioli–Garlic Flavored Mayonnaise

Place the yolks, salt, garlic, mustard and lemon juice in a blender. Run on low until smooth, about 8 seconds.

Turn up blender setting to medium-high. Pour in the oil very slowly at first, increasing the flow at the end.

Mix in pickled ginger, juice of pickled ginger and season to taste.

Trade Secret: I like to add freshly chopped tomato and green onion in my aioli, particularly when serving with crab cakes.

Yields: 1½ Cups
Preparation Time:
 10 Minutes

   3 **large egg yolks**
 ⅛ **tsp. salt**
   2 **garlic cloves, minced**
   2 **tsps. Dijon mustard**
   4 **Tbsps. fresh lemon**
     juice
1½ **cups vegetable oil**
   1 **tsp. imported sweet-**
     pickled ginger, minced
   3 **Tbsps. juice from the**
     pickled ginger bottle

David SooHoo
Chinois East West
Sacramento

☆

Avocado and Cilantro Salsa

Yield: 1½ Cups
Preparation Time:
  10 Minutes

 2 **large ripe avocados**
 3 **Roma tomatoes**
 4 **Tbsps. red onions, diced**
½ **bunch cilantro,**
  chopped fine
  Garlic to taste, chopped
  fine
  Jalapeño peppers to
  taste, chopped fine
 1 **Tbsp. tomato juice**
  Cayenne pepper
  Tabasco
  Lemon juice

 Peel avocados and tomatoes and dice into small chunks. Mix with onions, cilantro, garlic and jalapeño peppers.

Add tomato juice, cayenne pepper, Tabasco sauce and lemon juice to taste.

Trade Secret: The avocado and cilantro salsa is a wonderful accompaniment to a chicken quesadilla.

Joachim Splichal
Patina
Los Angeles

Chardonnay Cream Sauce

In a small heavy, non-aluminum saucepan, boil the Chardonnay with the shallot over high heat until only about 2 Tbsps. of liquid are left, 5 to 7 minutes. Add the cream, reduce the heat slightly and simmer until the sauce is thick and reduced by about half, 7 to 10 minutes more. Season to taste with salt, pepper, and a little lemon juice.

In a food processor, or with a hand-held blender, process the sauce until smooth, 1 to 2 minutes. Strain it through a fine-mesh sieve and return it to the pan to warm through gently. Adjust the seasonings to taste.

To keep the sauce warm, set the saucepan inside a bowl or larger pan of hot but not boiling water.

Trade Secret: I use this version of Chardonnay cream sauce with non-seafood pastas and main courses. It makes a wonderful sauce for poultry, meat or vegetables.

© Michael's Cookbook

Yield: 2 Cups
Preparation Time:
  25 Minutes

¾ **cup California**
  Chardonnay
1 **medium-size shallot,**
  finely chopped
2 **cups heavy cream**
  Salt and freshly ground
  white pepper
  Fresh lemon juice

Martin Garcia
Michael's
Santa Monica

China Moon Pickled Ginger

Yield: 2 Cups
Preparation Time:
  25 Minutes

  ½ **lb. fresh ginger, peeled**
1⅔ **cups Japanese rice**
    vinegar, unseasoned
  ½ **cup + 1 Tbsp. sugar**
  1 **Tbsp. + 1 tsp. kosher**
    salt

sing a thin-bladed knife, cut the ginger crosswise against the grain into paper-thin slices.

Cover the ginger with boiling water, let steep 2 minutes, stirring once or twice, then drain.

In a non-aluminum saucepan bring the vinegar, sugar and salt to a boil, stirring to dissolve the sugar and salt. Pour over the ginger. Cool in a clean glass container and refrigerate.

Trade Secret: For best flavor, wait a day or two before using. Pickled ginger keeps indefinitely, refrigerated. However, the juice turns murky after several weeks.

© *The China Moon Cookbook*

Barbara Tropp
China Moon Cafe
San Francisco

✩

Cucumber Relish

Peel the cucumber and julienne. Set aside. Wash cabbage well and julienne. Peel the onion and dice small. Core, seed and dice the tomato. Seed and chop the jalapeño chiles.

Mix all ingredients together and set aside for 30 minutes. Serve chilled.

Trade Secret: The cucumber relish makes a wonderful accompaniment to seafood tacos.

Serves 4
Preparation Time:
  45 Minutes

  9 **pickling cucumbers**
  ¼ **white cabbage**
  ½ **red onion**
  1 **large tomato**
  2 **jalapeño chiles**
    Juice from 2
    grapefruits
    Juice from 2 oranges
    Juice from 4 limes
1½ **Tbsps. salt**

Susan Feniger and Mary Sue Milliken
City and Border Grill
Los Angeles, Santa Monica

213

Evil Jungle Sauce

Yield: 2 Cups
Preparation Time:
15 Minutes

2 cans coconut milk,
Chaockoh brand
13.5 oz. each
1½ cups granulated sugar
4 Tbsps. Thai red curry
paste, Mae Ploy brand
½ cup white vinegar
2 tsps. fish sauce
1 Tbsp. oyster sauce
2 Tbsps. cornstarch
3 Tbsps. cold water
Unsalted butter
Fresh mint leaves or
fresh cilantro, chopped

immer together coconut milk, sugar, red curry paste, vinegar, fish sauce and oyster sauce and bring to a boil.

Mix cornstarch and water together and add to the coconut milk mixture to thicken. The sauce should be able to coat the back of a spoon.

Before serving, swirl in a little unsalted butter to make the sauce look glossy. Add some fresh mint leaves and/or fresh cilantro to sauce for color and taste.

Trade Secret: Ladle sauce over steamed or grilled meats. This sauce is particularly delicious over filet of salmon.

David SooHoo
Chinois East West
Sacramento

Tomato Coulis

Start a charcoal fire or heat the grill or broiler. Season and lightly coat the tomatoes with 2 Tbsps. olive oil. Place tomatoes on grill and cook until almost soft. Remove the seeds and strain to reserve juice. Chop the tomato pulp coarsely.

Place 2 Tbsps. of olive oil in a heavy-bottomed saucepan and heat over a moderate fire. Add the shallots and garlic and sauté for a few minutes, then add the tomato pulp and tomato juice. Blend well, then add the chiles, stock, bay leaf, wine and vinegar. Simmer for 30 minutes.

Strain coulis and discard tomato pulp and bay leaf. Place coulis back on the fire and reduce if necessary to 1½ cups. Cool coulis slightly and add the herbs. Season to taste with salt and pepper.

Yield: 1½ Cups
Preparation Time:
  45 Minutes

  4 **large tomatoes or**
    1 **28-ounce can**
    tomatoes
  4 **Tbsps. olive oil**
  ½ **cup shallots, sliced**
  5 **garlic cloves, slivered**
  2 **serrano chiles, peeled,**
    chopped fine
  ½ **cup light chicken stock**
    or duck stock
  ½ **bay leaf**
  ½ **cup Pinot Noir or**
    Zinfandel
  ¼ **cup balsamic vinegar**
  1 **Tbsp. basil, chopped**
  1 **Tbsp. parsley, chopped**
  1 **Tbsp. cilantro, chopped**
    Kosher salt to taste
    Cracked black pepper to
    taste

Bradley Ogden
Lark Creek Inn
Larkspur

Chile Vinaigrette

Yield: 2 Cups
Preparation Time:
  1½ Hours

½ **jalapeño chile, finely**
  chopped with a few
  seeds
½ **small red bell pepper,**
  chopped
½ **Tbsp. olive oil, to sauté**
  the peppers
½ **cup cider vinegar**
1 **shallot, minced**
1 **tsp. Dijon mustard**
1 **tsp. Worcestershire**
  sauce
  Salt and pepper to taste
1 **cup olive oil**
  Small bunch parsley,
  chopped
  Small bunch cilantro,
  chopped

 n a small pan, gently sauté the chopped jalapeño and bell peppers in the oil for a few minutes.

Combine the vinegar, shallot, mustard, Worcestershire, salt and pepper in a small mixing bowl. Whisk in the olive oil slowly. Add the parsley, cilantro and sautéed peppers. Allow to stand for at least 1 hour. Stir again and correct the seasonings if necessary. Depending on personal preference, you may want to add extra jalapeño peppers, but be careful.

Trade Secret: This recipe is intended for the steamed mussels, but it's a real treat served with avocado and oranges or even just with romaine lettuce salad.

John Downey
Downey's
Santa Barbara

Black Olive Vinaigrette

Pit olives and chop coarsely.
Roast, peel and seed the red peppers, then dice. Blend peppers with the olives, shallots, olive oil, vinegar and lemon. Season to taste with salt and pepper.

Trade Secret: This vinaigrette is excellent for grilled fish and poultry. It also goes well with steamed asparagus.

Serves 6
Preparation Time:
30 Minutes

24 oil-cured olives
 2 red peppers
 4 shallots, chopped
 1 cup olive oil
¼ cup red wine vinegar
   Juice of 1 lemon
   Salt and pepper

Cory Schreiber
Cypress Club
San Francisco

Apple cake
Chocolate decadence cake
Chocolate oblivion
Flourless chocolate pecan cake
Sponge cake
Tuscan cream cake
Carmel pot de crème
Chantilly cream
Apple clafouti with cider sauce
Ginger cookies
Spicy ginger moon cookies
Bittersweet chocolate crème brulée
Classic crème brulée
Raspberry passion fruit crêpes
Fresh fruit with English cream
Espresso granita
White chocolate mousse
Poached pears with crème anglaise
Key lime pie
Lime coconut pie
Chocolate croissant pudding
Rice pudding
Peach ravioli
Muscat grape sherbet
Strawberry shortcake
Lemon mousse soufflé
Fig-date strudel
Green apple and ricotta strudel
Taro with tapioca
Espresso brownie tart
Pear tart, cinnamon ice cream
Plum almond tart
Tiramisu with crème anglaise
Chestnut meringue torte
Chocolate raspberry ganache torte
Turtle torte
Walnuts and fresh figs
Zabaglione

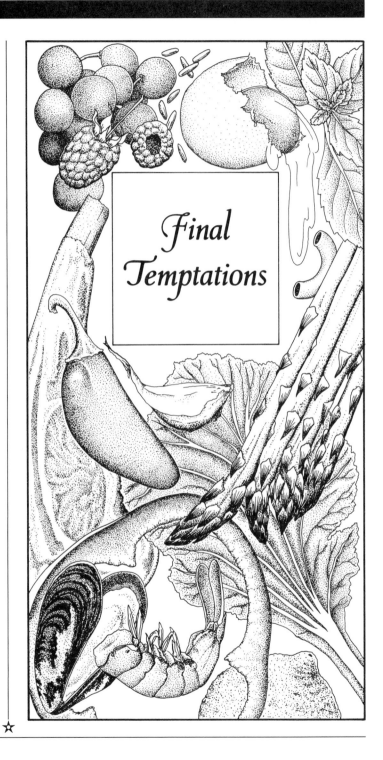

*Final
Temptations*

Apple Cake

Bake walnuts for 10 to 15 minutes. To remove the brown skin, place walnuts in a sieve or strainer and agitate them or rub them in a towel.

Sift together flour, baking soda, salt and cinnamon and set aside.

Beat eggs, white sugar, brown sugar, water, vanilla and corn oil. Add flour mixture and toasted nuts. When thoroughly blended, add apples and stir well.

Pour into a greased 9″ × 13″ pan and bake at 325° for 65 to 75 minutes. The cake will appear moist, but not wet.

Trade Secret: This is a spicy coffee cake dessert that can be dressed up with vanilla ice cream.

©*Cafe Beaujolais*

Serves 12
Preparation Time:
   1½ Hours
Pre-heat oven to 325°

1 cup walnuts, chopped
2 cups flour
2 tsps. baking soda
¾ tsp. salt
2 tsps. cinnamon
2 eggs, beaten
¼ cup white sugar
2 cups brown sugar
¼ cup water
1 tsp. pure vanilla extract
½ cup corn oil
4 cups apples, peeled, cored, cut into ½″ cubes

Margaret Fox
Cafe Beaujolais
Mendocino

Chocolate Decadence Cake

Yield: One 10″ cake
Preparation Time:
 1½ Hours
(note refrigeration time)
Pre-heat oven to 350°

1½ cups semisweet
   chocolate
 ½ cup unsweetened
   chocolate
1½ cups unsalted butter
1¾ cups sugar
 ½ cup water
 7 eggs
 1 cup heavy cream,
   whipped
   Extra chocolate to
   grate for garnish

ut chocolates and butter into small pieces. Put in a bowl.

Mix 1½ cups sugar with water in a saucepan and bring to a boil. Pour over chocolate and butter. Stir until melted.

Whip eggs and ¼ cup sugar in mixer until double in volume. Stir into chocolate mixture until no white streaks appear.

Pour batter into greased and paper-lined 10″ cake pan. Bake on a sheet pan with 1″ of water in it for about 40 to 50 minutes until it is set.

Cool cake and place in refrigerator overnight.

To release cake, dip pan in hot water and run knife carefully around the edge. Frost with whipped cream and decorate with grated chocolate.

Bradley Ogden
Lark Creek Inn
Larkspur

Chocolate Oblivion

Melt chocolate and butter together in a double boiler over low heat.

Whip eggs until volume triples. Fold eggs into the chocolate mixture.

Pour chocolate mixture into a loaf pan and bake in a sheet pan with 1″ of water in it for 5 minutes. Cover with foil and bake for another 10 minutes. Do not overcook.

Cool and chill in the refrigerator. Before serving, dust with unsweetened cocoa and garnish with strawberries.

Serves 12
Preparation Time:
  25 Minutes
(note refrigeration time)
Pre-heat oven to 350°

2 **lbs. bittersweet**
  chocolate
1 **lb. sweet butter**
12 **eggs**
  Unsweetened cocoa
  Strawberries for garnish

William Donnelly
Chez Melange
Redondo Beach

⭐

DAVID BECKWITH

Flourless Chocolate Pecan Cake

Yield: Two 10″ cakes
Pre-heat oven to 425°

½ lb. unsalted butter
¾ lbs. semisweet
chocolate
2 Tbsps. brandy
12 eggs, separated
1½ cups sugar
3 cups pecans, chopped

ombine butter, chocolate and brandy and melt in a double boiler or in a bowl over a pot of boiling water. Remove from heat.

In a large bowl, beat eggs yolks and 1 cup sugar together until light and fluffy. Fold in the melted chocolate and chopped pecans.

In a separate bowl, beat egg whites to a soft peak, slowly adding the remaining ½ cup sugar. Fold beaten egg whites into the batter. Do not over-stir.

Divide batter evenly between two 10″ greased springform pans.

Bake for 40 minutes or until a knife inserted in the center comes out clean.

Trade Secret: Serve with chocolate sauce, fresh berries and/or whipped cream.

David Beckwith
Central 159 Restaurant & Catering
Pacific Grove

Sponge Cake

ine the bottom of jelly roll pan with parchment paper.
Sift together the flour, baking powder and salt. Set aside.

Put the egg yolks and sugar in the bowl of an electric mixer. Using the whisk attachment, whip on high speed until thick and pale yellow. Reduce to medium speed and slowly add the water and the vanilla. Scrape the sides and bottom of the bowl. Return to high speed and continue whipping for about 5 minutes, until mixture is again thick and forms ribbons.

Fold the dry ingredients into the egg-sugar mixture.

Put the egg whites in a separate bowl of an electric mixer. With the clean whisk attachment, whip on high speed until soft peaks form. Fold half of the whipped whites into the batter and then fold in the remaining whites. Spread the batter evenly into the pan.

Bake the cake for about 15 minutes, until it is golden brown and springs back when lightly touched.

© *Stars Desserts*

Serves 6
Preparation Time:
 30 Minutes
Pre-heat oven to 350°

1¼ cups flour
2½ tsps. baking powder
 Pinch salt
 5 large eggs, separated
1¼ cups sugar
 5 Tbsps. boiling water
 1 tsp. vanilla extract
 An 11½" x 17½" jelly
 roll pan or sheet pan
 with 1" sides

Emily Luchetti
Stars
San Francisco

Tuscan Cream Cake

Serves 10
Preparation Time:
20 Minutes
(note refrigeration time)

1 recipe zabaglione,
see separate recipe
page 256
2 recipes sponge cake,
see separate recipe
page 223
1½ cups heavy whipping
cream
¼ cup sugar
1 cup chocolate shavings
¾ cup crushed amaretti
cookies
A 9″ springform pan

o assemble the cake, cut the sponge cakes into three 9″ circles and then cut each circle in half horizontally, to make six thinner 9″ circles. You will need only 5 layers for this cake. Freeze the extra cake pieces to use in trifles.

Put a cake circle in the bottom of a 9″ springform pan. Top the cake layer with 1¼ cups of zabaglione. Continue layering cake and zabaglione in this manner, ending with a layer of cake. You will have 5 layers of cake and 4 layers of zabaglione.

Refrigerate the cake for 1 to 2 hours to allow it to set.

Unmold the cake by running a hot dry knife around the edge of the pan and then releasing the latch on the springform.

Put the heavy cream and the sugar in the bowl of an electric mixer. With the whisk attachment, whip on high speed until soft peaks form. Frost the sides and top of the cake. Decorate the top with chocolate shavings and the sides with the crushed amaretti.

©Stars Desserts

Emily Luchetti
Stars
San Francisco

Caramel Pot de Crème with Caramel Sauce

Scald the milk and 2 cups cream with the vanilla bean. Keep the mixture warm.

In a heavy-bottomed saucepan, caramelize 1 cup sugar until it is a deep amber hue. Strain the warm cream and gradually and carefully add it into the caramelized sugar, whisking constantly. Be careful, as the caramel will foam up.

In a mixing bowl, beat the egg yolks. Gradually add the hot caramel cream and strain.

Ladle or gently pour the mixture into 8 ramekins. Skim the top surfaces to remove all bubbles.

Place the ramekins into a pan of hot water and cover the pan with foil. Bake for 40 minutes or until the custard is set. Remove from water and cool. Cover with plastic wrap and refrigerate. Bring to room temperature before serving. Top with the caramel sauce.

To make the caramel sauce, combine 2 cups sugar and lemon juice and cook the syrup over medium heat. Caramelize until golden brown.

In another pot, heat 1 cup heavy cream. Gradually add the cream to the caramelized sugar while stirring. Bring to a boil and stir in butter. If refrigerated before using, heat sauce over hot water before serving.

Serves 4
Preparation Time:
 1 Hour
Pre-heat oven to 300°

  2 cups milk
  3 cups heavy cream
  1 vanilla bean, cut in half
  3 cups sugar
12 egg yolks
    Juice of half lemon
  1 stick unsalted butter

Joyce Goldstein
Square One Restaurant
San Francisco

Chantilly Cream

Yield: 4½ Cups
Preparation Time:
  10 Minutes
(note refrigeration time)

2½ cups heavy whipping
   cream
 1 tsp. vanilla extract
1½ Tbsps. sugar
   Small pinch salt

ut all the ingredients together in a large stainless steel bowl. Whisk the cream just until it holds its shape.

Refrigerate the cream until ready to use.

Trade Secret: Chantilly cream should be used within an hour after it's made. If you wait longer to use it you may need to rewhip it slightly.

©*Stars Desserts*

Emily Luchetti
Stars
San Francisco

Apple Clafouti with Cider Sauce

Peel and slice apples. Melt butter in sauté pan and add apples, ¼ cup sugar and brandy. Stir and cook gently until just cooked through. Set aside.

In the blender, make the batter by combining ½ cup sugar, eggs, cream, vanilla, butter and flour. Set aside.

Put a large 10″ pie plate in a 375° oven to get hot. Brush hot pie plate with butter. Pour in half the batter. Add apples, saving a spoonful for the top. Add remaining batter. Top batter with saved apples and any juices. Sprinkle with sugar and cinnamon.

Bake 25–30 minutes or just until set.

To make the cider sauce, reduce the apple juice or cider by boiling juice rapidly in a wide pan until it is slightly thick or it coats a spoon. This amount will yield about 1 cup when reduced enough. It will thicken more when it cools.

Serve apple clafouti hot or cold with a little whipped cream and/or cider sauce spooned over the top.

Serves 4
Preparation Time:
  45 Minutes
Pre-heat oven to 375°

  6 cups Gravenstein or
     Golden Delicious apples
  ¼ cup butter
  ¾ cup sugar
  3 Tbsps. brandy
  3 eggs
  1 cup light cream
  1 tsp. vanilla
  3 Tbsps. butter, melted
  ⅔ cup flour
  1 Tbsp. powdered
     cinnamon
  2 qts. apple juice or cider
     Whipped cream,
     optional

Sally Schmitt
The French Laundry
Yountville

227

Ginger Cookies

Yield: 3 Dozen
Pre-heat oven to 325°

  1 **cup granulated sugar**
 ½ **cup firmly packed**
     light brown sugar
  2 **sticks soft sweet butter**
  1 **large egg**
 ⅓ **cup molasses**
  2 **tsps. ground ginger**
 ½ **tsp. ground allspice**
  1 **tsp. ground cinnamon**
  2 **tsps. baking soda**
 ½ **tsp. salt**
 ¼ **tsp. ground white**
     pepper
2¼ **cups flour**

ut ½ cup of granulated sugar, the brown sugar and the butter in the bowl of an electric mixer. With the paddle attachment, cream the butter on medium speed for 2 minutes, until the mixture is light and fluffy. Continuing to mix, beat in the egg and then the molasses. On low speed, add the dry ingredients and mix until incorporated. Refrigerate the dough for 30 minutes.

Roll the dough into ¾" balls and roll them in the remaining ½ cup of sugar. Line a baking sheet with parchment paper. Put the cookies 2 to 3 inches apart on the baking sheet. Flatten them slightly with 2 fingers.

Bake the cookies for about 12 minutes, until golden brown and set around the edges but still soft inside. Let them cool for 5 minutes and then remove them from the baking sheet.

©Stars Desserts

Emily Luchetti
Stars
San Francisco

Spicy Ginger Moons

With an electric mixer and flat beater attachment, cream the butter and sugar on low speed until smooth. Add the fresh and powdered ginger, vanilla, flour, baking soda and salt. Continue mixing until the dough comes together.

On a large, flour-dusted piece of parchment paper, roll the dough to an even ⅛" thickness, dusting the roller as needed to prevent sticking. Slip the parchment onto a cookie sheet, then refrigerate the dough until firm, about 1 hour.

Slide the chilled dough on its parchment back onto the work table. Place a fresh piece of parchment on the cookie sheet. Using a moon-shaped or a round cutter, cut the dough and place on the lined baking sheet. Give each moon a decorative "eye" by pressing a sliver of crystallized ginger into the dough.

Bake on the middle rack of the oven until the cookie edges are lightly golden, 10–12 minutes. Remove to a rack to cool.

Trade Secret: Cookies keep nicely up to a week, if sealed airtight, but flavor is keenest when freshly baked.

© *The China Moon Cookbook*

Yield: 5–7 Dozen
Preparation Time:
  25 Minutes
(note refrigeration time)
Pre-heat oven to 350°

  1 **stick unsalted butter**
  ½ **cup packed dark**
    brown sugar
  1 **Tbsp. fresh ginger,**
    finely minced
  1 **Tbsp. powdered ginger**
  ½ **tsp. vanilla**
  1¼ **cups all-purpose flour**
  ¼ **tsp. baking soda**
    Pinch of salt
  3 **pieces crystallized**
    ginger, cut into small
    pieces

Barbara Tropp
China Moon Cafe
San Francisco

Bittersweet Chocolate Crème Brulée with Caramelized Bananas

Serves 6
Preparation Time:
  1 Hour
Pre-heat oven to 275°

  ½ **cup milk**
1½ **cups cream**
  ½ **cup bittersweet**
    chocolate, chopped
    small
  5 **egg yolks**
  ⅓ **cup granulated sugar**
  ⅓ **cup golden brown**
    sugar
  4 **bananas**

 Bring the milk and the cream, mixed together, to a boil. Add the chopped chocolate into the milk mixture, set aside for 5 minutes.

In a mixing bowl, beat the egg yolks with the granulated sugar. Continue whipping the eggs while pouring in the milk mixture. Let cool.

Prepare 5 oz. round molds or soup bowls and pour into each 4 oz. of the chocolate brulée mixture. Place molds in a pan of water and poach in the oven for 40 minutes. When the crème brulées are cooked, transfer them to a sheet pan and let cool.

Decorate the top of each with 5 or 6 slices of bananas. Sprinkle with golden brown sugar and broil the crème brulées under a broiler until the sugar melts and turns into a golden caramel color.

Hubert Keller
Fleur de Lys
San Francisco

Classic Crème Brulée

Mix cream, milk and 3½ Tbsps. sugar together in a heavy-bottomed saucepan and bring to a boil. While cream mixture is heating, mix egg yolks and remaining sugar together in a separate bowl, beating until smooth. When cream has reached a boil, slowly whisk cream into egg mixture.

Divide into 4 shallow custard dishes. Place in a water bath and bake for 30–35 minutes at 275.° Remove to cool immediately.

When ready to serve, sprinkle remaining 2 Tbsps. sugar on top of brulée to caramelize under the broiler or with a butane torch.

Serves 4
Preparation Time:
   45 Minutes
Pre-heat oven to 275°

   1 pt. cream
   1 cup milk
5½ Tbsps. sugar
   7 egg yolks

Brian Whitmer
Pacific's Edge, Highlands Inn
Carmel
★

Raspberry Passion Fruit Crêpes

Serves 4
Preparation Time:
1½ Hours

2¼ **cups flour**
2 **Tbsps. sugar**
Pinch of salt
4 **eggs**
2¼ **cups milk, boiled and**
cooled
1⅞ **cups heavy cream**
¼ **tsp. vanilla bean seeds**
4 **fresh passion fruits,**
juice and pulp
2 **Tbsps. clarified butter**
Zest of 1 lemon
1 **pt. fresh strawberries**
Mint for garnish

ombine the flour, sugar and salt in a bowl and add the eggs, 2 at a time, mixing well with a spatula. Stir in ⅓ of the milk until you have a smooth batter. Pour in ⅞ cup of the cream and the rest of the milk. Leave batter to rest in a cool place for a least 1 hour before cooking the crêpes.

To cook, stir the batter and add the seeds from the vanilla bean, passion fruit pulp and juice.

Brush the skillet or crêpe pan with clarified butter and heat. Ladle a little batter onto the pan and cook for 1 or 2 minutes on each side, turning the crêpe with a metal spatula.

Whip 1 cup of heavy cream until peaks stiffen. Adjust sugar to taste and add lemon zest.

To serve, layer crêpes with whipped cream and top with lightly tossed sugared raspberries. Garnish with mint.

Alan Greeley
The Golden Truffle
Costa Mesa

Fresh Fruit with English Cream & Mint

Split vanilla beans in half. Scrape seeds. Add to milk and boil over medium heat. Remove from heat.

In a mixing bowl, blend egg yolks and sugar until color is light. Add ⅓ of the boiled milk to the egg mixture. Mix thoroughly.

Add the egg mixture to the remaining ⅔ of the milk and return to heat, boiling for 1 minute. Strain and cool.

Place mixed fruit in serving bowl and drizzle with sauce. Sprinkle with mint and serve.

Serves 8
Preparation Time:
  25 Minutes

1½ vanilla beans
 1 qt. milk
 8 egg yolks
 ¾ cups sugar
    Assorted seasonal
    fruit, sliced
    Mint leaves, julienne

Fred Halpert
Brava Terrace
St. Helena

Espresso Granita

Yields: 8 Cups
Preparation Time:
20 Minutes
(note refrigeration time)

8 cups cold espresso
3 cups superfine sugar
1 recipe chantilly cream,
  see separate recipe
  page 226
  Biscotti cookies, optional

our the espresso into a large bowl. Stir in the sugar. Pour the sweetened espresso into a shallow pan approximately 9″ × 13″ and place in the freezer. Every 30 minutes, roughly stir up the freezing mixture with a fork. This will give the granita a feathery and light icy texture.

Freeze the espresso until it is completely frozen, 8 hours to overnight, depending on your freezer.

Serve in tall glasses with chantilly cream and biscotti.

© *Stars Desserts*

Emily Luchetti
Stars
San Francisco

White Chocolate Mousse in an Almond Cookie Shell

To make the almond cookie shell, place 2 egg whites in bowl and beat briefly. Add ½ cup sugar and flour, then whisk and fold in butter. Stir almonds into mixture. Butter sheet pan and spoon tablespoons of mixture onto pan. Spread slightly with the back of a spoon to form circles about 2″ apart. Bake for 10–15 minutes or until golden brown.

Remove from oven and while still hot mold into small cups by placing over a rolling pin. Set aside to dry.

To make the mousse, in a saucepan, heat ½ cup sugar with 2 Tbsps. water or enough water until sugar forms a soft ball.

In the bowl of a mixer, put 8 egg whites and beat until medium stiff, beating first on medium then on high. Add the ball of sugar to the egg whites and continue to beat briefly until a stiff meringue is formed.

Place egg yolks and powdered sugar in a metal bowl and beat over heat in a double boiler with a whisk. Add the whipped cream, rum and crème de cacao and continue beating over heat. Gently fold in the warm melted chocolate. Refrigerate 3–4 hours.

To serve, scoop white chocolate mousse into each almond cookie shell. Garnish with raspberry purée and crème fraîche.

Serves 6
Preparation Time:
  1 Hour
(note refrigeration time)
Pre-heat oven to 350°

2 egg whites
1 cup sugar
2 Tbsps. flour
2 Tbsps. butter, melted
½ cup almonds, chopped fine
2 Tbsps. water
8 eggs, separated
¼ cup powdered sugar
2 cups cream, whipped
1 Tbsp. white rum
1 Tbsp. white crème de cacao
1 lb. white chocolate, melted
  Raspberry purée, garnish
  Crème fraîche, garnish

Julian Serrano
Masa's
San Francisco

Poached Pears with Ginger Crème Anglaise

Serves 6
Preparation Time:
  45 Minutes

  6 firm pears
2½ cups white wine
1½ cups sugar
  One 3-inch piece
  lemon zest
  2 vanilla beans, split or
  1 tsp. vanilla extract
½ cup mascarpone
¼ cup ginger root,
  peeled, chopped
¼ cup water
  2 cups half and half
  5 large egg yolks

Peel pears, leaving stems on, and core from underneath. In a saucepan just large enough to hold pears upright, combine wine, 1 cup sugar, lemon zest and 1 vanilla bean or ½ tsp. vanilla extract. Bring to a boil and simmer for 5 minutes. Add pears and poach for 10 minutes or until cooked through. A toothpick should pierce them easily. Allow pears to cool in the poaching liquid. Drain and stuff core cavity with mascarpone.

Prepare the ginger crème anglaise by placing the ginger, 2 Tbsps. sugar and water in a heavy-bottomed saucepan. Simmer until syrup becomes very thick, about 10 minutes. Do not allow syrup to turn color and caramelize. Add half and half and remaining vanilla bean or vanilla extract and bring to a boil. Remove from heat and let stand for 30 minutes.

Beat egg yolks with remaining sugar. Reheat cream mixture to simmering point and whisk into egg yolk mixture. Return entire mixture to pan and cook, stirring constantly, until thickened. Fill a large bowl with shaved ice and set a second bowl within it. Strain the custard into this bowl and cool, stirring occasionally.

To serve, pour a pool of crème anglaise onto each dessert plate. Top with a poached stuffed pear.

John Ash
John Ash & Co.
Santa Rosa

Key Lime Pie

Combine graham cracker crumbs with 3 Tbsps. sugar. Add butter and cinnamon. Press crust mixture into pie plate. Bake for 12 minutes then allow the crust to cool.

While crust is baking, prepare the filling by blending the condensed milk with the egg yolks. Add the lime juice and pour mixture into the cooled pie shell. Bake for 12 minutes to set the filling.

Whip the cream and 3 Tbsps. sugar together for the pie topping. Smooth it onto the top of the cooled pie. Refrigerate and serve chilled.

Trade Secret: If key limes are unavailable, use Bahamian or California limes.

Serves 4
Preparation time:
  30 Minutes
(note refrigeration time)
Pre-heat oven to 350°

1¼ cups graham cracker
  crumbs
6 Tbsps. sugar
¼ cup butter, melted
1 tsp. cinnamon
1 can condensed milk
4 egg yolks
2 Florida key limes, juice
  to equal 1 cup
1 cup whipping cream

Julio Ramirez
The Fishwife, El Cocodrilo
Pacific Grove

Lime Coconut Pie

Serves 8
Preparation Time:
1 Hour
(note refrigeration time)

1½ cups sugar cookie
    crumbs
 4 cups flaked coconut,
    loosely packed
 6 Tbsps. butter
 1 cup lime juice, freshly
    squeezed
 3 Tbsps. cornmeal
    Pinch of salt
1½ cups granulated sugar
 8 large egg yolks, reserve
    5 egg whites and set
    aside
 ¼ tsp. cream of tartar
    Grated rind of one lime

o make the crust, combine the cookie crumbs and coconut until blended. Use ⅔ of the coconut mix to line a 10″ glass pie plate, pressing mixture firmly to sides of pie pan. Reserve remaining coconut mix.

In a large saucepan, combine the butter, lime juice, cornmeal, salt and 1 cup sugar. Place over simmering water and heat, stirring frequently for 15 minutes or until curd is thickened. Add egg yolks and cook an additional 5 minutes. Cool.

Whip egg whites with cream of tartar until soft peaks form. Add ½ cup sugar and lime rind. Gently fold into curd and pour into coconut pie shell. Top with remaining coconut mix.

Bake at 300° for 30 minutes or until pie rises and coconut is toasted. Chill thoroughly and serve.

Susan Feniger & Mary Sue Milliken
Border Grill, City
Santa Monica, Los Angeles

☆

Chocolate Croissant Pudding with Wild Turkey Sauce

T o prepare the custard, mix 10 egg yolks together with ¼ cup sugar in a large mixing bowl. Add the vanilla bean and heavy cream.

In a large soup plate or individual soufflé molds, place croissant pieces and chocolate pieces together. Pour the custard over the chocolate mixture and cook in a bain marie or place molds in a larger baking pan filled with water, for 45 minutes or until firm.

Prepare the Wild Turkey sauce by bringing the half & half to a boil. Remove from heat.

In a mixing bowl, beat 5 egg yolks with ½ cup sugar and add to the hot cream. Return the cream to low heat and cook until cream thickens. Add Wild Turkey to taste. Cool, then refrigerate.

Serve the chilled sauce with the pudding.

Serves 4
Preparation Time:
  1 Hour
Pre-heat oven to 200°

15 **egg yolks**
¾ **cup sugar**
 1 **vanilla bean, chopped**
 1 **qt. heavy cream**
 1 **croissant, toasted, cut into pieces**
¼ **cup chocolate, chopped**
 1 **pt. half & half**
   Wild Turkey whiskey

Joachim Splichal
Patina
Los Angeles

239

Rice Pudding

Serves 6
Preparation Time:
  1½ Hours
(note refrigeration time)

    1 **cup white rice**
    5 **cups water**
    1 **cup sugar**
 1¼ **cups milk**
   ½ **stick cinnamon,**
     crumbled
    1 **tsp. lemon zest**
   ½ **tsp. vanilla**
   ⅓ **cup condensed milk**
     Whipped cream
     garnish
     Powdered cinnamon
     garnish

ut rice in 5 cups of boiling water, cover and cook until tender, then drain.

    Add the sugar, milk, cinnamon, lemon zest, vanilla and the condensed milk and cook over low heat until the rice mixture is thick. Remove from heat and put pudding into individual serving dishes, then refrigerate.

    To serve, top with whipped cream and powdered cinnamon.

Trade Secret: At specialty stores you can buy *cajeta*, goat's milk caramel, which can be substituted for the condensed milk.

Julio Ramirez
The Fishwife, El Cocodrilo
Pacific Grove

Peach Ravioli

Combine the eggs, flour, salt and olive oil to make the basic pasta ravioli recipe. Roll to almost transparent thickness. Cut eight identical circular shapes. Fill with fresh peach slices, then eggwash edges and seal with tops. Reserve 16 peach slices for garnish. Cover and refrigerate.

To prepare the sauce, bring champagne to a boil in saucepan. Add lemon, shallots and sugar. Boil until almost dry, then reduce heat. Carefully whisk in butter. Reserve and keep warm.

To serve, bring 2 qts. water to rapid boil and place ravioli in water for about 30 seconds. Drain and place two ravioli in center of each of four plates. Surround with sauce and garnish with peach slices. Serve immediately. You may add mint leaves and edible flowers for a colorful presentation.

Serves 4
Preparation Time:
 45 Minutes
(note refrigeration time)

2 eggs
2 cups flour
 Pinch of salt
1 Tbsp. olive oil
4 fresh, ripe peaches, peeled, sliced
1 egg for eggwash
1 bottle quality champagne
¼ cup fresh lemon juice
1 Tbsp. sugar
1 tsp. shallots, chopped
2 sticks of butter, cold
 Mint leaves, optional garnish
 Edible flowers, optional garnish

Jay Trubee
Dolly Cunard's
La Quinta

Muscat Grape Sherbet

Yield: 1 Quart
Preparation Time:
  45 Minutes
(note freezing time)

3½ lbs. Muscat grapes
 3 Tbsps. sugar
1⅓ Tbsps. corn syrup
 2 tsps. Muscat wine,
    such as Beaumes des
    Venise

ash the grapes and remove stems. Put the grapes in a saucepan, cover, and cook for 15 to 20 minutes, stirring occasionally, until they are soft and juicy.

Purée the grapes through a food mill, a blender or food processor into a bowl. Strain through a fine-mesh sieve. Measure 4 cups of the juice.

While still hot, stir in the sugar, corn syrup and wine. Mix until the sugar is dissolved. Chill.

Freeze in an ice cream maker. It is best to make this sherbet the same day it will be served.

Trade Secret: The Muscat grape is a large, meaty grape equally adaptable to wine making, table, or raisin use, and has a strong, easily distinguishable quality that is delicious all by itself.

©*Chez Panisse Cooking*

Alice Waters
Chez Panisse
Berkeley

Strawberry Shortcake with Crème Fraîche

Prepare the shortcake dough by combining in a mixer the flour, baking powder, salt, 3 Tbsps. sugar and butter until crumbly. Add ½ cup cream and ½ tsp. vanilla extract

Remove from mixer and roll out dough. Cut dough with a biscuit cutter, place on baking sheet and chill for 1 hour.

Bake at 350° for 15 minutes. Remove from oven and cool.

Mix together the crème fraîche, 1 cup cream, ⅓ cup sugar and ½ tsp. vanilla extract. Set aside.

Prepare the berry purée by combining 2 cups raspberry, lemon juice and 3 Tbsps. sugar in a blender. Purée and strain. Set aside.

Prepare the berry mixture by combining the strawberries, blueberries, 1 cup of raspberries, blackberries and powdered sugar together in a mixing bowl. Refrigerate.

To serve, cut shortcake in half. Place bottom half on plate and top with crème fraîche. Layer berry mixture on top and drizzle with the berry purée over the shortcake. Top with the other half of shortcake.

Serves 6
Preparation Time:
 45 Minutes
(note refrigeration time)

1½ **cups flour**
 ½ **tsp. baking powder**
 ¼ **tsp. salt**
 ½ **cup sugar**
 6 **Tbsps. butter, thinly sliced**
1½ **cups cream**
 1 **tsp. vanilla extract**
 2 **cups crème fraîche**
 3 **cups raspberries**
 1 **tsp. lemon juice**
 3 **cups strawberries, chopped**
 1 **cup blueberries, chopped**
 1 **cup blackberries, chopped**
 ½ **cup powdered sugar**

Hiroyoshi Sone
Terra Restaurant
St Helena

Lemon Mousse Soufflé with Blueberry Sauce

Serves 10
Preparation Time:
20 Minutes
(note refrigeration time)

8 egg yolks
½ cup sugar
 Juice and chopped zest
 of 3 lemons
3 tsps. unflavored gelatin
½ cup water
3 cups cream, whipped
2 bags (12 oz. each) frozen
 blueberries
2 Tbsps. honey
½ cup brandy
1 Tbsp. + 1 tsp. cornstarch

Prepare the soufflé by combining the yolks, sugar, lemon zest and lemon juice in a medium mixing bowl. Whisk over medium heat or over a pot of boiling water, until light and frothy.

Dissolve gelatin in water and stir gelatin into the egg mixture. Fold whipped cream into lemon mixture using soft gentle strokes.

Pour mousse into ungreased molds of your choice. Allow to set at least two hours for best results before serving.

In a heavy-bottomed saucepan, combine the blueberries, honey and brandy. Over medium heat, cook until blueberries are fully defrosted and you have a fair amount of juice in the saucepan. Reduce heat and whisk in cornstarch, stirring constantly for 2 minutes. Remove from heat, and cool until ready to serve.

To serve, unmold soufflé onto individual plates. Drizzle with the blueberry sauce.

Trade Secret: The sauce and soufflé can be prepared two days in advance and will stay fresh in the refrigerator for about 4 days.

David Beckwith
Central 159 Restaurant and Catering
Pacific Grove

Fig-Date Strudel with Vanilla-Mocha Sauce

Prepare the strudel dough by sifting the flour onto a smooth working surface. Make a groove in the middle and pour in the oil. Mix and knead by hand, adding water a little at a time until dough is smooth. Form a ball, rub oil all around and let rest for 1 hour.

In a large mixing bowl, combine the apples, figs, dates, ¼ cup sugar, rum, spices and vanilla. Set aside to marinate flavors.

On a flour-dusted work surface, pull strudel dough into one long thin shape. Brush strudel with ¾ of the melted butter. Spread half of the bread crumbs along one long line of strudel dough and top with the apple mixture, then walnuts, then remaining bread crumbs. Roll the strudel into a pinwheel, taking care not to pack it too tightly.

Place strudel in a buttered baking sheet and brush with remaining butter. Bake at 400° for about 25 minutes or until it is a light brown. Cool and cut into 1½″ slices.

Prepare the mocha-vanilla sauce by mixing together the egg yolks with ¼ cup sugar, cornstarch, vanilla scrapings and whipping cream until smooth and creamy. Bring coffee to a light boil and whisk quickly into yolk mixture. Remove from heat.

To serve, ladle sauce onto plates and place strudel on it. Dust with powdered sugar.

Serves 6
Preparation Time:
   1½ Hours

2 cups flour
⅓ cup oil
¾ cup warm water
2 large Granny Smith apples, cored, peeled, sliced
1 lb. dried figs
1 lb. dried dates
½ cup sugar
¾ cup rum
¼ tsp. cinnamon
¼ tsp. nutmeg
1 tsp. vanilla extract
   Pinch of ground cloves
1 stick sweet butter, melted
¾ cup walnuts, chopped fine
¾ cup bread crumbs, toasted, buttered, sweetened
4 egg yolks
1 Tbsp. cornstarch
   Scraping of 1 vanilla bean
1 cup whipping cream
1 cup strong coffee (espresso)
   Powdered confectioners sugar

Erna Kubin-Clanin
Erna's Elderberry House
Oakhurst

Green Apple and Ricotta Strudel

Serves 4
Preparation Time:
  1 Hour
Pre-heat oven to 350°

5 green apples, cored,
  chopped
2 Tbsps. butter
1 cup walnuts, chopped
1 cup pinenuts
1 cup raisins
1 cup sugar
3 Tbsps. vodka
1 cup ricotta cheese
1 cup ladyfinger cookies,
  crushed
3 egg yolks, beaten
1 egg, beaten
  One 16" × 16" frozen
  pastry dough, defrosted
  Powdered sugar

auté apples in butter for 5 minutes over low heat. Remove from heat to a large mixing bowl to cool. Add the walnuts, pinenuts, raisins, sugar, vodka, ricotta cheese, cookies and egg yolks, mixing well.

Take softened dough and flatten down to about ¼" thick. Top half of the dough with the apple-cheese mixture. Fold dough in half, pressing the ends together and brush with the beaten egg mixture.

Bake on a flat buttered sheet pan for 40 minutes. Let cool, then cut into ½" slices. Sprinkle with powdered sugar before serving.

Enrico Glaudo
Primi
Los Angeles

Taro with Tapioca

Soak tapioca overnight in 1 cup water. Steam taro until very soft, about 30 minutes and slice. Blend taro with milk and coconut milk to form a paste. Drain tapioca, place in a saucepan and add ½ cup fresh water. Bring to a boil, then simmer until soft and transparent, about 5 minutes. Let stand for a few minutes after cooking; it will become more jelly-like.

In a separate nonstick pan, combine sugar with 1 cup water and bring to a boil. Add taro paste and tapioca and bring to a boil again, stirring well. Season with sugar to taste.

Serve this soothing dessert warm, in small bowls.

Serves 4
Preparation Time:
  45 Minutes
(note overnight soaking time)

  ¼ **cup small pearl tapioca (not quick-cooking variety)**
2½ **cups water**
  ½ **lb. taro root, peeled**
  ½ **cup milk**
  6 **Tbsps. coconut milk**
  ¾ **cup sugar**

Philip Lo
Hong Kong Flower Lounge
Millbrae

Espresso Brownie Tart

Serves 8
Preparation Time:
 45 Minutes
Pre-heat oven to 350°

 1 **stick unsalted butter**
 ½ **cup cocoa powder**
 1 **cup semi-sweet**
   chocolate, roughly
   chopped
 ¼ **cup instant espresso or**
   coffee powder
1½ **cups sugar**
 3 **large eggs**
 ½ **cup all-purpose flour**
 ½ **tsp. baking soda**
 ¼ **tsp. salt**
 1 **cup walnuts, chopped**
   Confectioners sugar
   Whipped cream
   Chocolate shavings

Butter, then lightly dust a 9″ tart pan with cocoa powder.

Melt butter in a double boiler. When melted, stir in the chocolate, remaining cocoa and espresso powder and stir until smooth. Pour mixture into a mixer bowl and at low speed mix in sugar and eggs, one at a time. Continue mixing at low speed for 8 to 10 minutes.

In a separate bowl, sift together the flour, soda and salt. Fold the chocolate mixture into the dry ingredients along with the nuts. Pour into prepared tart pan and bake for 25 minutes.

To serve, cut into wedges and top with a sprinkling of confectioners sugar, lightly whipped cream and chocolate shavings.

Trade Secret: This tart is very gooey when hot and even when chilled will have a soft chewy center. Refrigerate at least 2 hours before serving cold.

John Ash
John Ash & Co.
Santa Rosa

Pear Tart with Cinnamon Ice Cream

Skin, core and slice each pear. Fan each pear into a nice design on puff pastry rounds. Sprinkle 1 Tbsp. sugar on each tart and dot each tart with butter. Place tarts on a cookie sheet and bake for 30 minutes. Glaze with apricot glaze.

To make the cinnamon ice cream, whisk egg yolks into ¾ cup sugar. Slowly whisk in hot milk and cinnamon.

Pour into a saucepan over medium heat, stirring until lightly thickened. Place saucepan in an ice bath to cool immediately. When cool, add the cream.

Pour mixture into an ice cream maker and follow the manufacturer's instructions.

To serve, place each warm tart on individual plates and scoop cinnamon ice cream on top.

Serves 4
Preparation Time:
  35 Minutes
Pre-heat oven to 375°

4 ripe pears
  Four 6" rounds of rolled
  out puff pastry
1 cup sugar
4 Tbsps. butter
4 Tbsps. apricot glaze,
  strained
6 egg yolks
2 cups milk, scalded
1 Tbsp. cinnamon
1 cup whipping cream

John McLaughlin
JW's Restaurant
Anaheim

Italian Plum Almond Tart

Serves 6
Preparation Time:
 1 Hour
Pre-heat oven to 375°

1 **cup all-purpose flour**
⅓ **cup + 2 Tbsps. sugar**
  Pinch of salt
¼ **cup almond paste**
9 **Tbsps. butter**
2 **egg yolks**
1 **cup almonds, sliced**
½ **tsp. orange zest, grated**
  Plum liqueur or kirsch
  to taste
2 **lbs. Italian prune plums,**
  sliced thin

repare the almond pastry shell by combining flour, 2 Tbsps. sugar, salt and almond paste in food processor bowl and pulse until blended.

Cut 6 Tbsps. cold butter into small pieces and add to mixture. Pulse again until mixture is blended. Add 1 egg yolk and pulse briefly until dough holds together when pinched.

Press dough into 9″ tart pan and bake until lightly brown. Set aside and cool.

Grind almonds finely in food processor. Set aside.

Beat 1 egg yolk, ⅓ cup sugar and orange zest. Mix in 3 Tbsps. melted butter and ground almonds. Add liqueur to taste.

Arrange plums on bottom of tart shell. Cover with almond filling, spreading with a spatula

Bake at 350° for 40 to 45 minutes, or until filling is set.

Annie Somerville
Greens
San Francisco

Tiramisu with Crème Anglaise

In a mixer, beat eggs, mascarpone and ¼ cup sugar until fluffy and creamy. Fold in whipped cream. Set aside.

Combine the coffee and rum. Dip each ladyfinger in the coffee rum mixture, sugar side down, for 1 second. Ladyfingers get soggy very quickly.

Layer ladyfingers in a 3" deep rectangular pan. Cover with mascarpone mixture. Repeat procedure until all the mascarpone and ladyfingers are used. Chill for 2 hours.

Prepare the crème anglaise in a mixing bowl, whisking together the egg yolks and ¼ cup sugar for about 2 minutes. Set aside.

In a double boiler, over medium heat, bring milk and vanilla to a boil. Add the egg mixture to the milk and whisk quickly so eggs don't curdle. Cook until 145° is reached. Cool.

Garnish ladyfingers with ground chocolate and crème anglaise before serving.

Serves 4
Preparation Time:
30 Minutes
(note refrigeration time)

- 3 **egg yolks**
- 1 **cup mascarpone cheese**
- ½ **cup sugar**
- ½ **cup cream, whipped**
- 1 **box ladyfingers (about 50 pieces)**
- 7 **cups espresso or strong coffee**
- ½ **cup dark rum**
- 7 **egg yolks**
- 2 **cups milk**
- 2 **tsps. vanilla extract**
- **Ground chocolate**

Donna Scala
Piatti Ristorante
Sacramento, Napa, Sonoma, Carmel, Montecito, La Jolla
★

Chestnut Meringue Torte with Apricot Champagne Sauce

Serves 6
Preparation Time:
  1½ Hours
(note refrigeration time)

 ⅓ cup dried apricots
 1 cup champagne
 1 cup fresh chestnuts
2½ cups heavy cream
 ½ cup white chocolate,
    chopped
 12 meringue rounds, flat,
    about 4″ diameter
    Cocoa powder

oak the apricots overnight in champagne. Purée in food processor fitted with steel blades. Season to taste and consistency with additional champagne. Set aside.

Make a cross-cut in the flat side of each chestnut. Roast in a 450° oven for about 15 minutes, until they open up.

Peel the chestnuts, then simmer in 1½ cups cream for 30 minutes. Remove chestnuts from cream and set aside.

Add chocolate chunks to cream and melt over low heat. When melted, blend the chocolate cream in a food processor and pour into a clean container to cool for several hours or overnight in the refrigerator.

When the white chocolate cream is thoroughly cold, add the remaining 1 cup of heavy cream and carefully whip until stiff. Do not overwhip.

Chop the cooked chestnuts and fold into the whipped chocolate cream. Spread the cream onto the uneven side of 6 meringues. Place the other meringues on top with their smooth side up. Smooth the sides with a palette knife. Dust the top with cocoa powder.

Serve the chestnut meringue torte on a pool of apricot sauce.

John Downey
Downey's
Santa Barbara

Chocolate Raspberry Ganache Torte

Serves 12
Preparation Time:
  1½ Hours
(note refrigeration time)
Pre-heat oven to 350°

3¾ cups dark semi-sweet
    chocolate, chopped
  6 Tbsps. butter
  8 egg yolks
  8 egg whites
  ½ cup sugar
2½ cups heavy cream
  ⅓ cup Chambord liqueur
  1 basket raspberries

Melt 1¼ cups chocolate and butter in a bowl over a double boiler. Let the chocolate mixture cool slightly and add the yolks without mixing them yet through the chocolate.

Whip the whites to soft peaks then add the sugar slowly to form stiff but not dry peaks.

Mix the yolks through the chocolate mixture and fold in the whites.

Spray a 10" × 4" deep cake pan with vegetable oil and dust it with flour. Pour in the cake mixture.

Bake the cake for 45 minutes to 1 hour. A cake tester should come out dry. Remove from the oven, allowing the cake to sit for 5 minutes inverted. Remove cake from pan, cool and refrigerate for at least 20 minutes. As the cake cools, the center should sink, creating a "well" for the raspberries and ganache.

Prepare the ganache by melting 1 cup chocolate in a mixing bowl over a double boiler. Add 1 cup cold cream and the Chambord and mix at high speed with a paddle until firm. The texture should be like a mousse.

Place the cake on a wire rack and fill the "well" with raspberries and top with ganache. Refrigerate until cool and firm.

Prepare the glaze by melting 1½ cups chocolate with 1½ cups cream. Mix together and pour over the cake. This should form a smooth even glaze over the cake. The excess chocolate should drip off the cake and through the wire rack.

Russell Armstrong
Trees
Corona del Mar
☆

Turtle Torte

Serves 12
Preparation Time:
20 Minutes
(note refrigeration time)
Pre-heat oven to 350°

2 sticks butter
4 cups pecans, chopped
1 cup sugar
½ tsp. salt
1 lb. bittersweet
   chocolate
2 cups heavy cream
¼ cup light corn syrup
   Caramel sauce
   Whole roasted pecans

 n a 10″ springform pan, spray vegetable oil and line with parchment paper. Set aside.

Prepare the nut crust by mixing together 1 stick of melted butter with the pecans, sugar and salt. Bake for 10 minutes, then cool.

In a double boiler, melt the chocolate, 1 stick of butter, cream and corn syrup over low heat. When chocolate mixture has cooled, pour into pecan crust.

Cool 8 hours or overnight. Top with caramel sauce and whole roasted pecans before serving.

William Donnelly
Chez Melange
Redondo Beach

Walnuts and Fresh Figs in Pernod Syrup

Combine the Pernod, water, sugar and walnuts in a medium pot. Bring to boil over medium heat and simmer until the liquid reduces and forms a medium-thick syrup.

Add figs and continue to cook, stirring for 1 minute. Pour into a bowl or container and refrigerate.

Place a scoop of ice cream in each of 4 dessert bowls, add the figs and spoon the walnuts and syrup over the top.

Trade Secret: Walnuts can be bitter and their bitterness is an important element in this dessert, the catalyst that changes the impression of the Pernod syrup.

Serves 4
Preparation Time:
  15 Minutes
(note refrigeration time)

1 cup Pernod
¼ cup water
⅓ cup sugar
1 cup walnuts
16 to 20 fresh mission figs
4 scoops vanilla ice cream

Michael Roberts
Trumps
Hollywood

Zabaglione

Serves 4
Preparation Time:
20 Minutes
(note refrigeration time)

  8 large egg yolks
 ½ **cup sugar**
    Pinch salt
 ¾ **cup marsala**
 ¼ **cup sherry**
1½ **cups heavy whipping**
    cream

ombine the egg yolks, sugar and salt in a large stainless steel bowl. Whisk in the marsala and sherry.

Fill a large bowl one quarter full of ice water and set aside.

Place the first bowl over a pot of boiling water and whisk the egg mixture vigorously for about 5 minutes, until it is thick and tripled in volume. The zabaglione should mound slightly when dropped from the whisk. Immediately put the bowl over the ice bath and whisk until cold.

Pour the cream into the bowl of an electric mixer. With the whisk attachment, whip on high speed until soft peaks form. Fold the cream into the zabaglione.

Refrigerate until ready to use.

©Stars Desserts

Emily Luchetti
Stars
San Francisco

Listen to the Chefs

Here are the finest chefs in California. They offer tips, advice, criticism and trade secrets. This is what they have to say.

My tips for cooks at home: Don't be afraid to try any recipe. Use your intuition. If something doesn't sound right, make changes to suit your taste. But be aware; many cooks overcook fish and meats. A good quick meal: Stir fries—you can use almost anything in the refrigerator or garden. I embrace the use of fresh ingredients and consider presentation as important as taste.

I became interested in cooking because of my grandmother, who was a great old-fashioned cook, and because of my interest in art. A great cook is someone who takes the time to seek first-rate ingredients. Cooks at home should be fearless, not afraid to make mistakes. Some of my best dishes came as a result of a "mistake." Many cooks make the mistake of using inferior utensils and are afraid to turn the heat up. The three ingredients I can't live without are Dijon mustard, balsamic vinegar and onions.

A great cook must have patience and a keen sense of curiosity about food. He or she must enjoy problem-solving. A good pair of comfortable shoes also helps. Be patient and organized. Pay attention to detail and read new recipes twice before attempting them. This will save you time and will give you a complete understanding of methods and techniques needed for the recipe. When I dine out, I prefer almost any type of ethnic food, as long as it's well prepared. There is so much honesty and tradition there—I find that very refreshing.

I got serious about cooking after moving to Sacramento 20 years ago and discovered that nobody here had the foggiest idea about authentic Italian food. Since I am often disappointed with other Italian restaurants, I generally opt for French, Chinese or California cooking. I look for recipes that set my gastric juices in motion and make me want to cook them. Good advice: Get to know the ingredients you are using. Once you understand them, you will know how and when to use them.

As a young boy, my grandmother did all the cooking and I always enjoyed watching her. That's how I got interested in cooking. When I dine out, I enjoy small tastings of the most interesting foods on the menu, from appetizers to dessert, with a vintage port to finish. A great cook needs passion, creativity and discipline. I have the utmost respect for home cooks, but here's a tip: don't overcook. I also find that many home cooks tend to over-spice their food. I call my cooking global cuisine. I believe in using the freshest produce indigenous to the areas of the world where the dish comes from.

There is no magic to being a good cook, you just have to care. Good tips: Don't overcook the fish! Remove it from the heat a little before it's cooked through, then let it rest a few minutes. In general, try to highlight natural flavors. And use fresh herbs freely. Go to the market first, then plan your menu. Don't be afraid to let a single ingredient stand alone—a simple head of broccoli, fresh and perfectly cooked, can be just fine without a lot of hollandaise sauce. Complicated dishes aren't necessarily better. Think simple and good.

A great cook is organized, someone who knows how to use fresh ingredients without complicating things. Simple is always best. I don't compromise on the quality and freshness of the ingredients. Remember, the presentation is essential to inviting the palate. It is the mixture of flavors and textures that makes a meal interesting and delicious. A good tip: Hire a maid to clean up.

A great cook is someone who loves to eat, is experimental, good with their hands, sensitive—and smart. When I dine out, I like Indian and Asian food the most; for lunch, Middle Eastern and Ethiopian are more and more of interest. Good tips for cooks at home: taste constantly while cooking, then stop and think about the food and adjust the taste. Also, use hot pans when sautéing. A good quick meal: feta, avocado, olive oil, bread and steamed artichoke. I like bold, strong flavors and appreciate the down-home or street food—the true kitchen of each country at its best.

Other restaurant: City Restaurant in Los Angeles

I got interested in cooking at an early age; I began baking cookies and cakes at the age of 8. When I dine out, I like simple, full-flavored food, not food that has been handled a thousand times and is not natural, like tomatoes cut into roses. Good tip for cooks at home: stay focused, even if something upsets your rhythm. A good quick meal: salad with mixed greens, tomatoes, cucumbers, with feta cheese and vinaigrette. Stick a roll or two in the oven and you're set. If time permits, sauté some chicken to top the salad.

A great cook is someone with an excellent palate, a curiosity about foods, a willingness to experiment and make mistakes—then make them right. I look for three things in a recipe: Complexity of flavors and textures, ease of preparation, and not-too-exotic ingredients. A good, quick meal: Polenta with sausages and steamed greens. Three ingredients I can't live without: Garlic, onions and chocolate—not all together, though. I care about putting out the best possible food, whether homey or fancy.

My father was a chef in Mexico and I always enjoyed good food, so I was naturally interested in cooking. I like clean, light, well thought out recipes. Some cooks handle the food too much and lose the ingredients' natural flavors. A good cook avoids conflicting ingredients that confuse the palate. Three ingredients I can't live without: wine, jalapeños and fresh veggies. When I dine out, I prefer Italian, French, Mexican, ethnic foods—I love them all.

My parents owned a restaurant when I was young, and everybody in my family cooked, so naturally I became interested in cooking at an early age. What do many cooks do wrong? Too many things on one plate. Some chefs think the more food on a plate, the better. Cooks at home should use simple recipes and pay attention to the look and presentation. I can't live without olive oil, herbs and fresh tomato. When I dine out, I prefer Chinese or Japanese food.

Other restaurant: Valentino, Santa Monica

What do I look for in a recipe? Clarity of organization, a point of view about flavor. Many home cooks don't plan ahead or have quality ingredients to begin with. They make poor substitutions and then wonder why the dish didn't come out. The three ingredients I can't live without: garlic, lemon and olive oil. And remember, don't try to do too much at one time. I try to understand the history behind the dish and how the flavors come together.

I have always loved the kitchen, even as a child. It started out being therapeutic, not just a job. Now it's a therapeutic job. Cooking is a state of mind—half romance and half application. When I dine out, I love almost everything: duck with turnips when it rains, grilled lobster with gazpacho when it's hot and everything else when it's not. Tips for cooks at home: always start with a glass of wine, don't sweat the small stuff, and always relax. The food knows if you're not having fun. Remain flexible.

A great cook needs a good palate, a repertoire of culinary skills and no fear of venturing away from what the recipe says. Conceptualize instead of gluing yourself to a recipe. Follow it, learn the idea, then deviate. Many home cooks don't trust their instincts when it comes to taste. Be comfortable and confident to try what you know tastes good. People have been eating for thousands of years. It's very difficult to create something entirely new. I enjoy revitalizing and renovating old classics and personalizing them with my own interpretation.

I usually do not use recipes other than for desserts. When I dine out, I prefer simply prepared food you can still distinguish as some form of its original state. Two things many cooks do wrong: over-season with herbs and under-season with salt and pepper. A good quick-meal: dried or fresh pasta, chopped tomatoes, fresh basil, balsamic vinegar, olive oil, salt and pepper. The three ingredients I can't live without: salt, white and black pepper, and chicken stock.

I got interested in cooking by looking at my grandmother when I was a kid. She was a much better cook than my mother—she used to make the perfect omelet soufflé. Cooks at home should keep it simple, but at the same time be adventurous and have fun. What do many cooks do wrong? Speaking for the professional cooks, they try to jump from one step to the other much too fast. A good, quick meal: champagne, caviar and good company. Three ingredients I can't live without: definitely ice cream, bread and coffee.

I look for innovation in a recipe—things that are different. I like exotic ingredients and colorful produce and sauces, cross-cultural cooking. A great cook is one who has the ability to taste and season and who can improvise. A good tip: trust yourself. If something tastes good to you, it will usually please everybody else. But don't take cooking too seriously. What many cooks do wrong: rush the cooking times, especially in reduction sauces. A good quick meal: angel hair pasta with tomato, basil, garlic, olive oil and a splash of sherry wine vinegar.

Other restaurants: Cafe Pacifica and Pacifica Grill in San Diego

I got interested in cooking because of the challenge and tremendous possibilities in combining art and good food. I look for balance of texture, flavors and color in a recipe. What makes a great cook? Love and dedication and dedication and dedication...and some talent. Some cooks are so concerned about following trends that they forget or are afraid to be uniquely themselves. Remain simple; use quality always. Three ingredients I can't live without: rain and sunshine and a good harvest.

I got interested in cooking by putting myself through college by working in restaurants. I look for recipes that are simple, not too fussy. When I dine out, I prefer Mexican food. A great cook must have a sense of taste and a sense of style. Many cooks go wrong by overcooking the meat and being afraid to use seasonings. Good tip: buy the freshest and best quality you can afford. Then, don't mess with it too much. Three ingredients I can't live without: garlic, fresh herbs, and tomatoes.

I look for presentation in a recipe: color, fragrance and taste. When I dine out, I prefer Japanese food. Many cooks make the mistake of not being attentive to the job. A good quick meal: steamed fish. Three ingredients I can't live without: oil, salt and sugar. Remember, presentation of a dish is very important. And always use ingredients that are easily available.

Other restaurant: Hong Kong Flower Lounge in San Francisco

A great cook is someone who is creative but holds on to tradition, an efficient person who is able to do a couple of things at once. Being highly organized certainly helps. Good tips: follow instructions in recipes but use your common sense. Don't be intimidated, just dig right in. Try a recipe once to see how it should work—then experiment. Life would not be the same without mascarpone, fresh berries and caramel. I don't make desserts too sweet; I try to give them maximum flavor. Desserts should taste incredible in order to be worth the calories.

I look for an interesting pairing of ingredients in a recipe. When I dine out, I prefer French food. A great cook is dedicated, self-disciplined, has imagination, flexibility and an open mind. A great cook is always learning. Many cooks make the mistake of not spending the few extra seconds to make a nice, clean presentation of even the most simple food. A good quick meal: I like to stir-fry whatever is fresh in my backyard vegetable garden. I always try to use fresh ingredients. I try to achieve a light, fresh taste.

My mother's passion for delicious and interesting food got me interested in cooking. Plus the enjoyment I get from working with my hands. I look for balanced flavors that make sense in a recipe. A great cook tastes often and imagines the experience of eating a whole dish of whatever she's tasting. Good tip for home cooks: follow your own tastes when adjusting a recipe. A good quick meal: shredded chicken salad. Three ingredients I can't live without: onions, pepper, olive oil—and, of course, salt.

Other restaurant: Border Grill in Santa Monica

When I dine out, I enjoy all kinds of food, I love variety and am always looking for new flavors. A great cook should constantly have his eyes and mind open and continuously improve. What many cooks do wrong: some cook too heavy; others don't update to match customers' changing desires. A good quick meal: pasta, salad and fish. I care about the outcome from A to Z —100% fresh fish, the correct amounts, flavors, temperature, proper balance and final presentation.

TODD MUIR ★ MADRONA MANOR ★ HEALDSBURG

When I look at recipes, I simply look for technique and ingredients suggested, and take it from there. When I dine out, my favorite food currently is Thai, because of its exotic ingredients and wonderfully sweet and hot combinations. A great cook possesses a well-grounded knowledge of cooking techniques, uses seasonal fresh ingredients with a light hand and can conceptualize flavor combinations. Cooks at home should have good quality equipment: knives, pans, etc. —and a few good general cookbooks.

BRADLEY OGDEN ★ LARK CREEK INN ★ LARKSPUR

The greatest influence on my cooking came from my early exposure to fresh, native American foods. Coming from the Midwest, I grew up with freshly caught trout, free-range chickens, and hand-picked fruits and vegetables. Good tips: keep it simple; use the freshest ingredients available and put them together in such a way that the flavors, colors and textures combine to bring out the best in each other.

I have been working in professional kitchens since I was 13. And the enjoyment of eating is what got me interested in cooking. My favorite food: all types. A great cook is someone who likes to eat. A good quick meal: order to-go food. Food should be fresh whenever possible, whatever the ingredients.

Other restaruants: Bix, Bistro Roti, Buckeye Roadhouse, Mustards, Tra Vigne, in San Francisco, Marin and Napa

My older brother was a chef in Italy and he gave me very good advice. I have always been very involved in cooking. A great chef has a steady personality, good training, a high knowledge of mixing certain ingredients together, and a lot of fantasy. Many cooks mix too many flavors in the same dish. Three ingredients I can't live without: salt, herbs, extra virgin olive oil. A good quick meal: angel hair pasta tossed with extra virgin olive oil, garlic, hot red pepper, a touch of Parmesan. A good tip: cook with love.

Other restaurants in San Francisco, Corte Madera, Palo Alto and Irvine

A great cook has to love and respect food for what it is—the basic nourishment of the body. The cook, like an artist, must have a sense of adventure and a feeling for the elements he's working with. He should be able to taste the food in his mind before he even starts. What many cooks do wrong: they won't taste the food. Three ingredients I can't live without: chiles, garlic, tomatoes. Cooking is a labor of love. It is taking the raw produce of the earth and by combining various elements and transforming them with fire, creating a gift to share with family and friends.

Other restaurant: El Cocodrilo in Pacific Grove

Eating first got me interested in cooking, then I discovered vanity—people love to be complimented, especially cooks. I look for recipes that are easy to prepare, with a clear idea of seasonings and not too many ingredients to spoil the pot. When I dine out, I prefer seafood and potatoes.

Many cooks are afraid of high heat, so they don't cook things quickly enough. Most cooks are afraid of spices and herbs. Don't try to be too complicated. Cook to please your guests, not yourself. Keep it clear—the ingredients should marry, not fight.

I became interested in cooking because of my grandfather; he had lots of restaurants. I look for simplicity, straightforward food in a recipe. One problem with many cooks: overcooking pasta. Good tips: use a good extra virgin olive oil whenever possible. A good quick meal: pasta with fresh tomato sauce. Three ingredients I can't live without: olive oil, tomatoes and garlic. What makes my cooking so special? It's simple food.

Other restaurants in Yountville, Carmel, Montecito, La Jolla and Sacramento

I read recipes for ideas and new techniques. I look for a new idea on an old classic or a classic that isn't in my repertoire. Good tips for cooks at home: read everything available and practice as much as possible. Remember that often the simplest things are the best. I buy almost no pre-prepared ingredients. Everything in our kitchen is done in small quantities and usually by hand. I really do use things in their proper season, when they are best in flavor and texture. Ingredients should be fresh, simple and of good quality.

When I dine out, I look for food that was carefully chosen and prepared, in a distinct style that shows some depth on the chef's part. A great chef needs good coordination and strength in all the senses, because cooking involves all five senses. Cooks at home should remember that recipes start in the market. They should also be willing to improvise. Many cooks over-complicate the processes in the kitchen. A good quick meal: whole roasted chicken with lemon and garlic, roasted potatoes and mixed green salad with some type of cheese.

When I read a recipe, I look for easy delivery and easy-to-find produce. Having a great recipe makes a great chef. Too many cooks put too many different flavors on a plate. Three ingredients I can't live without: oil, herbs and tomatoes. What makes my cooking so special? Dedication.

Cooking meals for the community Zen center and vegetarian food got me interested in cooking. When I dine out, I prefer Asian food. A great cook is one who has a great sense of taste, sensitivity to what's in season and a willingness to work with what's there. Some good tips for cooks at home: use fresh ingredients, grow or buy good produce, try a planter box with fresh herbs. A good quick meal: pasta, potatoes, polenta. What makes my cooking special is that I pay attention to all steps in a planning order. I put a tremendous amount of care into the finished product.

HIROYOSHI SONE ★ TERRA ★ ST. HELENA

In a recipe, I look for interesting combinations of ingredients that spark my imagination. A great cook has total recall of taste, artistic ability and basic classic cooking techniques. Good tips: get the best ingredients, always sharp knives, clean as you cook. Many cooks go wrong with the handling of ingredients: over-cooking, undercooking, seasoning, knowing when to grill, sauté, steam or bake. My Japanese heritage, combined with classic French, Italian and Chinese cooking techniques, allows me to create dishes using techniques from many cuisines.

DAVID SOOHOO ★ CHINOIS EAST/WEST ★ SACRAMENTO

I love improvisation and customizing specific meals for customers. We Chinese don't follow recipes or do much about writing them down. We create expressions and keep those. Too many cooks use inferior equipment, and stoves and ovens that aren't what they say they are. A good quick meal: ramen with extremely expensive lunch meats. Three ingredients I can't live without: hoisin sauce, oyster sauce, butter. I follow my philosophy of the Nine-Door Theory and use it to anchor my cooking's high level of excitement.

JOACHIM SPLICHAL ★ PATINA ★ LOS ANGELES

I got interested in cooking because my parents had a small inn in the Black Forest. When I dine out, I look for good food, whether it is Italian, Japanese, Chinese or French. Good tip for cooks at home: buy the best seasonal ingredients and you are half way there. A good quick meal: pasta with tomato and basil. Three ingredients I can't live without: potatoes, olive oil and tomatoes.

I look for new ingredients, something I haven't made before, in a recipe. Cooking is all heart! You have to love it. After years of cooking, you just know what ingredients work well together. Good tips: don't cook unless you enjoy it. Start with simple, easy recipes. A good quick meal: linguine with tomatoes, herbs, shallots, lemon and olive oil. My training was French. Then I moved to San Diego and discovered Mexican. I've combined French, Mexican and California cuisines to prepare light, clean, healthy Southwestern food that's cleverly presented.

A great cook needs taste, visual awareness, literacy and stamina. Recently, at a friend's house, I had a dinner that could not have been more perfect or satisfying. There was some braised lamb shoulder left over from two days before. There were a couple of tomatoes, some dried macaroni, an onion, a carrot, some herbs from the garden, and not much else. As it turned out, "not much" was enough. I cook American food using French cooking principles, a style of cooking which, in its influence and scope, drawing on bar and grill, brasserie, bistro and classic restaurant food, has become a new American classic.

I lived for two years in Taipei, Taiwan, in homes headed by wonderful, traditional (but eccentric!) cooks from northern and central China. That got me interested in cooking. I look for lively flavors and great color in a recipe. When I dine out, I prefer California-Italian food. Good tip: taste every ingredient you use, from salt to oil. If it doesn't taste good to you, try other brands. In this way, you develop your palate and confidence. A good quick meal: great bread and great cheese coupled with an excellent cured ham and a good smear of mustard.

When I dine out, I like all kinds of food. On my day off, I'm just happy not to have to cook and clean up. What makes a great cook: loving what you do, paying attention to detail, and a great staff.

Good tip: don't attempt ridiculously complex recipes; perfect your own specialties and then work up to more complex dishes. Too many cooks get in over their heads, don't do their homework and don't stick to things they know. Three ingredients I can't live without: salt, pepper and water.

ALICE WATERS ★ CHEZ PANISSE ★ BERKELEY

I was inspired to become a cook while traveling through France at the age of 19. When I look at a recipe, I look for inspiration from the main ingredients, not at the exact proportions or techniques. When I dine out, I prefer Indian food. A great cook must be close to the garden, must understand the ingredients. Good tip: shop first, get the ingredients, then decide on a recipe. Shop at the farmers market and buy what is in season. A good quick meal: grilled chicken on a bed of lettuces with lemon vinaigrette.

BRIAN WHITMER ★ HIGHLANDS INN ★ CARMEL

My mother's great cooking just drew me into a natural love of food—and cooking. What makes a great cook? Love of food, people and hard work. Good tip: cook with your heart and don't worry about changing someone's recipe a little. Many cooks make the error of trying to become chefs before they are really cooks. A good quick meal: great salad, a bowl of pasta and a fresh fruit tart. Three ingredients I can't live without: garlic, artichokes and basil.

How You Can Measure Up...

LIQUID MEASURES

1 dash	6 drops
1 teaspoon (tsp.)	⅓ tablespoon
1 tablespoon (Tbsp.)	3 teaspoons
1 tablespoon	½ fluid ounce
1 fluid ounce	2 tablespoons
1 cup	½ pint
1 cup	16 tablespoons
1 cup	8 fluid ounces
1 pint	2 cups
1 pint	16 fluid ounces

DRY MEASURES

1 dash	less than ⅛ teaspoon
1 teaspoon	⅓ tablespoon
1 tablespoon	3 teaspoons
¼ cup	4 tablespoons
⅓ cup	5 tablespoons plus 1 teaspoon
½ cup	8 tablespoons
⅔ cup	10 tablespoons plus 2 teaspoons
¾ cup	12 tablespoons
1 cup	16 tablespoons

VEGETABLES AND FRUITS

Apple (1 medium)	1 cup chopped
Avocado (1 medium)	1 cup mashed
Broccoli (1 stalk)	2 cups florets
Cabbage (1 large)	10 cups, chopped
Carrot (1 medium)	½ cup, diced
Celery (3 stalks)	1 cup, diced
Eggplant (1 medium)	4 cups, cubed
Lemon (1 medium)	2 tablespoons juice
Onion (1 medium)	1 cup, diced
Orange (1 medium)	½ cup juice
Parsley (1 bunch)	3 cups, chopped
Spinach (fresh), 12 cups, loosely packed	1 cup cooked
Tomato (1 medium)	¾ cup, diced
Zucchini (1 medium)	2 cups, diced

Mail Order Sources

If you are unable to locate some of the specialty food products used in "The Great California Cookbook," you can order them from the mail order sources listed below. These items are delivered by UPS, fully insured and at reasonable shipping costs.

SPICES AND HERBS

Penzey Spice House Limited
P.O. Box 1633
Milwaukee, WI 53201
(414) 768-8799
Fresh ground spices (saffron, cinnamon and peppers), bulk spices, seeds, and seasoning mixes.

Fox Hill Farm
444 West Michigan Avenue
P.O. Box 9
Parma, MI 49269
(517) 531-3179
Fresh-cut herb plants, topiaries, ornamental and medicinal herbs.

Old Southwest Trading Company
P.O. Box 7545
Albuquerque, NM 87194
(800) 748-2861
(505) 831-5144
Specializes in chiles, everything from dried chiles to canned chiles and other chile-related products.

Pecos Valley Spice Company
4371 Charlotte Highway 3 Heritage Park
Lake Wylie, SC 29710
(803) 831-0121
Dried peppers, mild to very hot.

Meadowbrook Herb Gardens
Route 138
Wyoming, RI 02898
(401) 539-7603
Organically grown herb seasonings, high quality spice and teas.

Rafal Spice Company
2521 Russell Street
Detroit, MI 48207
(800) 228-4276
(313) 259-6373
Seasoning mixtures, herbs, spices, oil, coffee beans and teas.

MEATS AND POULTRY

New Braunfels Smokehouse
P.O. Box 311159
New Braunfels, TX 78131-1159
(512) 625-7316
(800) 537-6932
A family-owned business since 1945, selling quality hickory smoked meats, poultry, and fish. They also sell lean summer sausages, bacon, and beef jerky.

Omaha Steaks International
P.O. Box 3300
Omaha, NE 68103
(800) 228-9055
Corn-fed Midwestern beef, filet mignon and boneless strips of sirloin.

Gerhard's Napa Valley Sausages
901 Enterprise Way
Napa, CA 94558
(707) 252-4116
Specializing in more than 26 types of fresh and smoked sausages: chicken apple, east Indian, turkey/chicken, Syrian lamb, kielbasa, Italian, Bavarian beerwurst, Cajun, duck with roasted almonds and much more. They do not use cereal fillers, MSG or artifical flavors.

Deer Valley Farm
R.D. #1
Guilford, NY 13780
(607) 764-8556
Organically raised chicken, beef and veal. These meats are very low in fat and high in flavor.

PASTRY AND BAKED GOODS

Cafe Beaujolais Bakery
P.O. Box 730
Mendocino, CA 95460
(707) 937-0443
Panfortes, almond and hazelnut pastries as well as fruit cakes, jam, chocolate and home-made cashew granola.

SPECIALTY FOODS AND FOOD GIFTS

Gazin's Inc.
P.O. Box 19221
New Orleans, LA 70179
(504) 482-0302
Specializing in Cajun, Creole and New Orleans foods.

Kozlowski Farms
5566 Gravenstein Highway
Forestville, CA 95436
(707) 887-1587
(800) 473-2767
Jams, jellies, barbecue and steak sauces, conserves, honey, salsas, chutneys and mustards. Some products are non-sugared, others are in the organic line. You can customize your order from 65 different products.

Knott's Berry Farm
8039 Beach Boulevard
Buena Park, CA 90620
(800) 877-6887
(714) 827-1776
Eleven types of jams and preserves, nine of which are non-sugar.

FRUIT

Timber Crest Farms
4791 Dry Creek Road
Healdsburg, CA 95448
(707) 433-8251
Domestic dried tomatoes and other unsulfured dried fruits and nuts.

Lee Anderson's Covalda Date Company
51-392 Harrison Street (Old Highway 86)
P.O. Box 908
Coachella, CA 92236-0908
(619) 398-3441
Organic dates, raw date sugar and other date products. Also dried fruits, nuts and seeds.

VINEGARS AND OILS

Williams-Sonoma
Mail Order Dept.
P.O. Box 7456
San Francisco, CA 94120-7456
(800) 541-2233 credit card orders
(800) 541-1262 customer service
Vinegars, oils, foods and kitchenware.

Community Kitchens
P.O. Box 2311, Dept. J-D
Baton Rouge, LA 70821-2311
(800) 535-9901
Vinegars and oil, in addition to meats, crawfish, coffees and teas.

Corti Brothers
5810 Folsom Blvd.
Sacramento, CA 95819
(916) 736-3800
Special gourmet items such as imported extra virgin olive oils, wines, exotic beans, egg pasta.

Festive Foods
9420 Arroyo Lane
Colorado Springs, CO 80908
(719) 495-2339
Spices and herbs, teas, oils, vinegars, chocolate
and baking ingredients.

Kimberly Wine Vinegar Works
290 Pierce Street
Daly City, CA 94015
(415) 755-0306
Fine wine vinegars and northern California
olive oil.

Select Orgins
Box N
Southhampton, NY 11968
(516) 288-1382
(800) 822-2092
Oils, vinegars and rice.

PASTA

Morisi's Pasta
John Morisi & Sons, Inc.
647 Fifth Avenue
Brooklyn, NY 11215
(718) 499-0146
(800) 253-6044
Over 250 varieties available from this 50-year
old, family-owned gourmet pasta business.

FLOURS AND GRAINS

The Vermont Country Store
P.O. Box 3000
Manchester Center, VT 05255-3000
(802) 362-2400 credit card orders
(802) 362-4647 customer service
Orders are taken 24 hours a day.
Many different varieties: whole wheat, sweet-
cracked, stone-ground rye, buckwheat,
cornmeal and many more. They also sell a
variety of items which are made in Vermont.

G.B. Ratto & Co. International Grocers
821 Washington Street
Oakland, CA 94607
(510) 832-6503
(800) 325-3483
Flours, rice, bulgar wheat, couscous, oils, and
sun-dried tomatoes.

DRIED BEANS AND PEAS

Baer's Best
154 Green Street
Reading, MA 01867
(617) 944-8719
Bulk or 1-pound packages of over 30 different
varieties of beans, common to exotic. No peas.

DRIED MUSHROOMS

Gourmet Treasure Hunters
10044 Adams Avenue, Suite 305
Huntington Beach, CA 92646
(714) 964-3355
Many kinds of dried mushrooms, specialty rices
(arborio and basmati), olives and olive oil, and
Japanese and Vietnamese ingredients.

SAFFRON

Vanilla Saffron Imports, Inc.
949 Valencia Street
San Francisco, CA 94110
(415) 648-8990
(415) 648-2240 fax
Saffron, vanilla beans and pure vanilla extract,
dried mushrooms as well as herbs.

NUTS

Gourmet Nut Center
1430 Railroad Avenue
Orland, CA 95963
(916) 865-5511
Almonds, pistachios and cashews.

Koinonia Partners
Route 2
Americus, GA 31709
(912) 924-0391
Shelled/unshelled, flavored pecans and peanuts in addition to chocolates and different varieties of fruitcakes.

COFFEE AND TEA

Brown & Jenkins Trading Co.
P.O. Box 2306
South Burlington, VT 05407-2306
(802) 862-2395
(800) 456-JAVA
Water-decaffeinated coffees featuring over 30 blends such as Brown & Jenkins Special blend, Vermont Breakfast blend and Haiwaiian Kona, in addition to 15 different flavors of teas.

Stash Tea Co.
P.O. Box 90
Portland, OR 97207
(503) 684-7944
(800) 826-4218
Earl Grey, herbal teas like peppermint, ruby mint, orange spice and licorice flavors.

SEEDS FOR GROWING HERBS AND VEGETABLES

Shepard's Garden Seeds
6116 Highway 9
Felton, CA 95018
(408) 335-6190
Excellent selection of vegetable and herb seeds with growing instructions.

Vermont Bean Seed Company
Computer Operations Center
Vacauluse, SC 29850
(802) 265-4212
Selling over 60 different varieties of beans, peas, corn, tomato and flower seeds.

VERMONT MAPLE SYRUP

Green Mountain Sugar House
R.F.D. #1
Ludlow, VT 05149
(802) 228-7151
(800) 647-7006
Different grades of maple syrup, maple cream and maple candies, in addition to cheese, fudge and creamed honey.

Butternut Mountain Farm
P.O. Box 381
Johnson, VT 05656
(802) 635-7483
(800) 828-2376
Different grades of maple syrup, also a variety of honey and fruit syrups such as raspberry and blueberry.

HONEY

Howard's Happy Honeybees
4828 Morro Drive
Bakersfield, CA 93307
(805) 366-4962
Unfiltered flavored honeys, such as orange blossom and sage honeys in addition to honey candy.

CHEESE

Crowley Cheese
Healdsville Road
Healdsville, VT 05758
(802) 259-2340
Smoked, mild, medium and sharp cheeses, plus spiced cheeses such as garlic, sage and hot pepper.

Tillamook County Creamery Association
P.O. Box 313
Tillamook, OR 97141
(503) 842-4481
(800) 542-7290
Over 30 types of cheeses, black wax cheese, and a hot jalapeño cheese.

CHOCOLATES AND CANDY

The Brigittine Monks Gourmet Confections
23300 Walker Lane
Amity, OR 97101
(503) 835-8080
Popular items are chocolate with nuts and pecan pralines.

FISH, CAVIAR AND SEAFOOD

Nelson Crab
Box 520
Tokeland, WA 98590
(206) 267-2911
(800) 262-0069
Fresh seafood as well as canned specialties like salmon, shrimp and tuna.

Legal Sea Foods
33 Everett Street
Boston, MA 02134
(617) 254-7000
(800) 343-5804
Live lobsters, fresh filets and seafood steaks, clam chowder, little neck steamer clams, shrimp, smoked Scottish salmon and Beluga caviar.

Glossary of Ingredients

ACHIOTE: a spice blend made from ground annatto seeds, garlic, cumin, vinegar and other spices.

ANAHEIM CHILE: elongated and cone-shaped chiles that are red or green with a mild flavor.

ANCHO CHILE: a shiny skinned red or green cone-shaped chile with medium heat.

ARBORIO RICE: a large-grained plump rice used for risotto; requires more cooking time than other rice varieties.

ARMENIAN CUCUMBER: a long pale green-ridged cucumber with an edible skin, also known as the English cucumber.

ARUGULA: also known as rocket or roquette, noted for its strong peppery taste.

BELGIAN ENDIVE: a white, yellow-edged bitter lettuce that is crunchy.

BOK CHOY: resembles Swiss chard with its long, thick-stemmed, light green stalks. The flavor is much like cabbage.

CAPERS: available in the gourmet food sections of supermarkets, capers are a small, green, pickled bud of a Mediterranean flowering plant; usually packed in brine.

CARDAMON: a sweetly pungent, aromatic cooking spice.

CHANTERELLE MUSHROOM: a trumpet-shaped mushroom that resembles an umbrella turned inside out. One of the more delicious wild mushrooms.

CHEVRE: cheese made from goat's milk; it is lower in fat and offers a delicate, slight and slightly earthy flavor.

CHICORY or CURLY ENDIVE: a crisp, curly green-leafed lettuce. Best when young. Tend to bitter with age.

CHILE OIL: a red oil available in Asian stores. Chile oil is also easily made at home by heating 1 cup of vegetable or peanut oil with 2 dozen small dried red chiles or 1 Tbsp. cayenne.

CHIPOTLE PEPPERS: ripened and smoky flavored jalapeño peppers have a fiery heat and delicious flavor.

COCONUT MILK: available in Asian markets, this milk is noted for its richly flavored, slightly sweet taste. Coconut milk can be made by placing 2 cups of finely grated chopped fresh coconut in 3 cups scalded milk. Stir and let stand until the milk cools to room temperature. Strain before using.

CRÈME FRAÎCHE: a bit richer than sour cream yet more tart than whipped heavy cream. It can be purchased in most supermarkets or made by whisking together ½ cup heavy or whipping cream, not ultra-pasteurized, with ½ cup sour cream. Pour the mixture into a jar, cover and let stand in a warm, dark area for 24 hours. This will yield 1 cup which can be kept in the refrigerator for about 10 days.

CRESS: resembles radish leaves, with a hot peppery flavor.

FISH SAUCE: a thin, salty, translucent brown sauce which is an extract of fermented fish. It has a distinctive flavor and an odor which disappears during cooking.

FRISEE: sweetest of the chicory family, with a mildly bitter taste. The leaves are a pale green, slender but curly.

FROMAGE BLANC CHEESE: fresh, day-old curds with some of the whey whipped back into the cheese. The texture is similar to ricotta cheese and is available in plain or flavored flavors.

GORGONZOLA CHEESE: a blue-veined creamy Italian cheese.

HABANERO CHILE: tiny fat neon orange-colored chiles that are hotter than the jalapeño chile.

HAZELNUT OIL: a lightly textured oil with a rich essence of hazelnut.

JALAPEÑO CHILE: these plump, thumb-size green chiles are known for wonderful flavor.

JICAMA: grows underground like a tuber yet is part of the legume family. Beneath the thick brown skin, the flesh is creamy white and sweet. Tastes like a cross between an apple and a potato.

KALAMATA OLIVE: intensely flavored, almond-shaped, dark purple Greek olive that is packed in brine.

LEMON GRASS: available in Asian food stores, this citrus-flavored herb can substitute for grated lemon peel.

MACHE: also known as lamb's lettuce, has a delicate, sweet-nutty taste. The lettuce is a deep green.

MESCULUN: a traditional French mixture of tiny lettuces, including curly endive, red lettuce, Romaine, oak-leaf, butter lettuce and rocket.

MISO: a fermented salty soy bean paste made by crushing boiled soybeans with barley.

MOREL MUSHROOM: a wild mushroom that is cone-shaped with a spongy beige cap. Has a nutty taste.

NAPA CABBAGE: also known as Chinese cabbage, looks like a cross between celery and lettuce, very much like romaine lettuce. The flavor is more delicate with a slight peppery taste.

NASTURTIUM FLOWERS: edible sweet and peppery flowers in a rainbow of colors. Nasturtiums are beautiful in salads and easy to grow.

OYSTER MUSHROOM: a beige colored fan-shaped wild mushroom with a mild flavor and soft texture.

PANCETTA: unsmoked, Italian bacon. If unavailable, use a high-quality, thinly sliced domestic bacon.

POLENTA: cornmeal—ground corn kernels, white or yellow, often enriched with butter and grated cheese. A staple of northern Italian cooking.

PORCINI MUSHROOM: the parasol-shaped mushroom cap has a thick stem, with a meaty, smoky flavor.

QUINOA: served like rice or a base for salads. Pale yellow in color and slightly larger than a mustard seed with a sweet flavor and soft texture.

RADICCHIO: this peppery-tasting lettuce has brilliant, ruby-colored leaves.

ROMAINE: known for a sweet nutty flavor, this lettuce has long, crisp, green or red leaves.

ROUX: a mixture of melted butter or oil and flour used to thicken sauces, soups and stews. Sprinkle flour into the melted, bubbling hot butter, whisking constantly over low heat, cooking at least 2 minutes.

SAFFRON: a bright yellow-colored strongly aromatic spice that imparts a unique flavor.

SAVOY CABBAGE: also known as curly cabbage, has lacy leaves with a white or reddish trim.

SERRANO CHILE: a fat squat red or green hot chile. They are milder roasted with the ribs and seeds removed.

SHIITAKE MUSHROOM: a Japanese mushroom sold fresh or dried which imparts a distinctively rich flavor to any dish.

SUN-DRIED TOMATOES: air-dried tomatoes sold in various forms such as marinated tomato halves which are packed in olive oil or a tapenade, which is puréed dried tomatoes in olive oil with garlic.

TAHINI: Middle Eastern in origin, tahini is made from crushed sesame seeds. Used mainly for its creamy, rich and nutty flavor as well as binding food together.

TEMPEH: made from cultured, fermented soybeans, comes in flat, light, grainy-looking cakes.

TOFU: a versatile fresh soybean curd, tofu is an excellent and inexpensive form of protein. It is characteristically bland in taste, but can be enhanced with seasonings.

TOMATILLOS: green husk tomatoes; small with a tart, citrus-like flavor.

WATERCRESS: this spicy flavored green is dark in color with glossy leaves.

Recipe Index

About the Author

KATHLEEN DEVANNA FISH, author of the popular "Secrets" series, is a gourmet cook who is always on the lookout for recipes with style and character.

In addition to "The Great California Cookbook," the California native has written "California Wine Country Cooking Secrets," "San Francisco's Secrets," "Monterey's Cooking Secrets" and "Cooking and Traveling Inn Style."

Before embarking on a writing and publishing career, she owned and operated three businesses in the travel and hospitality industry.

She and her husband, Robert, live on a boat in the Monterey harbor.

ROBERT FISH, award-winning photojournalist, produces the images that bring together the concept of the "Secrets" series.

In addition to taking the cover photographs, Robert explores the food and wine of each region, helping to develop the overview upon which each book is based.

Bon Vivant Press
P.O. Box 1994
Monterey, CA 93942
800-524-6826
408-373-0592
FAX 408-373-3567

Send _____ copies of "The Great California Cookbook" at $13.95 each.

Send _____ copies of "California Wine Country Cooking Secrets of Napa/Sonoma" at $13.95 each.

Send _____ copies of "San Francisco's Secrets" at $12.95 each.

Send _____ copies of "Monterey's Cooking Secrets" at $13.95 each.

Add $3.00 postage and handling for the first book ordered and $1.50 for each additional book. Please add $1.08 sales tax per book, for those books shipped to California addresses.

Please charge my ☐ Visa
                  ☐ Master Card # _____

Expiration date_____ Signature_____

Enclosed is my check for_____

Name_____

Address_____

City_____ State_____ Zip_____

☐ This is a gift. Send directly to:

Name_____

Address_____

City_____ State_____ Zip_____

☐ Autographed by the author
Autographed to_____